Another Chance

Postwar America, 1945–1985

R. Jackson Wilson, Editor
Smith College

Another Chance

Postwar America, 1945–1985

James Gilbert
University of Maryland

Second Edition　　1986

The Dorsey Press
Chicago, Illinois 60604

103246

ISBN 0-256-03542-3

Library of Congress Catalog Card No. 85-72253

Printed in the United States of America

1 2 3 4 5 6 7 8 9 0 MP 3 2 1 0 9 8 7 6

For Jenny and Simone

Foreword

A foreword is a type of ritual moment—the occasion for an editor to introduce an author to the public. In some ways, this moment resembles the introductions that masters of ceremonies give to their (invariably) distinguished guests. And when we hear the staged voices of those whose role it is merely to introduce, we are skeptical. There is a false ring to it all, usually, and we are likely to doubt the sincerity of the words "an honor" or "a great personal pleasure."

Because of this, it is uncomfortable to present someone we really *do* think is distinguished, and whom it really *does* give us pleasure to introduce to an audience. It is, in fact, an honor to help bring James Gilbert's *Another Chance* to publication. It is a fine book. It confronts a difficult task with intelligence, courage, and good sense, and it performs the task with quiet modesty.

The task is to make sense out of the experience of the men, women, and children of the United States during the four decades following World War II. *Another Chance* is the history of that experience, but it is history in a sense that differs somewhat from the usual and traditional meanings of the word: *Another Chance* tries to tell a complete story. It addresses more than the doings of politicians and diplomats, generals and labor leaders. These people are in the book, but they do not control it. James Gilbert has written the story not only of the powerful and the celebrated but also of "ordinary" people. He has attempted to understand what it meant to be a child or a mother in those years—or to be old or poor. *Another Chance* is the history of a whole society. It deals with the ways Americans governed each other. But it also attempts to understand something of how they worked, entertained themselves, married and divorced, got sick, and worried about their streets, their neighborhoods, and their schools. Perhaps most of all, *Another*

Chance tries to understand how Americans of all kinds thought and felt about their experience.

The notion of crisis has become debased. We live from crisis to crisis. Our presidents rise and fall in crises, and, in the end, there seems to be no normality against which to measure any new crisis. But however bankrupt the rhetoric of crisis may have become for Americans of the 1980s, there can be little doubt that the generation whose experience *Another Chance* interprets did come onto the scene at the end of a long period of crisis. The Great Depression and World War II had threatened their world more severely than any event since the Civil War. And the threat had lasted longer than any other, with possibilities of defeat much more disastrous than any their ancestors had confronted. In 1945, they did seem to have another chance.

But, as James Gilbert very wisely knows, the new chance was itself fraught with the possibilities of defeat and social collapse. The ways in which Americans learned to perceive these new dangers— and the often faulty means they attempted to devise to meet them—constitute a fascinating history. And *Another Chance* presents that history with real clarity and subtlety. From its pages we come away with an enlarged, and perhaps more sympathetic, picture of what (depending on our age) we, or our parents, or our grandparents were and did.

A French philosopher once observed that those who will not learn from the errors of the past are doomed to repeat them. But French philosophers have always had an unfortunate weakness for the clever phrase, the *bon mot*. The truth is that those who do try to learn from the mistakes of the past are probably doomed to invent their own new mistakes. The decent wisdom of *Another Chance* lies in its underlying awareness that those who will not learn from the past are really doomed to be solitary—to think that their times and crises, their lonely rendezvous with their private destinies, are unique. Because he has been able to understand so much of what ordinary Americans felt and experienced a generation ago, Gilbert is able to offer us the most valuable gift of the historian: a grasp of the fact that others have been here before and have passed through their incomplete trials and triumphs with the same stubbornly inconclusive results. Herein lies the fine irony of his title: History, as long as it continues to happen, is always another chance.

R. Jackson Wilson

Preface

The preface to a second edition is a welcome second chance to speculate about the meaning of an historical era. This is particularly a welcome occasion in revising a book that is so close to the present. In the previous edition of this work, I closed the narrative at the end of the 1960s, although I very much had the next decade in mind when I speculated that 1968 ended an important era in American history. I still believe this to be true, but in this edition I have disclosed my reasons by adding two chapters that chronicle the social, economic, and cultural changes in the decade and a half following that decisive year.

Quite briefly, I have argued that the political and social consensus guiding American development after World War II frayed in the late 1960s and 1970s. What emerged was not, of course, completely a new society and culture, but a critical examination of what had been accomplished and a decision to proceed with greater caution. In the future, many of these apparent changes will no doubt seem slighter than they appear today; we will recognize old traditions decked out in today's fashions. Yet, it seems to me that after the war the focus on inequities and the means to change them became sharper. Hence, we had another chance to resolve some of the basic, underlying problems of our society.

Writing from the perspective of the mid-1980s, three fundamental ways to characterize the shifts between eras come to mind. The first suggests that during the 20th century, American politics moved between two polarities that define most national activity. Generally, political movements have swung between an emphasis upon public institutions and then private institutions as the means to approach social and economic problems. The range between these emphases has not always been great, but the choices between them have had great influence on the way people have lived their lives and the nation has solved its problems. Second, there is a curious, almost cyclical lapse of attention paid to fundamental problems in American life. Sometimes the nation has focused upon the very difficult inequities of race, class, and gender. At other times it has not—despite the fact that these problems have not disappeared. Finally, it appears that some epochs have a moral consensus, and others exhibit contention and even moral confusion.

At the cost of great oversimplification, it appears that in the period immediately following World War II, American society achieved a consensus of sorts about using public institutions to change social priorities. After the mid-1960s, however, the impulse weakened, and a different sort of social agenda presented itself. In some respects this has amounted to a retrenchment. But in another sense, events of the very recent past have allowed us to probe the optimisms and apparent accomplishments of the postwar period. Thus there is a necessity to take positions on contemporary issues if only to shed light on the whole period, to see what is changing and what remains static.

Perhaps these propositions add up to nothing more than a suspicion of theories about social progress, but I think not; nor do I believe the alternative. History does not repeat itself so much as it changes more slowly than we imagine. For despite our inattention to it, the history of our culture defines our language, our memory, and our imagination. Perhaps it also defines our future.

Preface to First Edition

Looking back at the immediate past from the perspective of the present, like viewing a length of trail just hiked over, can be disorienting. Only as we move upward and away from the narrow track of the present do its shapes take on meaning, its switch-backs become obvious, and its paths criss-cross into clear patterns. It is, of course, too soon to make definitive judgments, but some of the major turnings in the path through the tangle of contemporary events are becoming clear.

At least two distinct periods can now be distinguished since 1945: one that began in the midst of World War II and extended into the late 1960s and another rather different one since then. This book explores the first, remarkable, postwar period, although it ends with a sketch of some of the forces and energies that have emerged since 1968 and have moved politics, social life, culture, and the economy in new directions.

The most important source of energy in the postwar world was America's undeniable economic success and stability. This achievement created opportunities as well as obligations for action in world affairs. On the domestic front, it offered previously excluded minorities of the American population a wider share in prosperity and the rights of citizenship than they had ever enjoyed. By the end of the 1960s, the United States played a leading role in the revolution of rising expectations at home and abroad—a role that was as uncomfortable as it was exciting.

Extraordinary political stability and continuity during this period underscored domestic confidence that federal and bureaucratic programs could and should be used to solve social problems and reduce inequalities. At the same time, attitudes toward these problems and their solutions changed in the context of a new urban and suburban culture that predominated after the war. Counterbalanced by frequent social and economic crises, economic success and new lifestyles and racial and sexual relationships accelerated the sense of change. Viewed increasingly through the new mass medium of television, culture appeared in a state of rapid and inexorable flux.

It is a challenging task to describe the economic, political, social, and cultural changes of postwar America and do justice to each. The method I have employed is thematic, attempting to demonstrate the relationship of social and cultural change to more commonly discussed subjects of economic and political trends. To this end, I have separated the chronology of presidential administrations from some of the broad social and cultural questions that preoccupied Americans during this period. I have examined these social and cultural topics at length. I have placed them, however, in such a way as to indicate their importance and relevance to political change. The result will be, I hope, a richer and broader picture of society, and one that will reflect some of the subtle tones of American culture during this period.

Many people have generously helped me in one way or another with this book, and I am delighted to acknowledge their assistance. The following persons read all or parts of the work: Herman Belz, George Callcott, Frank Freidel, William Graebner, Nelson Lichtenstein, and Larry Myers. Fellow researchers at the Library of Congress unwittingly helped me temper some of my ideas about the postwar period over lunch and coffee breaks. They include Cindy Aron, Kenneth S. Lynn, Carolyn L. Karcher, Dorothy Ross, and Jon Wakelyn.

I am especially grateful to R. Jackson Wilson, editor of the series of which this book is a part, who first persuaded me to undertake this work and then made the sorts of quiet comments that opened, and sometimes closed, the doors of speculation. Barry Karl gave me encouragement and criticism in exactly the right doses. Editors David Follmer and especially John Sturman offered suggestions. My typist Sue McLaughlin made order out of a chaos of revisions. Finally, I am deeply indebted to the libraries of various federal agencies in Washington, D.C., particularly the U.S. Army, for their help and generosity in supplying photographs.

James Gilbert

Contents

List of Tables

List of Maps

Another Chance

Postwar America, 1945–1985

Prologue
Rising Expectations

In September 1945, *Look* magazine published a photographic essay picturing the distinctive features of American society. Stressing an old theme, the essay disparaged the notion that "the frontier is gone." How foolish to dwell on limitations, it continued, when possibilities opened everywhere. "Here is a partial list of America's new frontiers," it concluded: "the modern house . . . the automatic washer . . . express highways . . . television . . . the private plane . . . quick freezing." Fifteen years later, in his campaign for the presidency, John Kennedy invoked the same idiom of expansion and promise, although he certainly had more in mind than *Look*'s shopping list. If anything, the sense of potential had deepened during the intervening years. Millions of Americans agreed with Kennedy; the decades following years of depression and war had renewed interrupted dreams and added new ambitions. As the *Reader's Digest* predicted in 1945, these were years when Americans had a precious "chance to make a second start."

People in every age probably think of themselves as exceptional—singular in their wisdom and experience and unique in the opportunities they have seized, the risks they have run. Certainly, postwar Americans portrayed themselves in this fashion. This generation took suburban living as its ideal at home and the Cold War as its ideology in foreign policy. It engendered a baby boom and then lived through a youth rebellion, but it was very much shaped by the heritage of the Depression of the 1930s and the unfinished business of World War II. In the marriage of existing American culture to the new world of 1945, the mass media, shifting sexual practices and family arrangements, mobility, and population and political changes were both old and new, with deep roots in the past. Yet, for all the persistence of past problems, the postwar world, more than any previous age, promised to fulfill ideals of American exceptionalism and the American dream. If ever there was a nation which believed in second chances, this was the nation and this was the age.

Age-old problems in race relations and poverty appeared just at the point of solution. The economy no longer rose and plunged in twenty-year waves of calm and storm. Emancipation from customary practices in culture and social life, so fervently predicted since the 1920s, now seemed real. Dread communicable diseases and the maladies of deprivation and malnutrition expired. Liberation, affluence, and technological progress made optimism the natural creed of many Americans.

The reasons for this optimism lie partly in the way the war ended. The United States emerged with the world at its feet. Power accumulated as the nation accelerated its economic and political penetration of developed and underdeveloped societies. In the relative vacuum left by the destruction of Europe, the expansion of the American economic system through links to raw materials producers and markets drew the United States into internationalism on an unprecedented scale. Thereafter, changing definitions of what counted in American survival focused the nation's attention on once obscure and remote places in Asia, Eastern Europe, and South America. The United States became the dominant nation on the planet.

More closely and rationally guided than ever before, the American economy achieved remarkable heights of production and breadth of distribution. Reform programs, social security, and, eventually, in the mid-1960s, subsidized medical care for the elderly softened inequalities and strengthened the purchasing power of all Americans, while contributing a critical element to the gross national product. As the economy shifted to services and consumer jobs, with less blue-collar work, more federal and state regulation, automation of the workplace, and expansion of credit-dependent family economies, Americans redefined their necessities to include what other ages had thought to be luxuries.

During the postwar years, and especially after 1960, American life-styles changed rapidly; indeed, the very term "life-style" signified the fluidity of social mores. The family structure shifted and relaxed. The decline of censorship and the impact of advertising, television, and other media made even private sexual fantasies the subject of mass culture. Toleration for once-repressed sexual practices, for new marital arrangements, for experiments in drug use changed the overt beliefs of many Americans. More important, shifts in the attitudes of blacks, other minorities, and women toward their own rights, and the general acceptance of these claims by the rest of society, allowed a minority of black Americans to enter the middle strata of employment and freed the vast majority from restrictions that had bound them since the beginning of the century. For women, equal pay for equal work became more commonplace.

Politically, these were years of Democratic party hegemony. The ideas, innovations, and coalitions that blossomed out of the arid ground of the 1930s returned, perennially, to ornament the political landscape of the 1950s and 1960s. Despite the interim of Republican presidencies, 1953–1960 and 1969–1976, the fundamental consensus of American politics derived from the practices of executive leadership, federal regulation, and interest-group coalitions developed by the Democratic leadership in the 1930s and 1940s. Even when out of national office, the Democratic party maintained its leading edge in politics by dominating Congress and a majority of state governments.

Viewed from the perspective of 1985, the years from 1945 to the end of the 1960s deserve recognition for their coherence as a period and for their social achievements. Even in the darkest years of the war in Vietnam, when the shouts of critics were loudest, the most ardent dissenters shaped their vision of the good society out of promises made in the recent past.

These almost tangible possibilities of harmony and success certainly did not die in the 1970s, but they did revert to the more familiar—and abstract—guise of aspirations and visions. Suddenly, problems that had existed, albeit obscurely, reemerged with force. The war in Vietnam, the riots in American cities, the weakening of presidential leadership and political parties exposed the underlying limitation of resources and the narrowness of consensus that optimism had once masked. From the time of the second Eisenhower administration in the 1950s, the terrain under American interests and alliances abroad began to shift. As the Soviet Union, Western Europe, and Japan rebuilt and modernized their economies and underdeveloped countries increasingly husbanded their natural resources, the United States saw its relative economic and political power shrink. By the 1970s, competition for markets and raw materials and the diffusion of technology and production created a world in which the United States was preponderant but not unique.

Just as striking was the transformation of American politics. After the election of 1968, political parties had increasing difficulty translating the contradictions of American society into national compromises. The existence of discredited and unpopular leaders in both parties coincided with a decline in shared goals. The growing importance of the media and political polling, on the one hand, emphasized narrowly defined and free-floating single-issue groups and, on the other, contributed to growing apathy and a feeling of remoteness in voters. Ironically, expansion of the means of communication eroded trust in the ability to communicate.

Victories in social reform, as some observers had warned, did not always break the tenacious grasp of old intolerances. The advances and successes in the struggle for equality for all Americans relaxed but could not release the hold of racism and sexism in society. Backlash, timidity, class conflict, as well as deep-seated custom and belief pushed the struggle for equality to a more complex plane. Abolition of segregation did not necessarily mean integration. Sex-divided job opportunities still existed despite the record number of working women. For every wrong corrected, a new puzzle had to be solved, with the rights of others to be adjusted.

During the 1970s, the divisions in society attracted increasing attention. Americans, more conscious of limitations, soberly appraised their society. From the perspective of the mid-1980s, division of the postwar era into two segments became all the more discernible. The strident optimism of the period from 1980 to 1985 rested upon a fragile hope that the unresolved problems of the previous decades would be pushed aside by the hidden hand of prosperity. The focus on private approaches and the insistent demands of the most ideological components of society suggested a nation defined by its peripheral elements and not by its center—the parts never adding up to the whole. It suggested a society divided about goals and uncertain about its future. Nothing in this state of affairs could be more distinct from the period of the first years following World War II, when the course still seemed clear: a generation about to embark on fulfilling its dreams and a nation about to be given a second chance after a decade of depression and four years of war.

1 Shaping the Things to Come

Sitting by the fireside of his Little White House retreat on Pine Mountain, Georgia, on April 12, 1945, President Franklin D. Roosevelt suddenly complained of a terrible headache. Shortly afterward, doctors pronounced him dead. Two hours later, the new President, Harry S Truman, swore the oath of office in Washington. For many Americans, it was hard to imagine a presidency without Roosevelt; he had presided over seven years of depression and five years of war. Hundreds of thousands of citizens lined the streets to watch his funeral cortege pass from Union Station to the White House. A young Texas representative, Lyndon Baines Johnson, interviewed by *The New York Times*, poignantly expressed his anguish: "I don't know that I'd ever have come to Congress if it hadn't been for him." He frankly wondered what would happen without F.D.R. "There are plenty of us left to try to block and run interference, as he had taught us, but the man who carried the ball is gone—gone." Others wondered too. In the Soviet Union, newspapers broke their tradition against placing foreign news on the first page, running a front-page, black-edged photograph of Roosevelt and editorials praising the leader of the nation's staunch ally.

In the springtime of 1945, the United States stood at the threshold of a great military victory. Victory, however, was a fragile trophy in a desperate and turbulent world. Beyond its own shores, America looked over a shattered and disorderly world. The major European powers—even the victors—had lost heavily in casualties, economic facilities, and military hardware. The Soviet Union sustained an awesome 22 to 24 million dead in the war; Germany lost 4.2 million. While France and Italy suffered relatively few casualties, the experience of Fascist regimes in both countries discredited old political institutions and former leaders. Each country emerged from the war in political and emotional confusion; each was torn by elements that supported or opposed a serious economic and political restructuring of its society along socialist lines. Disarray and weakness in the old European colonial powers aided African and Asian nationalists who sought to destroy colonial regimes and build their own independent nation-states.

In this disorderly world, the United States was the exception. Victory represented a triumph of order, planning, and production, not just an expenditure of blood. A Gallup poll, published in early 1945, confirmed this judgment. Only 36 percent of Americans represented admitted that they had made any real sacrifice for the war; and most of this minority mentioned the absence or death of a relative in the armed forces. The great majority replied that they felt no great loss or deprivation.

Despite extravagance, waste, and corruption, America's gross national product increased dramatically, from about $91 billion in 1939 to about $212 billion in 1945. Even the economic and social effects of fielding a huge army while increasing production were contained. Mobilization of a large army meant the transportation, training, and housing of millions of young men away from home. Their withdrawal from factories and farms left jobs to be filled by women, Southern blacks, and retired or very young workers. In general, this shift to a new working population occurred smoothly; federal institutions, like the War Manpower Commission, worked with local governments and industry to recruit and accommodate workers and ease their special problems.

There were many serious disagreements about what to do in the future, but few observers could deny that centralized control, social planning, and massive government stimulation of the economy had pulled the nation out of the Depression of the 1930s. This success, however, raised more questions than it settled. World War II generated a great social and economic experiment, but not everyone agreed on the lessons that had been learned. More important, because of its enormous financial power, the federal government affected every aspect of the economy—even when it refused to act. No one could ignore its future role.

Lack of comprehensive planning worried such figures as Henry Wallace, Vice-President (until 1944) and *bête noire* of conservative Democrats, but a favorite of liberal and labor segments in the Roosevelt political coalition. In his widely read book *The Century of the Common Man* (1943) Wallace wrote that American exceptionalism (the exemption from European-style social revolution) would not last beyond the end of the war. Without "vigorous" government actions, he said, a wave of economic storms would sweep the country: inflation, scarcities, bankruptcy, and possibly "violent revolution." Sounding very much as if he were predicting a crisis like the Great Depression of the 1930s, Wallace was only dramatizing fears shared by some economists, sociologists, and political leaders of the day.

Writing for a conference held in New York on the Scientific Spirit and Democratic Faith, philosopher Jerome Nathanson expressed a more common opinion about planning: "The chief problem of our time is how to plan our economic and social life without sacrificing freedom." This proposition was no mere rhetorical flourish. It went straight to the core of American hesitations about the role of state intervention. Most Americans in 1945 firmly believed in the inevitable antagonism between individualism and democracy, on the one hand, and planning and state activity on the other. The Depression and then the war temporarily suspended this belief, but it remained an overarching assumption.

The experience of the 1930s shaped the anticipations and actions of Americans in all walks of life. Although many people were untouched by the ravages of the Depression, it formed the central feature of the decade's topography. Economic insecurity, breadlines, Hoovervilles, and make-work relief hovered as uncomfortable memories. As late as 1939, official unemployment figures had been extremely high: 9 million or 17 percent of the work force. The Depression had broader effects than such statistics reveal; it disrupted the educational, marital, and child-rearing plans of many young Americans; it abruptly ended careers and forced many ablebodied men and women to question their own abilities and dignity; and it focused both culture and art upon those persistent elements of solidarity and community in the American experience. Most Americans emerged from the Depression with more, not less, faith in traditional institutions like the family. Security, not experimentation, was their aim. Thus a *Fortune* magazine survey of workers taken in 1943 found surprisingly few who would risk job security for an uncertain reward or advancement. Fifty-five percent preferred to keep a low-paying secure job. Only a few would opt for very high pay if the chances of failure were also great. Perhaps as educator James B. Conant wrote in 1940, the experience of the 1930s had shattered "the modern soul" and lowered expectations about the ability of industrial society to bring happiness to its citizens.

Few significant politicians—certainly not Roosevelt—advocated comprehensive government guidance of the economy. Most policymakers, economists, businessmen, and labor unions recognized that some forms of governmental interference in the economy were beneficial and in their own interests. But, they were unsure how far to go in the direction of federal planning. They did not agree about who should do the planning or who should benefit from social programs initiated by the state. Inevitably, government programs that emerged from the war were sometimes contradictory—shocking in their limitations or unprecedentedly generous in their comprehensiveness.

During the war, the federal government established one major planning organization, housed in the executive branch. It had a brief and controversial existence, however. First formed in 1933 as the National Planning Board, F.D.R. reorganized it as the National Resources Planning Board (NRPB) in 1939. Headed by F.D.R.'s uncle, Frederic Delano, the board began comprehensive discussions of the role of government in the postwar economy. In reports, conferences, and interdepartmental policy dinners, members of the Washington board discussed plans for demobilization, public services, social security, and financial and fiscal problems. Their overriding concern was unemployment. On this delicate issue, the Trends and Stabilization Section, directed by economist Paul A. Samuelson, suggested federal action to achieve full employment after the war. Other activities of the NRPB included regional planning conferences for demobilization and reconversion to peacetime production. Preliminary plans were drawn up for such regions as the "Niagara Frontier," Denver Metropolitan area, and the Puget Sound area.

Perhaps the most controversial proposal of the NRPB was its National Production and Employment Budget. This alternative budget was designed to be countercyclical, that is, it had built-in government spending and fiscal management elements triggered to work against the business cycle in order to prevent recessions or runaway booms. Its goal was full employment, but critics could only see it as a flagrant step toward socialism.

While F.D.R. may have approved some of the NRPB's goals, he would not fight to keep it in existence. When Congress voted to eliminate funds for the board in 1943, it rejected not just this body, but the only effective executive branch planning organization. Perhaps this was inevitable, for whatever Roosevelt's sympathies for the NRPB's work, his own style of administration was very different. Where he preferred to improvise and divide authority, planners hoped to anticipate and centralize.

The major bureaucratic agency of economic control during the war was the Office of War Mobilization, created in May 1943 and transformed into the Office of War Mobilization and Reconversion (OWMR) in October 1944. Headed by James F. Byrnes, this superagency coordinated personnel, production, and resource allocation and supervised specific federal agencies concerned directly with the economic war effort. As a central planning bureau, the OWMR might have formed the nucleus for postwar economic coordination, but there was no move to transfer its functions to peacetime. In fact, the major controversy inside the agency related to how quickly the United States economy should be allowed to convert to civilian production. After 1943, several important figures, led by Donald M. Nelson, the chairman of the War Production Board, fought with some success to begin peacetime conversion. From 1943 to August 1944, limited reconversion was allowed in consumer industries, but the serious reverses of the Battle of the Bulge in Belgium during that summer ended this limited experiment. Military planners who demanded full production of war material until the end of the war prevailed. Thus, when the OWMR disbanded in December 1946, no one thought to continue it as an economic planning agency.

Roosevelt's most fully articulated plans for postwar society suggest that he agreed with the goal of a speedy reconversion to private ownership and production and a dismantling of controls. In early 1944, the administration approved the Baruch Plan for Demobilization and Industry Reconversion. Drawn up by industrialist Bernard Baruch, head of the War and Postwar Adjustment Advisory Unit of the War Mobilization Board, the plans dictated speedy termination of government war contracts and quick reconversion to civilian production. They set up standard guidelines to facilitate rapid conversion to consumer production. Removal of price controls and limitations on scarce materials were deferred to the end of the conflict. Nonetheless, it is clear that Roosevelt intended to return the economic initiative to private business as soon as possible.

Congress made one last effort in 1946 to institute some form of federal planning in the Full Employment Bill. Debated in the midst of acrimonious strikes and intensifying difficulties abroad, the bill was eventually gutted of its mandatory investment features. When signed on February 20, 1946 by President Truman, the law had a less ambitious title, the Employment Law. It dropped specific reference to a National Production and Employment Budget, but it did commit the federal government to the goal of full employment, and it established a Presidential Council of Economic Advisers and a Congressional Joint Committee on the Economic Report. It required the President in conjunction with the advisers to issue an annual report on the economy. Thus, it retained the outlines of planning without specific powers. The federal government committed itself in theory to intervene actively in the economy, but that commitment remained fuzzy, ill-defined, and controversial.

This did not mean that the federal government took no role in the economy; on the contrary, its power grew throughout the next four decades. Up to the mid-1970s a growing number of key government advisers and economists accepted the basic tenets of Keynesian economics (named after the British economist John Maynard Keynes). Keynes had argued that in order to control growth and prevent depressions, the national government should intervene in the economy to maintain total demand for goods and services. Through taxation and deficit spending, the government could encourage overall investment, or it could dampen growth. Even when Keynes's ideas were eclipsed in the late 1970s by monetary theories, the basic commitment remained the same: Government must set and regulate the economic environment.

Despite congressional conservatism on the issue of comprehensive planning, Capitol Hill anticipated increased federal economic activity after the war. In the spring of 1943, the Senate considered several bills to prepare demobilization and postwar economic plans. An initiative proposed by Senator Walter F. George, of Georgia, passed the Senate in March 1943, establishing a Special Committee on Postwar Economic Policy and Planning.

Chaired by George, the committee investigated a number of anticipated postwar problems, such as troop demobilization, reconversion of war production, unemployment, highway development, postwar taxation, and housing and urban redevelopment. One of its most far-reaching suggestions came from its special housing subcommittee chaired by the conservative Republican Senator Robert A. Taft. Taft, working with the Banking, Education, and Labor Committees of the Senate, held hearings from June 1944 to February 1945, in which he called for a national commitment to good housing as "essential to a sound and stable democracy." Taft and his committee proposed federal commitment to slum clearance and rehousing. At least 6 million new housing units were required, and some of them would have to be public housing. Thus the Senate, in such hearings, prefigured several of the important social and economic programs undertaken later during the Truman administration.

One major reason for federal inertia in postwar economic planning was the attitude of organized labor and business groups. Organized labor was surprisingly quiet on the issues of postwar planning. Although congressional friends of labor often stood in the forefront of planning efforts, neither the AF of L nor the CIO evidenced much direct interest in the issue until 1943. By then, the AF of L had appointed a special postwar planning committee headed by Matthew Woll; the CIO was still, at this late date, only preparing to establish such a committee. Both committees did suggest minimal national planning, but the real interests of unions lay elsewhere. Labor preferred to preserve the gains made in collective bargaining and membership under the New Deal and especially during the war, rather than to embark on ambitious new programs.

American business leaders had mixed feelings about postwar planning. While these leaders adopted important internal measures of corporate planning largely unknown before the war (General Electric, for example, directed each of its departments to plan future employment and production needs), business leaders continued to be hostile to most federal planning. Business wished to anticipate future needs, and it was willing to let government take steps to protect the economy, but, by and large, its attitudes toward central planning were antagonistic.

During 1942 and 1943, in conferences, articles, and speeches, business leaders focused on postwar problems. The most pressing of these, they urged, would be dismantling government ownership and direction of war production, elimination of controls, prevention of unemployment, and reconversion. The National Association of Manufacturers (NAM), one of the most powerful American business organizations, held two War Congresses of American Industry in 1942 and 1943. At the first of these, it adopted a War Program of American Industry, outlining wartime goals and establishing a kind of Atlantic Charter for American business. Among its several points, the NAM proposed something for every class: a prosperous agriculture, employment in free enterprise for all who could work, a higher standard of living, and the right of small operators to go into business for themselves. The principal axiom, however, was undoubtedly the second, pledging salaries and profits to all "commensurate with their performance and usefulness to society." The NAM, in other words, promised a more efficient and better operating private economy.

At the same conference, Henry J. Kaiser, president of the Kaiser Aluminum Company, outlined social goals for American industry once the war ended. He estimated that 9 million new housing units would be required immediately after the war. To meet an anticipated increase in automobile transportation, he argued for a huge new highway system. Finally, he urged private business to help promote adequate medical care for every citizen. To achieve these goals, he suggested that automakers prepare 1945 models, that construction lobbyists begin a crusade for a modern "turnpike" system, and that the medical profession push private insurance systems to head off state or socialized medicine.

Kaiser's remarks suggest the degree to which business had successfully adopted market research and planning. The astute discussions sponsored by the NAM in 1942 and 1943 reveal foresight about the shape of postwar society and accuracy in identifying the leading sectors of development—highways, automobiles, housing and health care—that would fuel the postwar boom. Other organizations, like the American Chamber of Commerce, cautiously predicted a postwar boom once controls were abandoned. In 1943, the Chamber of Commerce urged industry to plan for investment and production so that both industry and government could avoid the disastrous rollercoaster boom and depression following World War I. Pent-up demand, availability of investment capital, and conversion to the use of new materials in manufacture would prevent economic dislocations.

☆   ☆   ☆

Beyond organizing and directing the wartime economy, the federal government profoundly affected the lives and salaries of millions of Americans. Federal policy had its greatest postwar impact on Americans in the labor force rather than on the direction of the economy. The draft of millions of soldiers in an economy reaching full production seriously depleted the white, male industrial working class. By necessity, federal policy altered the makeup of the industrial labor force and touched off a massive migration of families from South to North, from East to West, and from rural areas to cities. As with the issue of economic planning, the *fait accompli* of wartime labor policy became the center of controversy:

Could the changes of the war be undone? To what extent, after the war, should returning soldiers be given their old positions or preference in new places? What should be done with the millions of new black and female workers? In this area, federal policy, while it ignored some serious problems, underwent extensive discussion. Never before or since has the government intervened so seriously and successfully in the lives of Americans.

Recruiting women workers on the "Home Front" was a major task undertaken by the federal government. The actual numbers of women who entered nontraditional jobs can be overestimated, but the response to the call was striking. Campaigns directed at women urged them into new and high-paying jobs in shipbuilding and aircraft and munitions manufacture. Women answered the call of patriotic duty and the lure of high wages. Approximately 5 million new women workers joined the labor force from 1941 to 1945.

By 1942, about one of every three workers was female; during the next year, the figure rose to 36 percent. Women chose various sorts of work, from the "Woman's Land Army," organized to replace depleted farm labor, to defense work. By 1944, 1.25 million or about one-half of all employees in the aircraft industry were women. A good many of them labored at the intricate work of assembling B-29 bombers, the mainstay of the U.S. Air Force. Others took up welding and metallurgical work in shipbuilding. Black women, in particular, were concentrated in the ordnance industry, making small arms and ammunition. As a pamphlet published by the War Department summarized: "A woman is a substitute—like plastic instead of a metal. She has special characteristics that lend themselves to new and sometimes to such superior uses."

By the end of the war, many women refused to see themselves as substitutes. In 1946, a survey by the Federal Women's Bureau of women workers in ten major war production areas revealed that most female workers hoped to stay on the job, even after the troops came home. About 75 percent of the interviewees intended to continue working, and, of these, about 86 percent wanted to retain their current positions. They had made an indelible mark on the workplace, and only a concentrated drive could eliminate them. Factory buildings had been altered to accommodate women workers: extra restroom facilities, cafeterias, lightweight machine tools, and other special equipment, including plastic jigs, long-handled levers, and weight-lifting devices, had been adopted. In local communities, over 3,000 child-care centers were established to supervise the children of working women.

A Symington-Gould sand slinger at rest, Buffalo, New York, May 1943. Because of the serious labor shortage during the war, women moved into nontraditional jobs in heavy industry and manufacturing, where they found higher wages and often gained new self-confidence and independence. (Library of Congress, photo by Marjorie Collins)

The massive entrance of women into industrial employment and the positive publicity given to their efforts had other effects outside the factory. For one thing, their presence created a highly skilled labor pool: over 2 million women enrolled in some form of vocational training during the war. The public commitment to "womanpower" also raised broader issues of women's rights. Equality of pay and working conditions did not always accompany women into the workplace. Unions like the AF of L enlisted new women members "for the duration only." Some locals even kept separate seniority lists for men and women. Hostility between male and female workers sometimes flared, particularly when the latter first entered an industry. Some companies, like General Electric and Westinghouse, established "women's rates" that pegged pay below the prevailing wage for males doing the same work.

Unequal treatment led to a campaign to secure justice for women. The Republicans in 1940 and the Democrats in 1944 supported an Equal Rights Amendment to the Constitution in their campaign platforms, but support lagged in two important quarters. Both the CIO and the AF of L opposed such an amendment, and the two most powerful female political figures, Eleanor Roosevelt and Frances Perkins, the Secretary of Labor, refused to support it.

On another front, strong support developed in 1945 to empower the Federal Women's Bureau to investigate sex discrimination in employment. This suggested "Federal Wage Discrimination Act" of 1945, introduced by Senator Wayne Morse, of Oregon, and Senator Claude Pepper, of Florida, enjoyed substantial backing from women's groups, the CIO, and even the conservative Republican Senator Robert A. Taft, of Ohio. The proposed act, which tried to balance the interests of women and the "reemployment rights of returned veterans," failed to pass. Although the War Labor Board issued guidelines for equal pay for equal work in 1945, the failures of the Equal Rights Amendment and the Wage Discrimination Act were handwriting on the shop wall for women employees.

By the last months of the war, Secretary of Labor Perkins seemed more worried about potential GI unemployment than the rights of women workers. She suggested that workers over sixty-five and under twenty be encouraged to retire and that women who entered the job market only because of the war should leave the work force voluntarily. The War Manpower Commission assumed that women would retire, proposing that "the separation of women from industry should follow an orderly plan." At the same time, the Commission warned employers that some women needed work. William H. Stead, the Dean of the Washington University Business School, expressed what was probably a more typical viewpoint. The major postwar employment problem, he wrote, would be to get rid of temporary workers. If two-thirds of them were removed, it would be a "tremendous" achievement.

Black workers constituted another group viewed as temporary, and therefore a problem for postwar conversion. The discriminations and restrictions faced by black workers were both similar to and different from those of white women. As in World War I, employment opportunities and labor shortages in the industrial areas of the North and West compelled a strong migration of black men and women from the South. Their movement was not accomplished without bitterness and dispute. Finding large areas of employment closed and extensive wage and skills discrimination on the job, black leaders challenged the Roosevelt administration in early 1941 to act to ensure fair treatment. A. Philip Randolph, head of the Brotherhood of Sleeping Car Porters, a powerful black trade union, and Walter White of the NAACP, threatened a demonstration in Washington to highlight the plight of black workers. In the face of this potential embarrassment, President Roosevelt issued Executive Order #8802 on June 25, 1941, creating a Fair Employment Practices Committee (FEPC) designed to enforce the pledges of equal treatment given in the Executive Order. Henceforth, any company engaged in defense production would be required to hire without regard to race, creed, color, or national origin.

Roosevelt's initiative had immediate effect. In September 1941, Lockheed Aircraft, which employed 40,000 workers, hired its first black employees. Black workers, hearing of opportunities, streamed northward to cities like Chicago and Detroit, where in some cases they had been actively recruited by the federal government. In Detroit, trouble broke out between white and black defense workers. Acrimony turned to riot in early 1942 with white opposition to black occupancy of a specially constructed housing development. Occasional wildcat strikes erupted, until, in June 1943, isolated incidents burst into a full-scale race war. In three days of battle, thirty-four persons died, hundreds were injured, until federal troops restored order. In August of the same year, frustrations again boiled over into violence, this time in Harlem.

After a day of rioting, six persons had died and over 300 were injured in an angry protest over poor living conditions and the slow progress in racial equality.

Incidents such as these, plus the rumored existence of "Eleanor Clubs," named after Eleanor Roosevelt and purported to be groups of black domestics planning to strike the kitchens of white employers, persuaded F.D.R. to consider further actions to defuse racial tension. He explored, then rejected, the creation of a Commission on Race Relations. Thus, the most strenuous wartime activity on behalf of blacks remained the FEPC. And even this body was attacked in Congress in 1944. By the end of the war, with Roosevelt dead, the new President, Truman, issued Executive Order #9664 on December 20, 1945, which removed the power of the FEPC and transformed it into an advisory body. It was finally dissolved in June 1946.

This faltering federal commitment to the rights of black Americans came at a particularly difficult time for them. Returning black GIs demanded the right to vote in the deep-South states of Mississippi, Alabama, and Georgia, where a variety of legal subterfuges deprived them of the suffrage. Racial tension after demobilization increased rapidly, and white backlash precipitated local revivals of the Ku Klux Klan. Incidents abounded, particularly one in Columbia, Tennessee, where the Klan, with the complicity of local law enforcement officials, terrorized the local black community. When the smoke cleared, twenty-eight blacks had been arrested and two killed.

Incidents such as these led to the creation of the National Emergency Committee Against Mob Violence headed by Eleanor Roosevelt and Dr. Channing Tobias. Pressure from this group, plus loss of control of Congress to the Republicans in November 1946, convinced President Truman to act. On December 5, 1946, under executive order, he created a Presidential Civil Rights Committee designed to explore the problems of black Americans and to suggest remedial legislative programs. Like many other pressing internal social problems, the need to correct century-long injustices to black Americans got caught in the whirligig of demobilization. Such problems took second place to presidential and congressional preoccupation with dismantling regulations and controls over the private economy. Only when political pressure built up to the bursting point did significant action occur.

One group, however, emerged from the war with a grant of privileges and advantages practically unheard of in American history. In its case, federal planning was extensive, comprehensive, and favorable. Memories of the Depression and the troubled demobilization of 1919 focused attention on returning GIs. The American government had traditionally rewarded soldiers with cash bonuses, and sentiment ran strongly in favor of some monetary reward for World War II veterans. Many Americans felt that the sacrifice of several years' service placed returning soldiers in a poor competitive position: They had lost seniority on the job and missed crucial years in school or apprenticeship training. Possibilities of renewed depression added further worries. If returning GIs attempted to reenter the labor market simultaneously, the United States risked massive unemployment.

Planning for a GI bill was foreshadowed in the Selective Service Act of 1940, which contained a reemployment provision committing the federal government to aid returning soldiers seeking employment. Administration planners quickly realized the immensity of this commitment. They estimated that by 1945, about one-quarter of the work force would be demobilized veterans. Pressure to pass what became the Servicemen's Readjustment Act came from many quarters. More than 600 bills relating to returning GIs were introduced into the Congress during the war years. Citizen groups, particularly the American Legion, organized support for liberal grants of financial and educational benefits.

Roosevelt lent his support to this aspect of planning for the future. At first, he turned to the National Resources Planning Board to direct work on a GI bill. This body, in turn, set up a Postwar Manpower Conference incorporating representatives from educational, defense, and organized labor establishments. Their resulting recommendations favored subsidized education to compensate for time spent in the armed forces. Written with the aim of preventing postwar unemployment, the conference report revealed both the worries and the expectations of the Roosevelt administration.

At the same time, Roosevelt also created an Armed Forces Committee on Postwar Educational Opportunities, known as the Osborn Committee, after its chairman Brigadier General Frederick H. Osborn. This committee, consisting also of General Lewis Hershey of the Selective Service, of officials from the army, navy, and U.S. Office of Education, and of leading educators, published recommendations in 1943 that became the basis for the administration's bill, introduced in November by Senator Elbert

Thomas, of Utah. After a good deal of debate and effective lobbying for increased benefits by the American Legion, the Servicemen's Readjustment Act, also known as the Veterans Act or the GI Bill, was passed and signed into law on June 22, 1944.

The Veterans Act worked a revolution in American society that became increasingly obvious with the passage of time. Its effects were probably unanticipated, but GI educational grants, home and business loans, and employment preferences touched off the immense expansion of higher education that followed the war, helped to subsidize the building of suburbia, and aided thousands of young men in local and federal government careers. The GI Bill encouraged a generation to view privilege as its right, giving returning soldiers a competitive edge in education and employment that deeply affected the relative status of women and black Americans. Their advantage operated for two crucial reasons. While a few hundred thousand women in the armed services were eligible to use veterans' privileges, this number represented only a tiny percentage of American women. The opportunities for returning black GIs were theoretically more favorable, but in practice, black GIs had restricted opportunities because of continued segregation in private and state-funded colleges and universities, discrimination in state and federal hiring, and limited access to VA-approved housing because of restricted covenants widely adhered to by real estate interests and enforced by the courts during the 1940s.

The rationale for the World War II GI Bill registered worries about potential depression, but its generous provisions indicate the popularity of World War II. (The Korean War GI Bill and the Cold War GI Bill were far less generous.) The best publicized portion of the act, Title 2, dealt with higher education. Originally, the law provided that veterans under twenty-five at the day of entry into military service, who remained for ninety days or more, would receive one year's subsidized education. Two years' service earned three years of schooling. All tuition fees would be paid to the college chosen by the veteran, plus a monthly subsistence of $50 for single and $75 for married GIs.

Although some educators from elite universities like Harvard and the University of Chicago worried over the potential harm of admitting a flood of returning soldiers, most colleges and universities welcomed the additional enrollment and financing brought by their new students. Pressure on better public institutions mounted; Rutgers University in New Jersey, for example, enrolled more than twice as many students (many of them GIs) in 1948 as in 1939. New York, lacking a comprehensive state educational system, suffered serious overcrowding. In 1945, Republican Governor Thomas E. Dewey and the Democratic party both advocated a new university system. The resulting system—the State University of New York (SUNY)—developed after 1948 into one of the largest, most extensive, and best-funded systems of undergraduate, graduate, and professional training in the nation. By 1947–1948, the Veterans Administration was paying the bills for almost 50 percent of the male students in institutions of higher learning. In all, some 2,232,000 veterans attended college under the first GI Bill.

Returning soldiers, who traded in their uniforms for an academic mortarboard, changed campus life. As an older generation of students, almost half of them were married. Housing was a severe problem, and temporary "vetsvilles" mushroomed around state universities. In these communities, veterans developed a subculture of food co-ops, nursery schools, and wives' organizations. For the returning soldier, classroom offerings were often inappropriate; worse still, *in loco parentis* rules designating dating customs, hours outside dormitories, and dress codes seemed onerous or silly. As a result, many schools revised curriculum offerings and eliminated some of the more restrictive social codes.

Despite inevitable cases of graft and inefficiency, the educational provisions of the GI Bill were a huge success. Thousands of young men, who might otherwise have settled immediately into industrial jobs, attended colleges and universities. Beyond the expectations of most experts, GIs did well in schools, thereby adding to those forces pushing for democratization and expansion of higher education. Federal largesse to universities became a major staple in educational planning. By 1962, because of the additional Korean GI Bill passed in 1952, colleges and universities had received over 5 billion dollars in tuition contributions, and veterans had received over 10 billion in subsistence allowances. Simultaneous grants from state programs for veterans enlarged the opportunities of the returning GIs. State governments, such as that of Wisconsin, replicated federal spending in providing additional scholarships and subsistence programs for vets.

Part of the Servicemen's Readjustment Act set up a GI loan system. Administered by the Veterans Administration, a large fund was available to GIs for mortgage and business loan credits.

With little or no down payment, veterans could purchase homes using a VA loan for down payment. Originally limited to $2,000 or 50 percent of the total loan, veterans' credit for home mortgages was frequently revised upward to keep up with inflation and changes in the housing market. Business and farm loans were also available through the VA.

By 1961, the annual report of the Veterans Administration recorded a total of 6 million loans (5.6 million for housing under the World War II and Korean War GI Bills). This government generosity stimulated private home ownership. By 1961, over 60 percent of all American families owned their own homes compared to only 44 percent in 1940; GI loans had undoubtedly been a key factor. Of 33 million owner-occupied dwellings in 1961, one out of every six had been financed by VA loans. And, during the 1950s, one out of every five new housing units was purchased with VA help.

A further advantage given to veterans came in preferential hiring in federal and state civil service jobs. This custom of granting "veterans' preference" dated back to the World War I demobilization, but the practice after World War II was more extensive. As a result of joint work by veterans' organizations and the Federal Civil Service Commission, a Veterans' Preference Act was passed in 1944, voted unanimously by the Senate with only one dissenting vote in the House. The act applied to all federal executive branch positions, permanent or temporary. In civil service examinations, veterans would receive five extra points on their scores. Disabled veterans and certain wives, widows, or mothers of disabled or deceased veterans would receive ten points. In addition, the law established a "rule of three." In choosing from a list of three finalists for a position, the selecting official could only pass over a veteran with permission from the Civil Service Commission. In making job cutbacks, veterans were to be retained over nonveterans.

State governments followed suit. California and Kansas awarded ten and fifteen points respectively to state civil service scores of veterans. Others, such as New York and Iowa, gave veterans preference in promotion, and New Jersey exempted decorated veterans from appointment and promotion competitions. Even labor unions promised reinstatement of former members with accumulated seniority for years spent in the armed services. And the Ford Motor Company set up Camp Legion at Dearborn, Michigan, for occupational rehabilitation, medical treatment, and job training for handicapped veterans.

Programs for demobilized GIs more than answered the gravest fears of American policymakers about the possible return of economic depression. The GI Bill poured millions of dollars into training and education, contributed to the promotion of private home ownership, and granted preferential hiring for government positions. By the mid 1960s, expenditures for veterans, including hospital and disablement pay, constituted the fifth largest item of the federal budget. Millions of Americans were touched in some fashion by these programs—as much as half of the population. Veterans' organizations, like the American Legion, the Veterans of Foreign Wars (VFW), Disabled American Veterans, exercised powerful lobbies in Washington. Because, by 1959, more than 50 percent of the federal work force was veterans, a good deal of bureaucratic sympathy for continuing programs operated inside of government. By the end of the 1960s, VA reports demonstrated the effects of such programs. Even for males of equal education, income levels of veterans were significantly higher.

Male Income by Education Level: 1971

Education level	Veterans	Nonveterans
Less than high school	$ 5,700	$3,740
Some high school	7,810	6,070
High school graduate	8,740	7,470
Some college	9,610	5,940*
College graduate	13,610	9,720

*Many still attending.
Source: Administrator of Veterans Affairs, Annual Report (1971), p. 3.

☆　　　　　☆　　　　　☆

Despite extensive attention to the problems of veterans and serious thought given to the problem of a possible return to economic depression, the United States did not end the war with a clear vision of social policy. Unity had been achieved, as Kate Smith's phenomenally successful war-bond radio drive revealed in September 1943. Broadcasting for hours without break, Smith begged, threatened, and harmonized her vast radio audience into purchasing bonds. But unity for victory did not mean consensus about the future. Americans still thought very much in terms of the 1930s; haunted by a fear of depression, they still viewed big government as a temporary fixture. Few could even begin to predict the effects of the war on American society. Still children of unemployment and insecurity, Americans in 1945 were largely unaware of the extent to which their lives had been put on a different course by four years of world conflict. As late as 1946, a *Fortune* magazine survey of 1,500 business leaders found that a large majority believed a major depression with large-scale unemployment would recur within the next ten years. The face of society had yet to reflect the prosperity and mobility generated by the war. America and Americans looked very much like it and they had in the early 1930s. Indeed, through 1946 the image of war continued to dominate America's leading pictoral journals, such as *Life* magazine.

Automobiles and railroads still dominated travel inside the United States. The number of civilian aircraft passengers increased rapidly after the war to approximately 12 million per year in 1946 and 1947. But the boom in building aircraft, in increasing average speeds, in upgrading landing and airport facilities, and in transferring freight from ground to air carriers did not occur until the later 1940s and early 1950s.

Patterns of energy consumption during and immediately after the war changed rapidly, although in 1945, the United States remained a coal-dependent society. In 1940, coal provided 52 percent of the nation's energy, with oil, natural gas, and electricity supplying smaller percentages. During and after the war, relative production of coal fell, and consumption from other sources rapidly increased, so that by 1950, oil and natural gas clearly dominated power sources. Coal declined in use in electrical generating: transportation carriers that burned gasoline and oil proliferated; railroads converted to diesel power; and home heating converted to oil and gas. At the same time, per capita expenditure of energy accelerated, primarily because of the boom in automobile use. Still a society dependent upon traditional sources of energy in 1945, the United States in a few years converted to seemingly clean-burning and limitless sources of fossil fuels. Few could anticipate the future price tag of pollution in the nation and political turmoil in the Middle East that this transformation would exact.

In 1945, the United States was still primarily a nation of makers and movers, not of sellers and bureaucrats. It stood on the verge of transformation into a society that consumed goods and information at a rate that would stagger the imagination of the frugal Depression decade. Work in manufacturing, .transportation, and mining continued to dominate the economy, but job offerings in these fields increased only marginally after the war. In the case of mining, the number of jobs fell in subsequent decades. The greatest new job opportunities appeared in wholesale and retail work, in state and local government (where employment in twenty-five years more than tripled), in construction, and in finance and insurance.

The geographic distribution of the American population also began a rapid transition in 1945. The Northeast and north central sections of the country still dominated the cultural, economic, and political life of the nation. Large manufacturing cities of the East and Midwest, in turn, dominated these regions. Most of the national political debates centered on traditional battles between urban, ethnic coalitions and disproportionately powerful rural or upstate areas. Although the solid South was the political tail that frequently wagged the Democratic donkey, the financial power associated with New York, Chicago, Cleveland, and other traditional business centers continued to direct the American economy.

Nonetheless, shifts in population, first apparent in the 1920s, became particularly clear after the war. While all regions of the nation experienced growth after 1945, the South and particularly the West greatly increased in population. Population in the West, for example, increased by 40 percent from 1940 to 1950, while the old Northeast gained only about 10 percent. In part, this change resulted from war dislocations—the positioning of military installations and industries in the warmer climates of the South and West made easier by the rapid adoption of home, office, and industrial air conditioning after the war. Perhaps it was also the traditional lure of the West (California always shows up as the place Americans would prefer to live). Possibly it was a combination of all these things. But its one certain effect was the diminished power and importance of the industrial East.

While Americans began to live in new places, they also lived longer. The year 1945 marked the midpoint in a decade of one of the greatest advances in average life expectancy of most Americans. In 1940, the average expectancy for males was about 61 years; for women it was 65. In 1950, this rose to 65.5 years for men and 71 years for women. For black Americans, figures were significantly lower, 51 and 55 in 1940, and 59 and 63 in 1950, although these figures too improved during the period. This increase in longevity touched off important life-cycle changes. For all populations, it meant that large numbers of adults would survive beyond the age of active work into retirement. Although the war intervened to disguise the impact of this increasing longevity, its unexpected effects began to register later in the decade. One reason for increased longevity was the rapid improvement of medicine during the war. Delivery of medical care and drug discoveries revolutionized the treatment of diseases. By World War II, most, if not all, nutritional diseases were under control. After 1945, for example, pellagra and beriberi were no longer a serious threat to life except in isolated pockets of the country. The properties of certain antibiotics like penicillin had been known to scientists before the war, but medical research and production of such wonder drugs increased rapidly after 1941. In 1942, there was barely enough penicillin manufactured in the United States to treat 100 patients. By late 1943, enough existed to supply all of the Allied armies. During the war, production of streptomycin, first isolated in 1943, also began. By 1945, this drug proved successful in treating cases of tuberculosis and other perennial killers.

Part of this medical success story can be attributed to the entrance of the federal government into research and the diffusion of medical technology. The American armed forces, for example, immunized and treated millions of American men and provided rudimentary instruction in hygiene and the prevention of certain maladies like venereal disease. Federal financing of primary research increased rapidly after the war with reorganization of the National Institutes of Health in 1948 and the National Institute of Mental Health in 1949. Delivery of health care was increasingly shouldered by the federal government after passage of the 1946 Hill-Burton Act, which provided funds for the construction of hospitals—facilities that, unfortunately, remained racially segregated until 1964.

Beyond funding and research, the federal government also extended its record-keeping facilities relating to disease control. The Center for Disease Control in Atlanta, Georgia, took on the task of monitoring the progress and incidence of infectious diseases. Originally called the Communicable Disease Center when it was created in July, 1946, the institution had grown out of a World War II agency specializing in malaria control.

American medicine during and after the war had to treat dis-

abled soldiers. A large number of the patients in VA hospitals after
the war were confined for psychiatric disorders—estimates of these
run as high as 60 percent. With the need to care for such persons,
federal agencies dramatically increased spending for research on
problems of mental health. For example, only 2.5 million dollars
were spent on research into psychiatry in 1946. By 1947, 27 million were being expended for the same purposes. Facilities for
mental patients also rapidly increased; in fact, about 80 percent of
all existing psychiatric units in general hospitals were constructed
after the war.

Inevitably, during the 1950s and 1960s, American attitudes toward life and death changed under the impact of the medical
revolution begun in the war. Wonder drugs, new vaccinations
against such diseases as infantile paralysis, and better general
health care and delivery systems helped to prolong life. Ironically,
however, along with new technologies to cure patients, the waste
products of industrial society increasingly took their toll in human-
induced diseases such as cancer. Liberated from certain traditional
killers, Americans found themselves faced with new diseases in
epidemic proportions.

    ☆   ☆   ☆

While American society in 1945 physically resembled a hard-
working, manufacturing and industrial society, whose most serious
problems were periodic, capitalist depressions, the war unleashed
forces that were incomprehensible to the prewar world. In three
domestic areas—technology and communications, the articulation
of new social goals, and the aggrandizement of federal institutions—Americans had to face challenges more serious than demobilization or reconversion to consumer production. Undoubtedly, most Americans wanted to return to what they imagined had
been the security and good life of the past. This was both impossible and a deceptive aspiration. The war laid the foundations for a
new stage of social development for which old solutions had little
relevance.

Postwar society—even the shape and uses of consumer items—
reflected the technological triumphs of World War II production.
The civilian application of wartime discoveries often had to await
the end of hostilities; nonetheless, new materials and new energy
sources and communication systems designed to help defeat the
Axis powers revolutionized peacetime production.

The most important new material developed during the war was plastic. Derived from a variety of sources, plastics had long been used for ornamental objects, like combs and billiard balls. New fabrics like nylon first appeared in 1938, and scientists created clear vinyl plastics in the 1930s. However, their wide application as practical substitutes for metal, wood, and rubber was stimulated by wartime shortages of traditional materials and by demands for lighter, but strong and flexible objects. The United States military forces used a wide variety of objects, from synthetic rubber to foamed-plastic bubbles used in submarine buoys to Teflon, Saran, and styrenes. Thus, when Edward Stettinius, Jr., Priorities Director for the Federal Government, and later, Secretary of State, ordered the substitution of plastics for strategic materials in 1941, he was helping to determine the shape of postwar production. By the end of the war, civilian industries were well under way in planning to use plastic substitutes for metals. In 1945, Henry Ford dramatically made this point for the press when he wielded an ax against a plastic experimental car to demonstrate its toughness and resilience.

A new source of energy developed during the war also had wide potential for application. Although its immediate purpose was military, research on a controlled splitting of the uranium atom was kept secret from Vice-President Truman and America's allies, the Russians. Scientists scattered across the United States worked on isolated aspects of harnessing atomic power. Officially called the Manhattan Project and tightly run by Washington bureaucrats, the program successfully achieved a self-sustaining nuclear chain reaction in the laboratory at Stagg Field at the University of Chicago on December 12, 1942. Completion of a workable bomb took two-and-a-half more years; the peacetime application of atomic energy to power generation awaited the 1950s. But the atomic age was born during the war beneath this unused football field.

War also accelerated the invention of new information-retrieval instruments. The war exaggerated the need to compute rapidly, to store and recall information, and to solve complicated mathematical problems. Although work on mechanical calculation began before World War II, several technological breakthroughs occurred after 1939. The binary digit—the basis of computer language—was developed in the 1930s. International Business Machines Corporation (IBM) secured important bookkeeping contracts during the 1930s, including keeping the records of the Social Security Sys-

The ENIAC computer, developed in 1946. This first large electronic digital computer had 18,000 vacuum tubes and used 140,000 watts of electricity. It used punched cards and plugged wires like those on a telephone switchboard. A quarter-inch computer chip today has far more capacity than the original ENIAC. (*Smithsonian Institution*)

tem. During the war, it extended its government operations, working on such defense projects as building a code-breaking machine. By 1944, IBM created its first Automatic Sequence Controlled Calculator, the Mark I, a huge, complicated machine with 500 miles of wires. Only four years later, the company marketed its first commercial electronic computer. The proliferation of information devices and their miniaturization quickly followed, burgeoning into one of the most important postwar industries.

☆   ☆   ☆

By most measures, Americans were unprepared to face the world taking shape during the war in the laboratories and production lines of industry and around the conference tables of the federal government. At best, most people hoped that the terrifying, swerving world of the 1930s would end in a smooth, safe ride into prosperity.

In some respects they were right. Worry about a return to depression was inappropriate after World War II. Despite a flurry of predictions in popular magazines like *Time* and *Life*, the Depression did not recur. Pent-up demand in the form of wartime savings overwhelmed a consumer market shrunken by scarcities. Wage earners, who had saved their salaries because of rationing of consumer goods during the war, bought and ordered goods much faster than they could be produced. For the immediate postwar period, the greatest problems were lagging production and inflation.

Polls taken in 1945 gave no indication of the social and moral convulsions in store for American society. For example, George Gallup estimated that a majority of Americans desired no serious change in the social order once the war ended. Yet, change characterized the new postwar world. A few significant observers saw beyond the status quo when they looked out across American society. They were anything but pleased with the rush to demobilize and reconvert and its attendant emphasis upon restoring traditional values. To the Swedish sociologist and economist Gunnar Myrdal America was approaching an abrupt turning point where the problem of solving racial discrimination could no longer be postponed. This was the hypothesis of his widely discussed work *The American Dilemma*. Undertaken in 1938 with financing by the Carnegie Foundation, Myrdal's study, published in 1944, described a yawning disparity between the promise of American ideals and the experience of black citizens. This, Myrdal wrote, constituted an intolerable burden that must be cast off. Perhaps better than he knew, Myrdal warned that America had developed a defeatist attitude toward social legislation and attempts to improve society through planning and conscious direction. The nation, he wrote in 1944, suffered from "moral overstrain."

Perhaps Myrdal was right about the exhaustion of reform efforts and planning, but this did not mean that Americans were afraid or pessimistic about the future. Writing in 1941 for his publication *Life* magazine, Henry Luce had proclaimed the advent of the "American Century." Viewed from America's shores, the rest of the world lay in ruin. But the world in disarray meant opportunity, not danger, to Luce. Living passionately by its ideals, he advised the United States to feed the world and ply it with the tools of modern technology. The World War remained a world problem, but the solution to world problems belonged to America. There was little need to transform America: We must undertake to be "the Good Samaritan of the entire world."

John Hersey wove the same advice into his bestselling novel of 1944, *A Bell for Adano*. The story focused on Major Victor Jopollo, the American military commander of the small Italian town of Adano. Administering American-style justice in the confused aftermath of Fascism, Joppolo also carefully observed local customs. Although removed by a capricious superior, the commander "represented in miniature what America can and cannot do in Europe." For Hersey, the potential for generosity and optimism hung in the balance. Would America be able to offer the war-weary world the care and good humor of its Major Joppolos?

2 A Spoiled Victory

On November 5, Vice-President-elect Harry Truman rushed an enthusiastic telegram to Franklin Delano Roosevelt, his running mate on the Democratic ticket of 1944: "I am very happy over the overwhelming endorsement which you received. Isolationism is dead. Hope to see you soon." Truman was right, if premature. The anxious vigilance of the 1930s was disappearing with every casualty on the beaches of the Pacific Islands, and with every death in European foxholes. It receded a little more at every Allied conference, lost force because of every joint military communiqué and operation, and dimmed after every Voice of America newscast proclaiming America's intention to create a new peaceful world order. Roosevelt had successfully set national policy on a course of internationalism, although it would be several years before this was fully apparent.

As for Truman's veiled request to see the President, nothing much would come of it. F.D.R. brushed off his enthusiastic Vice-President, fully intending to pursue and hold power as he had always done: by sharing it with no one. Truman, like most Vice-Presidents, dwelt in the obscurity of a functionary's job, anxious to participate but kept in the dark about the secrets of policymaking. And the Missourian was right about who had won the election. It was Roosevelt's victory in the same way that it was Roosevelt's war.

The transition to full-blown internationalism after 1945 was a gradual process involving much more than treaties or declarations of intent. The men who made and articulated American foreign policy in the White House, the State Department, the military, and the Congress first had to be convinced that a broad system of international political agreements could achieve foreign policy aims. The revolution in their thinking during these years amounted to this: a new belief that the United States must pursue its diplomacy in concert with other nations. Perhaps this was the price of predominance, for the exercise of power brought added responsibilities. The internationalism to which Truman alluded coincided with an enormous expenditure of American power everywhere in the world. Before the war, in 1938, the United States had no military alliances, no troops stationed in foreign countries, and a minuscule defense budget. By the end of the 1960s, the United States' military budget approached 80 billion dollars annually. There were over a million-and-a-half military personnel in over 100 countries, and the nation was tied by defense agreements to the destinies of 48 other nations.

The internationalism of World War II emerged from the task of supplying Allied nations and defeating the Axis powers. In the desperate phase of battle, potential American disagreements with the French, English, and especially the Russians faded. The American postwar position, however, gradually became clear. The United States would have both a dependent and an imperial relationship to other nations, dependent in the sense that what happened abroad politically or economically had profound domestic repercussions, and imperial in the sense that the United States became determined to exercise its new power in its own interest.

Postwar internationalism centered on four broad aims. Fundamental was the promotion of the American economic system, through open access to raw materials, secure foreign investments, multilateral trade, and a stable world currency. A corollary of this aim was to support political democracy and economic liberalism where possible. Third was the prevention of the spread of Communism, Socialism, or various forms of economic nationalism that might disrupt the first two goals. A fourth broad aim emerged only gradually, at first as a means of achieving world stability, and then as an end in itself. This was the maintenance of military superiority over the Soviet Union. Of course, foreign policymakers argued over how to achieve these goals. But their general agreement made events that occurred in Berlin, Korea, along the Mekong River in Indochina, or Santiago, Chile, as important as what happened in New York, San Diego, or Kalamazoo, Michigan.

Policies that developed over time did not spring full-blown from the minds of diplomats. Yet, over the years in Washington, distinct patterns of leadership emerged. A remarkable continuity of policy advisers led by Averell Harriman, Clark Clifford, Dean Acheson, John Foster Dulles, Senator Arthur H. Vandenberg, and others developed a coherent view of America's role in world politics. Policy once followed tended to perpetuate itself. Once decided upon, a program of economic and military aid to embattled Greece in 1947, for example, could easily be replicated and expanded in other programs, such as the Marshall Plan for Europe of 1948 or Point Four Aid to underdeveloped countries in 1950.

☆ ☆ ☆

During the war, Franklin Roosevelt kept close and jealous control of foreign policy decisions. Wearing three hats—as military commander in chief, as domestic leader, and as head of America's foreign policy apparatus—F.D.R. left a legacy of treaties and agreements as well as a frustrating tradition of ambiguity and postponement. Inactive where he could afford to put off a decision, acutely aware of potential domestic opposition to agreements with the Russians, and determined not to repeat the mistakes of Woodrow Wilson with which he was personally familiar, F.D.R. was more concerned about ending the war than sketching blueprints for a permanent peace. As Dean Acheson, Secretary of State under Harry Truman, later wrote, the President procrastinated in making important foreign policy decisions; he divided administrative power so as to concentrate it in his own hands. He also unrealistically believed in the potential of international universal organizations like the United Nations. From hindsight, Acheson was arguing that, where he had one, Roosevelt's policy exuded optimism. And in a sense, Acheson was right. Wherever Roosevelt did articulate a general policy, in his support for the United Nations or for the Atlantic Charter, he echoed the twenty-five-year-old idealism of Woodrow Wilson's Fourteen Points.

The most important wartime statement setting forth American war aims was drawn up in August 1941, before the United States officially entered the conflict. Partly in fear that the British and Russians, then jointly fighting Hitler, might agree to divide the world into spheres of interest, Roosevelt met with Winston Churchill, the British Prime Minister, at Argenta Harbor, Newfoundland. There, they agreed on an eight-point declaration of principles known as the Atlantic Charter. Beyond a joint commitment to defeat the Nazis, the eight points included support for free trade (except in areas subject to British Empire restrictions), renunciation of war and aggression, and the promotion of world peace, prosperity, and growth. The heart of the document, however, betrayed potential conflicts, and the Russians, when they came to sign it, appended a caveat that certain "historic peculiarities of particular countries" would exempt them from following all eight points. The Soviets had points two and three in mind because these rejected "territorial changes that do not accord with the freely expressed wishes of the peoples concerned" and defended "the right of all peoples to choose the form of government under which they will live."

The Russians never really deviated from this position. Time and again they announced they would not tolerate hostile governments in power along their Eastern European borders, no matter how they came to power or what support they enjoyed. More broadly, perhaps, they realized that the two Atlantic Charter points committed signatories to a policy that foreclosed the possibility of revolution. But from America's point of view, they were equally unrealistic. These two points were practically meaningless in a world beset by nationalism and economic chaos after the war. Beyond a few countries with a working tradition of parliamentary democracy, modern communications, and economic stability, it is difficult to imagine where the solemn words about self-government used by the framers of the Atlantic Charter might have applied.

In effect, Roosevelt's support for the Atlantic Charter and his public proclamation of the Four Freedoms for the world (freedom of speech, freedom of religion, freedom from want, and freedom from fear) had little specific content. However, in other areas of war strategy, Roosevelt greatly affected the shape of the postwar world. The unconditional surrender of the Axis powers; a United Nations organization to preserve world peace; bipartisanship (meaning Republican agreement) in foreign policy; and a victory in Europe first, with a minimum expenditure of U.S. casualties, were all policies with far-reaching effects. Working with advisers Harry Hopkins, Henry Stimson, Secretary of War General George C. Marshall, and others, Roosevelt often bypassed his Secretary of State Cordell Hull and the State Department bureaucracy. The President preferred personal diplomacy with face-to-face meetings, allowing him to assess the power and intelligence of world leaders, such as Churchill, Stalin, and Chiang Kai-shek of China. This afforded him maneuverability and personal power ordinarily limited by emissaries. But it also meant that the President's policy decisions belonged to him. While he might reap the rewards of success, he would surely also be caught in the whirlwinds of failure.

Several practical decisions flowed from F.D.R.'s support of unconditional surrender proclaimed at the Casablanca Conference with Churchill in January 1943. For example, despite rumors of secret American negotiations in 1945 with German General Wolff for surrender of the Nazi armies in northern Italy, the unconditional surrender pledge preserved the Russian-British-American alliance. When Stalin angrily protested the activities of Allen Dulles in forwarding German peace feelers to Washington in April, F.D.R. quite rightly replied that the United States and Britain would never consider a separate peace. Also, Roosevelt's decision to build the atomic bomb came partly from his belief that the Allies faced an implacable enemy with whom negotiations were futile. When Roosevelt agreed to American production of a nuclear bomb, he assumed it would be used to put a speedy end to the war. If successful, this awesome weapon would save American lives and bring the Japanese and German regimes to their knees.

Roosevelt's attitude toward atomic research demonstrates his style of leadership and hints at what his postwar foreign policy might have been. He was willing to accept limited participation of the British, but even they were acceptable only as junior colleagues. Despite the urging of scientists such as Niels Bohr, a Danish refugee instrumental in developing atomic theory, F.D.R. refused to share nuclear information with the Soviets or even inform them of American plans to build a bomb. Roosevelt clearly felt he held a strong hand, and he had no desire to deal away his winning cards.

Roosevelt's commitment to minimizing American casualties also directly affected policy toward the Russians, for it helped shift the burden of defeating the Nazis to the Soviet army. Desperate, as his forces crumbled before the armored divisions of the Germans, Stalin begged Roosevelt and Churchill to open a second European front in order to divert Axis troops from the East. Roosevelt seemed to agree in May 1942, during a Washington conference with Vyacheslav Molotov, the Russian envoy. But lack of preparations, risks, and British losses in their North African colonies diverted the American effort. The Germans pushed into the industrial heartland of the Soviet Union while the United States sped Lend-Lease supplies through submarine-infested waters to Russian ports. But F.D.R. would not agree to a Channel crossing until vast preparations had been completed in 1944. By this time, north Africa (that is, French and British colonies) had been reconquered;

Italy had ceded to the Allies; and the Soviets had hurled back the German Wehrmacht.

When the Soviets reversed the tide of battle at Stalingrad and Leningrad and then began painfully to recapture territory, circumstances changed. Once Russian forces began to push into Poland in early 1944, many of the questions about the shape of Eastern Europe, which worried diplomats at Teheran in 1943 and later at the Yalta Conference in 1945, became academic. The alliance of convenience cemented by common opposition to Hitler showed signs of disintegration as victory approached.

Roosevelt's reluctance to articulate war aims or to strike a lasting and meaningful bargain with the Russians came in part from his fear of political opposition at home. The President's decision to don the cap of "Dr.-Win-the-War" did not save the Democratic party from a close brush with defeat in the 1942 congressional elections. The new 77th Congress was in no mood to listen to liberal promises about world peace or to vote for domestic reform programs. From this situation, F.D.R. concluded he needed Republican support to achieve approval of United States participation in a United Nations organization. As the President wrote to Stalin in 1945, "You are, I am sure, aware that genuine popular support in the United States is required to carry out any government policy, foreign or domestic."

The unlikely source of crucial bipartisan support came from Senator Arthur Vandenberg, Republican from Michigan. First elected to the Senate in 1928, Vandenberg was a native son of Grand Rapids. He had been a successful editor of the *Grand Rapids Herald* and author of two books on Alexander Hamilton. A determined conservative, he was one of only two senators to oppose recognizing the Soviet Union in 1933. In 1940, he had been, he recalled, "an unsuccessful nonactive, *isolationist* candidate for the presidential nomination." Crediting Pearl Harbor for his conversion to internationalism, he was also reborn as a supporter of bipartisanship in foreign policy during the winter of 1943–1944. Vandenberg's growing importance to F.D.R. and then to Truman placed him in the right spot at the right time to affect policy.

These dual conversions in no way established him as a liberal. They simply made his conservatism more relevant. His prominence among foreign policy supporters gave him power to dampen what enthusiasm existed in the Democratic party to accommodate

Stalin. He firmly opposed "appeasing" Stalin, and he said so vigorously at the United Nations Conference in San Francisco in April 1945, and in the Senate. Whether his attitude stemmed from long-held positions or his desire to please large Polish constituencies in Michigan or his general distaste for the political left, he bitterly opposed Soviet activities in Eastern Europe. The man who wrote in 1946 that the Labour Party victory in England so disgusted him that he would "seriously consider getting out of this miserable business" would never accept Communist revolutions in countries occupied by the Red Army.

Bipartisanship in foreign policy epitomized a political turn in the Roosevelt administration during the early days of the war. The President took a decisive step in deciding to dump Vice-President Wallace in favor of Harry Truman in 1944. Although widely praised for his senatorial investigations into inefficiency in war production, Truman was a relative unknown politically—in other words, he had not impressed fellow senators or the press with his views. Many knew him best as a politico associated with the Missouri Democratic party machine run by boss Thomas Pendergast. Others found him to be a loyal New Deal supporter, but lacking in initiative.

Other representatives of the new administrative order brought to Washington by F.D.R. included Secretary of War Henry L. Stimson; James Forrestal, former president of Dillon, Read and Company; John J. McCloy, member of a New York law firm; and Bernard Baruch, the elder statesman of high finance. While the President kept many of his New Deal advisers—Wallace was designated Secretary of Commerce in 1944, for example—his appointments after 1940 identified his administration with the political center.

Roosevelt edged toward the political middle in order to disarm potential critics. Primarily, he hoped to prevent a recurrence of the debacle of 1919 when Woodrow Wilson returned to the United States with a peace treaty unacceptable to Congress. Roosevelt's postwar hopes—like Wilson's—resided in an international peace-keeping organization. A tentative United Nations organization emerged in January 1942, in Washington, when the twenty-six nations fighting the Axis powers declared themselves an alliance devoted to the permanent suppression of aggression. In Moscow, next year, at an October conference of "Four Nations on General Security," China, the U.S.S.R., England, and the United States pledged to create an international organization of sovereign "peace-loving" nations dedicated to the maintenance of international security. By August 1944, plans had progressed sufficiently to hold a conference at Dumbarton Oaks mansion in Washington, D.C., where Britain, the U.S.S.R., the United States, and eventually China agreed upon a general structure (the General Assembly) with equal representation for all nations and a council (the Security Council) with permanent Great Power members and revolving elected members from other countries. In effect, this arrangement acknowledged the predominance of the principal nations of the wartime alliance. Precise details of voting and membership were postponed until the Yalta Conference, where it was agreed that all the great powers could veto nonprocedural actions before the Security Council. General Assembly membership extended to all nations that declared war on the Axis powers by March 1, 1945.

A final conference, held in San Francisco in April 1945, proved to be acrimonious. The Soviet Union demanded Assembly membership for the Ukraine and Byelorussia. Stalin also let it be known that he desired a veto even on procedural matters in the Security Council, a claim he gave up after talking to Harry Hopkins, who rushed to Moscow to negotiate this point. On the other hand, the United States urged membership for Argentina, a nation that had curried favor with the Axis powers. And, the Americans pressed for the right to preserve regional organizations, such as the inter-American defense system in the Western Hemisphere. When the compromise charter was signed, Argentina, Soviet Byelorussia, and the Ukraine were among its signatories. Article 52, preserving the right to create regional treaties, became the justification for several regional alliances established during the Cold War by the United States and its allies.

Despite American press outrage over Russian demands, the United States initialed the U.N. Treaty on June 26, 1945. It passed through the United States Senate two days later with almost no dissent. Woodrow Wilson's dream of a covenant of nations devoted to peace was finally achieved, but, by that time, the man most responsible for this victory and a personal link between the two historic efforts to secure it—Franklin Roosevelt—was dead.

Like the Atlantic Charter, the United Nations organization perpetuated the wartime alliance of Great Powers: England, the United States, the U.S.S.R., France, and China. No gathering of equals, the organization reflected a realistic appraisal of world power relationships. Two institutions existed in one: a democratic General Assembly and a Security Council dominated by the Big-Five Alliance. This structure preserved the big power diplomacy of the Allies in postwar international relations.

Other important international institutions to develop from the wartime alliance included the international financial organizations created by the Bretton Woods Agreements of 1944. Secluded for a twenty-two-day conference at Mt. Washington Hotel in Bretton Woods, New Hampshire, delegates from over forty countries discussed serious international financial and economic dislocations. The conference anticipated two principal problems after the war: huge North American balance-of-payments surpluses (the United States in 1944 held about two-thirds of the world's monetary gold stock) and enormous European deficits. Aware that economic depression and inflation following World War I had undermined world political stability in the 1920s and 1930s, Secretary of the Treasury Henry Morgenthau, who presided over the conference, and other American delegates, such as Harry Dexter White, Assistant Secretary of the Treasury, pushed plans to stabilize currency values and international trade. Also conspicuously present was John Maynard Keynes, the distinguished British economist whose theories provided a generation of postwar leaders with fiscal tools to prevent or to control recessions and booms. After World War I, Keynes had published his ominous *Economic Consequences of the Peace* in which he accurately forecast serious economic problems. At Bretton Woods, however, he showed more optimism. He hoped that the International Monetary Fund, for alleviation of balance-of-payments problems between trading nations, and the International Bank for Reconstruction and Development (the World Bank), designed to grant loans to devastated areas, would restore and improve world monetary and trade conditions.

The American delegates encountered reluctance from other allies. First the British and then the Russians made proposals to fit their national needs. Harry Dexter White, of the Treasury Department, developed the American proposals. White's plan aimed to facilitate convertability and to stabilize world currencies with a monetary fund joined by nations who contributed gold and currency to its stocks. In times of serious trade imbalance, members could borrow from this fund. Votes in the governing body would reflect the contribution made by each nation. As White estimated, this would give 25 percent of the vote to the United States and 35 percent to Latin America, so that the Western Hemisphere would have a controlling interest of about 60 percent. The British would control 17 percent and the Russians about 3 percent.

The Russians were reluctant to enter any scheme for international currency stabilization, because Stalin feared interference with Soviet economic autonomy and increased Western influence. Thus, the Russians participated in negotiations and stubbornly wrung concessions from the participants. No doubt Stalin, who wanted to keep Lend-Lease supplies flowing and the Russian-American alliance intact, was delighted by news, which Morgenthau circulated, about the possibility of a $10 billion postwar loan for the U.S.S.R. But, by December 31, 1945, with the war over, Foreign Minister Molotov announced that the Soviets would not participate in the Monetary Fund or the World Bank. Thus, these institutions remained under the control of Western Europe and the United States.

A final aspect of wartime policymaking machinery bequeathed by Roosevelt to his untutored Vice-President was his personal diplomatic style. Like a bright thread, it ran through almost every agreement and policy. Personal diplomacy undoubtedly reflected the President's political acumen, but it was also a policy fraught with confusion. For example, Roosevelt indicated he might agree to a division of the world into spheres of interest, where each major power dominated its designated area, but he refused to commit himself, even though Churchill, fighting for preservation of the British Empire, and Stalin, anxious to assert hegemony over bordering countries, might have preferred such an arrangment.

In the key area of contention and negotiation, then, Roosevelt remained noncommittal. Nonetheless, the problems of Eastern Europe, and particularly of Poland, required solutions. Poland was the terrain on which World War II began and traditionally the corridor of invasion into Russia. For millions of American voters, it was their nostalgic homeland. Roosevelt tried to put off any firm decisions about borders or the composition of a future government. For the Russians, however, settlement of the Polish question formed the bedrock of their policy; they insisted on retaining the boundaries adjusted by the 1939 Russian-German Nonagression Pact, and they demanded a government friendly to the U.S.S.R. Such a settlement would inevitably enrage Polish nationalists, for it changed old boundaries and would suppress political expression of hostility toward the Russians. Aside from strong sentimental ties, the United States had few economic or political interests in that nation. The fate of Poland, however, quickly came to symbolize the fate of all Eastern Europe. As Senator Vandenberg said in a speech on April 2, 1944, Poland was a test case for Soviet cooperation; it was a signal lamp "on these new horizons of our destiny."

In May 1945, Stalin wrote to Churchill his definitive views on Poland: "We insist . . . that only people who have demonstrated by deeds their friendly attitude to the Soviet Union, who are willing . . . to cooperate with the Soviet State, should be consulted on the formation of a future Polish Government." The Soviets never budged from this position. At first, the dispute over Poland centered around who should rule after the war: the refugee government-in-exile in London or the Polish refugees in Moscow. The London Emigrés received Churchill's support, but their relations with the Soviets were cool. In April 1943, when the Germans announced that they had discovered the corpses of thousands of Polish officers buried in Katyn Forest, purportedly murdered by Russian soldiers in 1940, the London Poles denounced the Soviets. The Russians angrily demanded a retraction. When this did not come, they broke all relations with the London government-in-exile, accusing it of fascist collaboration. A month before, however, the Russians had formed the Union of Polish Patriots, around which it began to assemble its own government-in-exile.

At first, neither F.D.R. nor Averell Harriman, the Ambassador to Moscow, reacted strongly to these events. However, in August 1944, as the Red Armies approached the Vistula River near Warsaw, the London Poles, anticipating liberation, called upon their supporters to rise up against the Germans. Suddenly, the Russian drive stalled. Virtually without weapons or supplies, the Warsaw fighters waged a losing battle. Furious and desperate, the London government-in-exile pleaded with Stalin to advance, but he refused, citing a German counteroffensive. When the Russians captured Warsaw, the ranks of Polish supporters loyal to the London government had been decimated.

For American policymakers, these events stood as dramatic proof of Soviet intentions. At one time, more tolerant of Russian aims, Harriman emerged a confirmed cold warrior. George Kennan, recently arrived in the Russian capital, recorded in his memoirs that the uprising was "the most arrogant and unmistakable demonstration of Soviet determination to control Eastern Europe in the post war period." Indeed, by this time, Kennan urged that the United States threaten to cut off Lend-Lease supplies to Russia unless Stalin made major concessions in Poland and other Eastern European countries.

Roosevelt responded to the quickly developing crisis in Eastern Europe by negotiating, compromising, and procrastinating. He postponed action for several reasons, not the least of which was the lack of American power in the region. At the Teheran Conference in 1943 and later at Yalta in February 1945, he sought Stalin's personal assurances of cooperation in Europe. Short of threats to the Soviets, he could do little else, but he also was pursuing his policy of winning the war with as few American casualties as possible, and he wanted Stalin's continued cooperation to end the war against Japan.

In his face-to-face encounters with Stalin and Churchill at Teheran and Yalta, Roosevelt attempted to maintain maneuverability in a rapidly shrinking space. Meeting in late November of 1943 in Iran, Roosevelt tried to convince Stalin to cooperate with American aims and the dictates of the Atlantic Charter. But, he indicated he would not oppose border changes for Poland. Citing his upcoming electoral problems with immigrant American voters, he suggested that Stalin allow the Baltic states of Lithuania, Latvia, and Estonia the right to plebiscite elections before incorporating them into the Soviet Union. In effect, the President seemed to signal that the United States would not fight for self-determination in Eastern Europe.

A year-and-a-half later at Yalta, at the last meeting of Roosevelt with Stalin and Churchill, the Soviets had already recognized their own government in Warsaw, the Lublin regime. Soviet troops occupied much of Eastern Europe and were rushing toward Berlin. American and British troops, after a massive Channel crossing, pushed back the Germans in the West. Roosevelt, however, was still bargaining to get the Russians into the war in Asia, and he and Churchill conceded Stalin's claims to Northern Sakhalin Island and the Kuriles (both north of Japan) as part of the price. Regarding Poland, the Russian leader signed a vague protocol promising free elections and participation by "all democratic and anti-Nazi parties." These ambiguous words left different interpretations open to both sides: thus the legacy of misunderstanding and recrimination. What Stalin thought he had achieved and what the Americans hoped he had promised were two different things. In retrospect, American policymakers often cited the Polish question as the beginning of the Cold War. According to Dean Acheson, Stalin began his "offensive" against the United States in Poland.

On March 30, 1945, Roosevelt, obviously ill and desperately fatigued by his Yalta trip, left for Warm Springs, Georgia, his favorite vacation retreat. Thirteen days later, in the afternoon, Harry Truman entered House Speaker Sam Rayburn's office for a meeting. The Speaker told him to call Presidential Press Secretary Steve Early immediately. Summoned to the White House, Truman undoubtedly suspected he was also being summoned to the Presidency. Roosevelt was dead.

Roosevelt's death in the spring of 1945, when the United States stood one month away from victory in Europe and five months away from V-J Day in the Asian war, created a leadership vacuum. His legacy of half-formulated postwar policy depended on personal understandings with Stalin and Churchill. He left behind nascent institutions: both the Bretton Woods agreements and the United Nations organization had yet to be implemented. The shape of German occupation remained undecided. Issues of loans, war reparations, the extent of Russian influence in Eastern Europe, the nature of governments in formerly hostile countries in the West all required resolution.

In Washington, Roosevelt left an internally divided administration. Secretary of the Treasury Morgenthau, for example, favored the pastoralization or permanent industrial and military dismemberment of Germany. Other cabinet members, including Henry Wallace of Commerce, favored accommodating the Russians. Still others proposed a tough policy toward Stalin and the aggressive use of American economic and military might to bend Russian policy. By and large, Roosevelt knew how to balance these opinions: disagreements kept his options open. For Truman, however, policy meant making decisions.

In the spring of 1945, when Truman was sworn in as President, he had little experience in foreign affairs and scant knowledge of negotiations with the Russians or other allies. Perforce, he had to rely on his advisers; he could not afford the luxury of F.D.R.'s intentional ambiguity. Truman felt that he needed to act quickly and decisively to establish continuity of government and leadership in an inherited administration made up of people having great wealth, prestige, and influence. Truman initially chose firmness with the Russians, delighting those in the administration pressing for a tougher policy. On April 20, Averell Harriman, just returned from the Soviet Union, met with Truman, Secretary of State Edward Stettinius (Cordell Hull had resigned in late 1944), Under Secretary of State Joseph C. Grew, and Charles E. Bohlen, the Department's Russian expert. Harriman advised a firm policy toward Stalin. He warned that the Russians stubbornly believed that the United States, fearing a depression, would make large concessions to them. The ambassador predicted a "barbarian invasion of Europe"; as evidence, he cited Russian activities in propping up the Lublin government in Poland. The United States, he concluded, should demand the letter of agreements signed at Yalta. Truman assured Harriman that he agreed. The United States would make "no concession from American principles or traditions in order to win their favor." Nor would the President shrink from taking firm control of foreign policy.

Two days later, Soviet Secretary of State Molotov arrived in Washington, en route to the U.N. convention in San Francisco. His first meeting with Truman was cordial. But, pressed by Stettinius, Stimson, and Navy Secretary James Forrestal, Truman decided to raise the Polish question. After opening statements the next day, Truman blamed Russia for disputes over Poland: the U.S.S.R. had violated the Yalta agreements and had scuttled free elections. When Molotov tried to explain his country's position, Truman cut him short. The Russian complained, "I have never been talked to like that in my life." The President snapped, "Carry out your agreements and you won't get talked to like that."

Undoubtedly, Truman reached his majority in this exchange; he demonstrated toughness and quickness, and he signaled the Russians that his administration would be different from its predecessor. But his pugnacious stance—although it helped him plug a domestic leadership vacuum and raise his stock among a distinguished coterie of anti-Soviet advisers—did damage to the precarious relations between the United States and the Soviets. And after initially flexing his diplomatic muscles, Truman himself began to realize some of the complexity of the issues he first tried to bluster through.

The closing moments of the war brought a rush of decision-making and international conferences. To aid him, Truman continued to rely upon Harriman, Forrestal, Stimson, and others, but he also brought in his own men who were generally not associated with the New Deal or were even hostile to it. Among these were South Carolina's James F. Byrnes, Dean Acheson, the Attorney General Tom C. Clark, and Kentucky congressman Fred Vinson. Several old New Dealers either jumped the administration ship or, like Henry Wallace, walked the plank of dismissal. This transition was more or less permanent. Truman's appointments in the State Department, especially, remained in office for many years. One member of his generation referred to himself and others as the "old contemptibles."

In dismissing Wallace on September 20, 1946, Truman furnished another sign of his determination to run foreign policy. Many observers also assumed he had declared independence from F.D.R. In late 1945 and 1946, Wallace openly criticized Truman's firm line with the Soviet Union, first at Cabinet meetings and then in public. At issue was the change he detected in American policy since the death of F.D.R.: the United States was on a collision course with the U.S.S.R.

At the conference at Potsdam, Germany, on July 3, 1945, Truman crossed the threshold of deteriorating relations. With Germany prostrate, the Allies had to settle issues of reparations. In the eyes of Truman and Secretary Byrnes, the Russians demanded far too much—$20 billion in reparations from Germany and a shift in Poland's boundaries that would push the western frontier of that nation to the Oder and Western Neisse rivers. The bargain struck at Potsdam was a tenuous compromise, with the question of boundaries unsettled. Occupying forces in each sector of Germany could exact reparations from the territory they occupied, with additional materials promised to Russia in industrial capital from the Anglo-American zones.

Other issues were more or less settled. Stalin agreed to enter the war against Japan, but he remained less cooperative about reversing his policy toward Eastern Europe. Truman's negotiating style was equally tough, influenced in part by the stubborn stance of Stalin and in part by the President's knowledge (received on July 16, 1945) that the United States had successfully exploded a nuclear bomb. These results greatly heartened the Americans, but when Truman briefly alluded to the successful test, Stalin dismissed the news with hopes that the weapon would be used against the Japanese. As everyone realized, however, atomic power was no minor matter. When Truman authorized the use of the bomb against Hiroshima and Nagasaki a few days after the Potsdam Con-

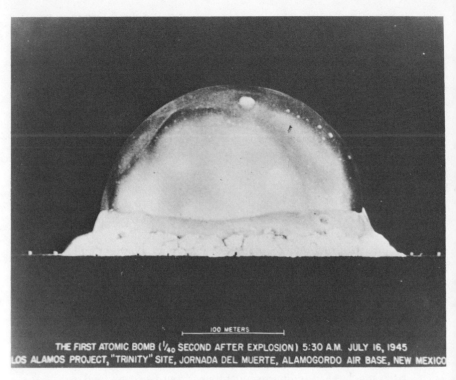

100 METERS

THE FIRST ATOMIC BOMB (1/40 SECOND AFTER EXPLOSION) 5:30 A.M. JULY 16, 1945
LOS ALAMOS PROJECT, "TRINITY" SITE, JORNADA DEL MUERTE, ALAMOGORDO AIR BASE, NEW MEXICO

The first atomic bomb 1/40 second after explosion, 5:30 A.M., July 16, 1945, Los Alamos Project, 'Trinity' Site, Jornada Del Muerte, Alamogordo Air Force Base, New Mexico. (Library of Congress)

ference, he did so with the intention of terminating the war. But his timing, coinciding with Russia's entry into the Asian war, convinced some observers—among them the Russians—that the United States intended to exploit the political advantages of its nuclear monopoly.

Although the President and some members of his entourage, particularly Secretary of War Stimson, anguished over atomic energy, Truman probably never seriously considered abandoning America's monopoly of atomic weaponry, except under circumstances the United States could control. The Baruch Plan, offered to the United Nations in 1946 by the aging South Carolina millionaire, proposed to place international nuclear disarmament under the aegis of the Security Council, with one important proviso: No veto of atomic energy policy would be allowed; until full control over nuclear weaponry went into effect, the United States would retain its monopoly. As expected, the Russians rejected the plan, exercising their Security Council veto. Instead, they embarked on a crash program to develop their own nuclear bombs.

Signs of deteriorating relations appeared elsewhere. After initial flexibility toward governments under its control in Hungary, for example, the Soviet Union began to tighten its grip in Eastern Europe. Moreover, in a speech in February 1946, Stalin warned of the possibility of future capitalist wars, and he announced a new five-year plan of military and heavy industry expansion. Cited by many American observers as a declaration of Cold War, the speech was quickly followed by news of the discovery of a nuclear spy ring operating in Canada. Many American policymakers were convinced that Stalin had shown his hand.

Two developments on the American side, which occurred almost simultaneously, indicated a new United States policy. In reality, however, they only gave intellectual shape and attention to existing American practice. The first was George Kennan's famous telegram, solicited by the State Department in February 1946. This long message proved, beyond the expectations of its author, to be enormously influential; it was widely circulated in administration circles and published later in *Foreign Affairs* under an anonymous signature. The other event was public. Winston Churchill, now out of office, responded enthusiastically to Truman's invitation to deliver an address in Fulton, Missouri, on March 5, 1946. He issued a tough, resounding call to confront the Russians.

Using a phrase he had employed many times before, the English-man denounced the "Iron Curtain" that had descended across all of Eastern Europe. Truman, sitting on the speaker's dais, and with prior knowledge of the speech's content, seemed to approve his words.

In effect, Kennan's telegram and Churchill's memorable phrases were two variations of the same theme. The first was safer, more hesitant and accommodating; the second was harsh and bellicose. But they marked the parameters of American foreign policy think-ing and indicated the relatively narrow kind of assumptions that guided American strategies of containment in the Cold War.

Composed in haste, the X telegram summarized Kennan's experi-ence since 1944 in the Soviet Union. In sections, "all neatly divided, like an eighteenth century Protestant sermon," he recalled that he had wanted to convince the leaders of the United States to oppose Russian feints and maneuvers, to block infiltrations and shore up weak spots: in effect, to contain expansion. This last idea meant, in his words, to maintain, "a long-term, patient but firm and vigilant containment of Russian expansive tendencies." This American coun-terforce would mellow aggressive tendencies in the U.S.S.R. Some-what later, Kennan claimed that policymakers distorted his mean-ing by emphasizing only military containment, but some of the blame must be his. The essay bristled with expressions like "fanati-cism" and "the innate antagonism between capitalism and socialism" and presented an extraordinary picture of Communists all over the world, drawn from the old RCA advertisement: "Like the white dog before the phonograph, they hear only the 'master's voice.'" Stripped of its subtleties, Kennan's essay probably said what many policymakers had already decided: Russian and Communist pene-tration into any new area in the world must be stopped. Further-more, it assumed that all Communists, whatever their nationality, only obeyed their master's voice from the Kremlin. Finally, the es-say offered the hope of future resolution in the struggle: the Soviets would finally relent.

Churchill's speech at Fulton, on the other hand, was simple and militant. The deposed British Prime Minister demanded an En-glish-American alliance to defend "Christian civilization." Equating Fascism and Communism, he stressed military opposition to Rus-sian policy. It would be a dangerous and awe-inspiring moment, he believed, but "the United States stands at this time at the pinnacle of world power." He hoped that power would join in service to his crusade.

Cold War Europe, 1950

The Iron Curtain speech had a remarkable success in defining the purposes of American foreign policy. Kennan's essay, published in July 1947, also drew widespread praise. But there were still dissenters who felt that even the Mister X article was far too harsh. Most notable among these was political columnist Walter Lippmann. In several essays, Lippmann sharply rebuked Kennan for his lack of realism. Containment as proposed and practiced, he wrote, was "fundamentally unsound," yet he feared this represented the best of State Department thinking. Remarkably prescient, he stated that containment would require too much planning and bureaucracy and would incur huge military expenditures that would revolutionize American society. Moreover, the policy seemed conservative and negative. Instead of pursuing peace first, it would assert power, and in areas where the United States could least afford to extend itself. Finally, he wrote, it was folly for the United States to try to make "Jeffersonian democrats out of the peasants of eastern Europe, the tribal chieftains, the feudal lords, the pashas, and the warlords of the Middle East and Asia."

Right in so many of his criticisms, Lippmann also understood that the Truman administration had chosen containment, not accommodation, by 1946. Occasionally, the administration doubted the wisdom of this choice, but the general direction had been set. Roosevelt's wartime internationalism evolved from a tenuous partnership of great powers into a policy that was perhaps implicit all the while: a redefinition of the world into spheres of interest. This is precisely what most policymakers had strenuously opposed, but it is what containment inevitably meant. Because containment implied limiting Soviet influence to its contiguous areas, the American sphere of interest remained huge and amorphous, encompassing Western Europe, Latin America, and many of the former Asian and African colonies of Britain and France. Unfortunately, this extended strategy defined every revolt, or nationalist revolution, and every attack on private property as a threat to American policy.

☆   ☆   ☆

World War II ended with one of the most decisive military victories in modern history. Yet, for all the good will generated in the heroic struggle against the Axis, the alliance between the Americans and the Russians degenerated into a squabble over the spoils. Good relations corroded rapidly into suspicions and antagonistic opposition. Perhaps this icy bath might never have been drawn, but only the magnanimity, understanding, and generosity possessed by few men could have altered the course of Cold War events. A different United States policy would have meant treating the Soviet Union more as a partner and less as a conquered nation. It would have demanded a degree of political sophistication probably undeveloped at the time. And, it would have demanded a degree of cooperation and understanding from the Soviet side that is very difficult to imagine. Had F.D.R. lived longer into the postwar period, American policy might have remained more flexible. But in reality, both sides came to feel that a hard line expressed their national interest.

As developed in acts and policy statements, the Cold War policy of the United States after Truman varied from time to time and place to place. Presidents Eisenhower, Kennedy, and Johnson, who followed its basic tenets, varied their approaches. In the 1970s there were false hopes that it might end—although in the 1980s, its premises were restated vigorously by President Reagan. Whole areas of the world escaped the Cold War and competition between superpowers. In Western Europe, American Cold War policy encouraged a remarkable reconstruction. Frequently, however, American policy was rigid and supportive of petty tyrants and dictators, such as Batista in Cuba, Duvalier in Haiti, the Shah of Iran, and Ngo Dinh Diem of South Vietnam. Over the years, the policy seemed to lose the subtleties and purposes enunciated by Kennan, until two overweening assumptions remained: support for American business interests and opposition to Communism.

Ironically, the division of the world was precisely what containment hoped to prevent; the United States itself promoted the polarization of the world into Communist and capitalist parties. Despite rumblings in Congress and bellicose campaign promises, the United States could not prevent the spread of Communism. Peace eluded Truman and those fellow practitioners of Cold War policies who followed him. The United States in 1950 found itself mired in a Korean War it could not win, and in the 1960s, in a struggle in Vietnam it had neither the heart nor the energy to conclude. The prosperity and economic stability sought by containing Russian influence was a glittering prize brought home in the 1950s and 1960s. But gilt-edged American economic success could not disguise the fact that, by the measure of its own goals, Cold War policy did not prevent the division of the world into two hostile camps.

3 Family Culture

In the last scene of the epochal film *Giant* (1956), an elderly Texas couple, played by Elizabeth Taylor and Rock Hudson, relax for the first time in 201 minutes. Recalling their good life together, they look approvingly at the baby crib at the end of the room. Here, two grandchildren, one obviously Anglo-Saxon, the other Mexican, smile into the camera. And, behind them, through the open window, the camera brings into focus another symbol of integration, a white sheep and a black Angus calf standing side by side. Thus, George Stevens's remarkably successful film ends in a vision of marriage and the perpetuation of the family as the solution to immense social problems.

This family ideology figured in a thousand ways in Hollywood movies in the 1940s and 1950s. Countless films ended in the same fashion, as if to say that romance, marriage, and children were sufficient goals for Americans: If only Americans strengthened the bonds of kinship, then the frightening transformations of modern life could be comprehended. Thus, in *Giant*, the struggle over racial integration becomes an episode in the renewal of family ties. In that film, East merges with West, civilization is united to the frontier, and two races join in marriage in a visual hymn to the American family.

During the same years, however, Hollywood made as many films that focused on the unraveling of the American family structure, in which divorce, extramarital love, alcoholism, and juvenile delinquency shattered the ideal of bliss and turned American men, women, and children into hostile, warring generations. James Dean, who played a grown-up delinquent in *Giant*, had only one year earlier achieved his first acting triumph in *East of Eden*. In that movie, the message was simple, but reversed: The American family was deeply troubled; parents lacked understanding. The result was tormented youth and generational conflict.

Americans have long lived with contradictory attitudes about the success of the family as a social institution. This immense subject has been a staple of modern culture in novels, films, and popular psychology and sociology. Yet the period after World War II owes some of its special character to unique developments in the social and cultural history of the family.

From the 1940s to the 1960s, Americans looked at the family with double vision: with optimism and despair. In one of the most popular novels of the period, J. D. Salinger's *Catcher in the Rye*, published in 1951, both visions exist. The contradictory attitudes of his society toward the family confuse the adolescent hero, Holden Caulfield. In his search for authenticity, he discovers only "phoniness"; instead of fathers, he finds betrayers. Yet Salinger's much-censored book ends affirmatively. After scrambling down the rungs of his private hell, Holden returns home with a larger, more tolerant view of society. He decides to live with contradiction.

A sense of the importance of—and a tone of worry about—the family and of the changing roles of parents and children was pervasive, even tingeing child-rearing and baby-care books. The remarkable sales of Dr. Benjamin Spock's *Baby and Child Care* book reveal a deep popular concern for family health in the decades following 1945. Between 1946, when it was published, and 1976, the pocket edition of this work sold over 23 million copies. Only the Bible and the combined works of Mickey Spillane and of Dr. Seuss sold significantly more copies. Spock's work was not entirely new, for it built upon previous child-rearing advice books, but the author was one of the first to popularize the theories of Sigmund Freud and of the American philosopher John Dewey. From these thinkers, Spock drew a theory of child-rearing designed to create well-adjusted individuals—a generation of guiltless, happy adults who could move easily into a modern world of large, socialized institutions. As he put it: "How happily a person gets along as an adult in his job, in his family and social life, depends a great deal on how he got along with other children when he was young." Early behavior depended upon mothers and fathers. In most cases, Spock advised, parents should follow their instincts with their children: "Trust your own instincts, and follow the directions that your doctor gives you." In many cases, a child could indicate what was best for him. As for parenting roles, the bulk of the obligation should fall to the mother, although a father might change diapers or make formula on Sundays.

It is difficult to measure the influence of Spock's advice on the parents who read the baby book. Many, if not most, probably got no further in the index than "measles symptoms" or "diaper rash." Yet Spock fully intended to help liberate the modern family from the long, repressive reach of tradition. Publication of his book signaled the important ideal of a child-centered, family-centered America on the verge of unprecedented prosperity and optimism. The fact that he updated and changed it frequently underscores his serious interest in affecting the family by writing about the baby.

Although the most popular, Benjamin Spock was not the only child-rearing expert in this era. The psychologist B. F. Skinner offered a remarkably different notion of the American family and of child-rearing for those who carefully read his utopian novel *Walden Two* (1948). In his books following World War II, Skinner proved himself to be one of the most inventive and controversial of modern behaviorist psychologists. In this period, he developed two significant inventions: the teaching machine and the "air crib." These instruments, intended to replace or aid teachers and parents, suggest the implicit direction of his thinking about child-rearing. The hopes of rationality and traditional religion had been dashed in Fascism, depression, and world war. Skinner proposed to raise a new generation of Americans, unaffected by guilt or misguided by false beliefs in religion and reason, which had been wrongly instilled by indulgent parents.

Walden Two, named after Henry David Thoreau's famous nineteenth-century book, described a perfected society incorporating management practices, equality, elimination of the family, and behavioral conditioning of children. Skinner suggested that the community, not the biological parents, assume the risks and rewards of child-rearing. He implied that excessive parental love was a key to the failure of Americans to adjust to modern society.

Both Spock and Skinner, in their own ways, responded to strong forces reshaping the American family. Some of these encouraged the view that family stability was increasing. Other trends appeared to threaten the very existence of the institution. As the economy changed, as more women sought full-time employment, as trends in marriage, birth, and divorce rates and in family size shifted rapidly, the shape of the family seemed to be evolving in several directions at once. No wonder, then, that American culture reflected contradictory attitudes toward this institution.

☆   ☆   ☆

After the war, the American family experienced the inconveniences and stresses of reconversion to peacetime living. Millions of women with absent husbands and children with absent fathers suddenly confronted returning GIs. Readjustment often proved difficult for both men and women. Demobilized soldiers had jobs or careers to resume or possibly several years of school under the generous provisions of the GI Bill. In industry, returning GIs resumed seniority in unions and took up jobs on the production line or in offices. This was not always an easy readjustment, as William Wyler's sympathetic film *The Best Years of Our Lives* depicted in 1946. Yet the problems faced by women were probably as disruptive. Returning soldiers and closed munitions plants spelled fewer jobs for women. While many of these workers intended to stay on the job, millions were forced out of the factory and into the home.

An enormous surge in divorce rates in 1946 suggests that these problems sometimes became too serious to settle. The year 1946 was an extraordinary year: 18.2 percent of existing marriages were dissolved, a rate significantly higher than the years on either side of this date. Although the divorce rate rose during the war to around 14 percent, 1946 represented the peak year, for the rate gradually dropped back to about 10 percent in 1950, where it remained stable for several years. As the two tables following show, the divorce rate rose sharply after the war, declined to a plane fifteen years in length, and then rose abruptly after 1968. Only post-1973 divorce rates equaled the high percentage that prevailed briefly in 1945 and 1946.

The impact of the war on family life also registered in marriage rates. Most countries fighting in World War II had significant in-

Divorce as a Percentage of Existing Marriages

Year	Percentage	Year	Percentage
1942	10.0%	1947	13.9%
1943	10.9	1948	11.6
1944	12.3	1949	10.6
1945	14.3	1950	10.2
1946	18.2	1951	9.9

Source: *Paul Jacobson,* American Marriage and Divorce (*New York: Rinehart, 1959*), p. 90.

Marriage and Divorce Rates per 1,000 Population, 1945–1980

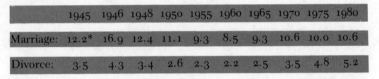

	1945	1946	1948	1950	1955	1960	1965	1970	1975	1980
Marriage:	12.2*	16.9	12.4	11.1	9.3	8.5	9.3	10.6	10.0	10.6
Divorce:	3.5	4.3	3.4	2.6	2.3	2.2	2.5	3.5	4.8	5.2

The best way to read these figures is to compare them. Thus, the marriage rate in 1945 is more than three times the divorce rate. In 1980, it is about twice the divorce rate.

Source: Statistical Abstract of the United States *(1984)*, pp. 84–86.

creases in postwar marriage rates, but the United States showed a particularly striking percentage of persons over fifteen who married. From 1944 to 1948, the United States had the highest marriage rate of any reporting country in the world, except Egypt. This statistic means that a higher percentage of Americans married than before or since that interval. Almost 70 percent of males and 67 percent of females over fifteen were married in 1950. Compared to figures collected during the Depression, this statistic represents a large increase. In 1946, the number of eligible persons who married during that year was almost twice the proportion joined in wedlock during 1932.

The consequence of the marriage boom and of lower average marriage ages was a baby boom: More marriages meant more children. The number of live births also increased because of other factors. The illegitimacy rate rose much faster than in previous periods, although this increase occurred in tandem with the higher rates for legitimate births from 1940 to 1957. The infant mortality rate (fetal death ratio) dropped significantly after World War II, reflecting major advances in obstetrics and also a rapid increase in the percentage of births in hospitals.

The American desire for larger families also pushed the baby boom. Translated into statistics, this desire of parents for more children showed up in an exceptional upward curve in the generally downward trend toward fewer children and smaller families typical of most of the twentieth century. Birthrate figures illustrate this trend.

The war-induced postponements of marriage and children partly account for the precipitate rise in family formation and births. Another factor was the undoubted prosperity that many Americans

Percentage of Hospital Births by Year and Race

White		Nonwhite	
Year	Percentage	Year	Percentage
1940	59.9%	1940	27.0%
1950	84.3	1950	57.9
1967	99.4	1967	92.9

Source: *National Center for Health Statistics*, Natality Statistics
Analysis, U.S., 1965–1967, *p. 20.*

experienced. (The gross national product doubled between 1945
and 1962.) Because of the postwar employment boom and few new
immigrants, many Americans increased the size of their families in
anticipation of continued economic stability. Although unmeasur-
able, the widespread emphasis upon family values, plus federal
economic stimulation in areas like home ownership, undoubtedly
registered in these statistics. After the Depression, the years following the war seemed to fulfill a middle-class dream of prosperity
and security.

More intensely involved than ever before in marital arrange-

Birth Rate per 1,000 Population
(by 2-year intervals)

Date	Percentage	Date	Percentage
1940	19.4%	1956	25.2%
1942	22.2	1958	24.5
1944	21.2	1960	24.0
1946	24.1	1962	23.3
1948	24.9	1964	21.7
1950	24.1	1966	19.4
1952	25.1	1968	17.4
1954	25.3		

Source: *National Center for Health Statistics*, Natality Statistics
Analysis, U.S., 1965–1967, *p. 2.*

An American view of women in the 1950s: "American women are struggling to fill new functions and responsibilities, to work out a new way of life in response to changing conditions: the daylong absence of the modern husband from the home; the lack of household servants; the public expectation that women will act as members of their communities and the world, as well as of their families; and the idealistic American conception of the wife's role that only the rare woman could fulfill. With the feminists' battle long behind them, U.S. women are less interested in being poets and statesmen then they were 25 years ago, and more interested in domesticity."

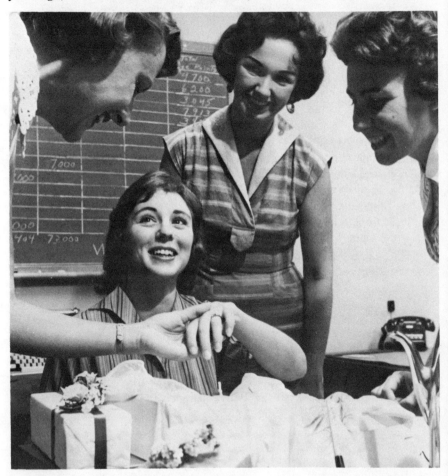

"Thirty-five percent of U.S. women hold daily jobs outside the home. The working woman may be an executive, but, eighteen times oftener, is a subordinate. And many a girl's happiest day at the office is the day she leaves to get married."   (National Archives)

"The Glorified American Girl is a prime element in U.S. mythology, but American men continue to marry 'the girl next door,' who bears only a family resemblance to the love goddess." *(National Archives)*

ments, Americans also talked, thought, and debated about the stability and future of this institution, sometimes as if the future of society or even victory in the Cold War depended upon it. New institutions to deal with family problems, developed by psychologists, indicated widespread concern for the continued health of the family.

Although the profession of marriage counseling appeared in the 1930s, it expanded enormously after the war in concert with a general increased interest in psychology. Up to the Depression, the mental health movement concerned itself primarily with individual adjustment and therapy. After the war, interest began to shift to the context of the family. In the 1950s, this attention became an organized movement. Beginning in 1950, with the formation of the Committee on the Family as part of the Group for the Advancement of Psychiatry headed by the noted psychologist William C. Menninger, the practice of family therapists spread in psychological circles. By 1956, this approach had become respectable and established.

Public opinion also reflected keen interest in the health of the family unit. Just after the war, the Gallup poll published a survey indicating that about 35 percent of Americans desired stricter divorce laws, 31 percent felt they should be unchanged, and only 9 percent thought they should be relaxed. Although some differences of opinion reflected age groups, with older people supporting a stricter marriage code, other surveys uncovered majoritarian conservative attitudes that disapproved of women wearing slacks or shorts in public or occupying public office.

Conservative attitudes toward the family, particularly enunciated by the Catholic Church, made legislators and health officials reluctant to legalize or disseminate information about birth-control devices. For the first two decades following the war, federal and state laws generally prohibited easy access to methods of family planning and limitation. This prohibition did not prevent widespread recourse to contraceptives and illegal abortions, but it did express and uphold an older, religiously sanctioned view of the family.

Nonetheless, during the 1950s, rapid progress marked the technology of birth control: The intrauterine device was reinvented, and researchers developed oral contraceptives from women. Although opposed by the official hierarchy of the Catholic Church, contraception by birth-control devices was promoted by Protestants. In 1961, for example, the National Council of Churches reported favorably on family planning schemes. Those states, such as Connecticut and New York, with legislative bans on the sale of contraceptives gradually eased their restrictions. The result was a franker and more open discussion of birth control and sexuality, increased activities by planned parenthood associations, and the legal use of contraceptives. By the middle 1960s, a number of population experts could realistically envision a drastic cut in the birthrate to effect zero growth in population.

As a method of birth control, abortion remained illegal throughout the United States until well into the 1970s. The problem of widespread illegal abortions, however, received widespread attention as early as 1955 at a conference on abortion sponsored by the Planned Parenthood Federation of America. Four years later, the American Law Institute, in its Model Penal Code, proposed revision of state bans on abortions for reasons of health, for risk of deformity, or for conception resulting from rape or incest. Although some states, such as Maryland, enacted such legislation, not until January 1973, when the United States Supreme Court in *Roe* v. *Wade* struck down the abortion laws on the grounds of invasion of privacy, did therapeutic termination become universally legal.

With so much attention given to child-rearing, the role of women in marriage attracted a great deal of discussion. Many American women held jobs after the war—over 2 million more in 1946 than in 1940—but others were forced out of work or voluntarily returned to the family. They were encouraged to do so by a popular culture that pictured domesticity as the most rewarding goal in life. From the nostalgic view of child-rearing in the best-selling family biography *Cheaper by the Dozen* to the pages of ladies' magazines, the message remained the same: House and garden were the ideal environment for American women. A good example of this ideology appeared in *McCall's Complete Book of Bazaars*, an advice book for holding a successful charity gathering. Obviously aimed at the middle-class suburban housewife, the book promised that a successful bazaar would create a feeling of "identification" in the community, as well as uncover hidden talent of neighbors. "A bazaar," the tract solemnly proclaimed, "can be a miniature world of its own, for the potentialities and challenges it offers are manifold."

The middle-class ideal for the family required prosperous suburban living. Success rested upon the ingenuity of the wife, who had to master different and conflicting roles. As mother, she guided the socialization of her children; as family manager, she directed the consumption of new household products; as sexual partner and seductress, she cemented the loyalty and attention of her husband. While certainly a stereotype, this view of women's roles existed in countless popular women's magazines that filled their pages with cooking tips, household cleaning advice, and short, romantic stories stressing the rewards of female sacrifice. Dubbed "the feminine mystique" by writer Betty Friedan in 1963, this ideology operated as a powerful justification for believing that the family was the most important institution in society. Because being a housewife was the most rewarding career, those women who worked or remained single risked guilt and neurosis.

Friedan's negative description of the miniature world of suburban housewifery probably exaggerated the pervasiveness and the uniqueness of the feminine mystique, but it did accurately reflect the picture of women in popular culture. While the idealized family was obviously a middle-class institution, even those few explicit portrayals of the working class, such as Jackie Gleason's *The Honeymooners,* expressed variations on the same theme. The majority of television programs indulged America's love affair with family life. By the mid-1950s, television had replaced the movies as the basic medium of family entertainment. As film companies in desperation began to aim their product toward specialized audiences, such as teenagers, television captured the family and adopted a conservative model of the institution.

Early television's most perfect family was the Andersons of *Father Knows Best,* a series that ran for eight years after 1954 on CBS and NBC and then survived in reruns on ABC. Although exhibiting a timeless quality, *Father Knows Best* mirrored postwar America. As if to signal the end of the Depression and the war era and the beginning of a hopeful and secure age, the producers of the show chose a title song, "Just Around the Corner There's a Rainbow in the Sky."

Initially a radio program begun in 1949, the series explored the troubles and triumphs of an American middle-class family, presided over by a wise and kindly father played by Robert Young. The town and characters were as typical and idealized as a Norman Rockwell cover for the *Saturday Evening Post*: Maple Street, Springfield, was an address with countless resonances in the col-

In this publicity still from Father Knows Best, *the mirror image of actor Robert Young serves to emphasize the importance of the character he played.* (NYPL Picture Collection)

lective memory and literary imagination. As manager of the General Insurance Company, Jim Anderson exercised his patient and benign rule over his wife, Margaret, and three children. So seriously did Robert Young take this role as paternal protector of the American family, that he sometimes stepped across the fictional frontier into real life. Thus, in 1950, he began an extensive campaign for safe driving, using his show to convince teenagers to modify their driving habits.

A comic variation on the ideal family and television's most popular production of the 1950s was the *I Love Lucy Show*. From its beginning in 1951, the show enjoyed an enormous success. The setting was apartment life in New York City; the two main characters were Lucy and her Cuban-born (and real-life) husband, Ricky Ricardo. Although the couple had no children initially, an upstairs couple, Fred and Ethel Mertz, acted sometimes as friends, sometimes as grandparents. When Lucille Ball became pregnant, the pregnancy and birth were written into the show. On Monday, January 19, 1953, one of the largest television audiences ever assembled heard the announcement of the birth of a son.

The premises of the show were comic, and the situations Lucy found herself in varied considerably, but each episode renewed the battle of the sexes. Ricardo was a popular bandleader. And whatever she did, Lucy could never achieve her greatest goal: to be an actor, a singer, a dancer, a star equal to her husband. Her aspirations always ended in chaos and comic hopelessness. The "situation" always resolved itself, however, as she resigned herself to being a housewife and helpmate.

The show ended in real-life divorce in 1960 (since 1957, the series had been replaced by hourly specials). In 1962, however, Lucille Ball returned with Vivian Vance on the *Lucy Show* in a situation without husbands. Their new series also proved to be enormously popular, and its success suggested that the television comedy format could do far more than reflect the traditional boundaries of home life. Its success indicated that the paternal, nuclear family was not the only living arrangement acceptable to Americans. The reality of American family life had become far broader, looser, and diverse than an ideal mother, father, and children living in pleasant harmony. Americans were well aware of this fact in the early 1960s. By the end of the 1960s, the broken family appeared as a staple in popular culture.

☆   ☆   ☆

Contrary to the postwar hopes of a great many Americans, the family also sustained changes that threatened to alter its traditional form. These changes appeared in two varieties: some threatened the traditional nuclear family, while others fundamentally altered relationships within the institution. Divorce, long the most ominous threat to the family, began to increase after 1958, rising rapidly in the late 1960s and 1970s. Pressure on relationships inside the family mounted with the steady increase in the number and percentage of married working women. By the end of the 1960s, the American family began to assume the characteristics of a dual nuclear family, with two centers: a husband and wife sharing both the task of breadwinner and the prerogatives of the role.

Although, from one perspective, the statistical profile of the family revealed stability and continuity in the period after 1945, a number of disruptive trends also emerged shortly after 1945. Early marriages and births out of wedlock increased rapidly. In 1940, the median age at the time of a first marriage for men was 24.3 years; for women, it was 21.5. By 1968, this figure fell to 23.1 and 20.8 years, respectively. In real terms, this meant many marriages with one or both partners who were still teenagers.

The rapid rise in illegitimacy rates—quadrupling between 1940 and 1970—enormously increased the number of single-parent family arrangements, most of them headed by women. While the number of households headed by women by no means approached the number headed by men, their growth was approximately twice the rate of two-parent families after 1940. These changes were especially striking in the black population. By 1974, about 29 percent of all households headed by women were black, even though the percentage of black households in the population was only about 11. Such disproportionate figures gave rise to a sociology of broken families and cultural deprivation affirming that single-parent families breed delinquency and criminality. As the 1955 report of the Congressional Joint Committee on the Economic Report said: "Broken families are more common in the low-income group. One seventh of the low-income urban families included one adult and one or more children but only one-twentieth of the middle income families were of similar structure." To some sociologists, this set of facts explained higher incidences of crime, unemployment, and other social ills among poorer populations.

If the feminine mystique aimed at creating competent, happy

women devoted to child-rearing, then rising juvenile delinquency figures, especially in the suburbs, suggested their failure. After 1948, official juvenile court case records and FBI arrest tallies for children under eighteen years old recorded a sharp increase in apprehensions and trials of young people. Almost every year, police arrested more children for crimes ranging from breaking curfews and smashing windows to criminal theft and murder. Crime rates for adults increased as rapidly, but teenage delinquency particularly worried social workers, sociologists, criminologists, and psychologists, all of whom agreed that the broken family breeds delinquency. For all the beneficial influences of suburban living—the idealized family, "togetherness," and permissive upbringing—children appeared to suffer acute alienation from their parents that they expressed in antisocial acts. And, as the average age of the American population plunged in the late 1950s and early 1960s, this trend threatened to persist.

Working women changed the family most significantly in this period. Over a ninety-year period, the percentage of women working rose from about 19 in 1890 to 43 in 1970. Most of this increase came from the entry of married women into the labor market. This group rose from a mere 5 percent in 1890 to around 41 percent in 1970. Significantly, one of the largest increases in women's employment occurred during the 1950s, a fact that may help explain the prosperity felt by many American families. (Increased employment did not necessarily mean increased career opportunity. This fact can be illustrated by changing percentages of women receiving master's and doctoral degrees. In the mid-1930s, women received 13 percent of Ph.D. and 37 percent of M.A. degrees. By the mid-1950s, this portion had shrunk to 9 percent of Ph.D. and only 33 percent of M.A. degrees.) The effects of this change in women's employment, of course, were experienced differently by different classes and in different regions of the United States. Nonetheless, rising employment provided a major key in the development of a strong women's movement in the 1960s.

A final large demographic shift that altered the basis of the traditional nuclear family was increased longevity. The average age expectancy increased by about five years between 1945 and 1970. This was a change of some significance. It meant that many more people could hope to live several years beyond retirement. Looked at comparatively, it also meant that women outlived men by an average of seven years in 1970 as opposed to four years in 1945. Another comparison indicates that blacks increased their longevity by a much higher percentage than whites, so that by 1970, this segment of the population lived, on the average, to sixty-five years.

Altogether, these figures point to an increasing part of the population that was either childless or characterized by the absence of one spouse through death or divorce. This extended period of later life, referred to by the French as the "third age," became increasingly important after the war, although its effects were temporarily masked by the marriage boom and baby boom. Despite the focus on youth in the 1950s and 1960s, the American population grew steadily older. The percentage of married persons living beyond sixty-five years of age increased after 1940, and the absolute numbers of single, elderly people increased. Among elderly Americans, widowed women constituted by far the largest group, with almost 30 percent surviving beyond sixty-five.

Political power of aged Americans first emerged during the 1930s in the Townsendites, a grass-roots movement that promised to end poverty among the retired. The passage of the Social Security Act in 1935 and its subsequent modifications, however, established policy for dealing with America's elderly. Primarily a strategy to convince workers to retire by providing income security, the program succeeded, but not without controversy. Millions of workers retired with some steady income; at the same time, inadequate funds for medical care, unemployment, boredom, and alienation plagued older Americans. The Golden Age movement, beginning in 1940, tried to confront these problems, as did the *Senior Citizen*, a journal first published in January 1955. Despite these efforts, the addition of large numbers of citizens in the third age created a group whose primary interests were neither marriage nor children. Many of them felt out of place in a family-oriented society, living a precarious existence in the retirement or nursing homes that spread rapidly after the war.

Modifications in laws concerning the status of families reflected the changing structure of American family life. Sociologists and anthropologists called the resulting legal institution a "companionship family," or sometimes, a "democratic family." In essence, this language implied increased freedom—sanctioned by law—ensuring individuals more latitude in choosing a marriage partner or in deciding to break off a relationship. Where the community and parents once severely curbed individual freedom, the state established liberal guidelines for divorce, inheritance, legitimacy, and the selection of marriage partners. At the same time, society more readily invaded family privacy. For example, in 1971, the United States Supreme Court, in *Wyman* v. *James*, ruled that social workers could enter the home in the interests of a child member, against the wishes of the parents. In this case, the rights of one member of the family were ajudged superior to the interests of the whole: Rights of individuals increased at the expense of the family unit.

Many Americans sensed doom in such postwar modifications of American family life. "Declining" moral standards and juvenile delinquency symbolized this danger, and a vast sociological literature sprang up to explain changes in behavior and morals. Alfred Kinsey's bestselling *Sexual Behavior in the Human Male*, published in January 1948, proved to be one of the most sensational of these works. Undertaken in 1940, Kinsey's questionnaire research into the sexual habits of American men attracted wide attention and comment in the press. It elicited stern jeremiads from conservative religious leaders, but celebrations from liberal psychologists, who delighted in Kinsey's frank approach. The report became the subject of intellectual round-table discussions, cocktail party witticisms, *New Yorker* cartoons, and a great deal of uninformed speculation. From 12,000 individual case histories, Kinsey and his fellow researchers concluded that sexual practices could be explained best by linking them to socioeconomic factors, race, age, occupation, and region. They found, for example, that upper-level economic groups tended to encourage kissing and masturbation but frowned on nonmarital intercourse. Lower-level economic groups were more prudish about kissing but did not worry terribly about nonmarital intercourse. Differences occurred in other groups with different taboos.

Most important, this relativistic approach to sexual practice challenged the notion of a single, prevailing moral standard for all Americans. Kinsey discussed every variety of sexual activity dispassionately. He categorized behavior by types of sexual outlets: self-stimulation, heterosexual petting or intercourse—including marital, premarital, and extramarital—and homosexual activities. Making no moral distinction between types, Kinsey seemed to define normality as a combination of normal and "abnormal" acts. He wrote, for example, that one-third of all American males had participated in serious homosexual activities at one time or another, but affirmed that this case no doubt on their identity as heterosexuals. Also, simply by reporting widespread extramarital practices, Kinsey appeared to be legitimizing them.

His second publication, *Sexual Behavior in the Human Female* (1953), again a best-seller, continued his exploration of the same rich but controversial vein. Widely discussed in the media and made the explicit subject of several Hollywood films, including *Two Plus Two*, these books invoked a wide debate about American sexual practices. They became the starting place for an attack on older standards of morality. Liberals cited Kinsey's works when challenging film and book censorship or when pushing for revocation of city and state blue laws. Actual sexual practices, they claimed, differed enormously from the unrealistic laws that were meant to control them.

Sexual liberalism aimed not just at debunking normality and accepted standards; it also pursued public sensuousness for profit. In October 1953, a young Chicago writer and cartoonist, Hugh Hefner, on a shoestring budget and the fortuitous acquisition of the rights to publish a nude photograph of movie star Marilyn Monroe, launched *Playboy,* a new men's magazine. An immediate success, the magazine combined carefully circumscribed pornography with sophisticated articles and stories. Hefner made a bunny in a tuxedo and the monthly centerfold nude, complete with rouged and powdered breasts, the symbols of a new public sensuality.

By the 1960s, Hefner presided over a commercial empire of sex. *Playboy* reached a circulation of over 800,000 in 1959. By this time a celebrity, Hefner turned his private life into further entrepreneurial ventures. His renowned parties were telecast in 1959 as the *Playboy Penthouse Show.* In 1960, he opened the first Playboy Club in Chicago. And, from 1963 to 1966, he published the "Playboy Philosophy," attacking repression and Puritanism in American culture, in his magazine. Greeted initially with considerable outrage, *Playboy* had become so accepted by 1976 that the future president, Jimmy Carter, confessed his private sexual fantasies in its pages without any permanent damage to his candidacy.

☆   ☆   ☆

When critics began to reflect on American expectations about family life, they often questioned the glorification of the housewife.

Philip Wylie's 1942 diatribe, *Generation of Vipers*, anticipated
later views of "Momism." Wylie blamed every social ill he could
imagine on the frustrations of women trapped in the home. This
misogynist handbook of epithets described women as raging, quar-
reling, murdering Cinderellas, responsible for civic corruption,
smuggling, bribery, theft, and murder. Dr. Vincent A. Strecker
repeated these charges in a more moderate guise in two books,
Their Mother's Sons, published in 1951, and *Their Mother's
Daughters*, published in 1956 with Vincent T. Lathbury. Here
too, the authors blamed a variety of ills on the "life-wrecking crew
of wives."

These pictures of enraged women trapped in unrewarding marriages constituted a small part of the criticism of the family.
Throughout the 1950s and into the 1960s, there were countless
other bleak portrayals of the American family. Perhaps the finest
writer to test the brittle metal of the postwar marriage ideal was
John Updike. Almost all of Updike's novels dwelt upon sexual
satisfaction, or lack of it, in marriage. *Couples*, a heralded novel
published in 1968, explores the loveless marriages and casual sexual encounters of couples who possess children but have no family
life. Husbands and wives are pretty much interchangeable. While
they can find no real existence outside marriages, they find no
salvation within their relationships either. Marriage appears as a
customary but hollow institution, an impermanent interlude in the
eternal struggle to achieve sexual conquest.

☆   ☆   ☆

The literature of the shattered family in the 1950s and 1960s was
extensive, frank, and sometimes brutal. Its counterpart in describing the younger generation is almost as wide and foreboding. In
fact, popular culture seemed to be obsessed with the problems of
youth. From the film *The Bad Seed*, in which innocence and youth
disguise a brutal murderer, to *Rebel Without a Cause*, to the ominous *Wild One*, starring Marlon Brando, Hollywood repeatedly
examined the angry and destructive lives of young people.

Of all the teenage juvenile delinquency films, perhaps the most
interesting is *Rebel Without a Cause*. In this enormously successful movie, James Dean portrays a middle-class boy whose arrival at
a new high school triggers events that end in tragedy and death.
The three main characters, all fated to participate in the final
destruction, live in broken or misshapen families. In Dean's fami-

ly, the mother dominates a passive father; in the second, the father is overbearing; in the third, the family scarcely exists, and the young man runs wild in search of love and security. These stereotyped broken families became a standard explanation for every variety of juvenile misbehavior. Not only were these truisms repeated just in popular culture, but they also became a staple of politics.

Many of the witnesses who appeared before the special Senate Judiciary Subcommittee set up to investigate juvenile delinquency in 1953 repeated the charge that the American family had bred a generation of young criminals. Under the leadership of Senator Robert C. Hendrickson, of New Jersey, and Senator Estes Kefauver, of Tennessee, the committee held extensive and widely publicized hearings during 1955 and 1956 exploring the causes of delinquency. The committee even subpoenaed the publishers of crime comic books and leading film and television producers to answer charges about the influence of media on young people. Although the committee generally supported the position of academics and social workers, who stressed the complexity of the issue, its hearings helped popularize the notion that the United States suffered from a tidal wave of delinquency. Sensationalized news reports of violent and brutal incidents involving teenage delinquents underscored this national concern.

Kefauver's own feelings about the causes of delinquency probably paralleled the reaction of most Americans: He blamed the American family. But recriminations did not end at the fireside. Parents tended to blame schools; the media portrayed parents as weak and vacillating and child-care institutions as callous and brutalizing. The Gallup poll, however, repeatedly found that most Americans blamed declining discipline and loose family ties for youthful misbehavior.

The misbehavior that shocked some observers expressed freedom to others. Jack Kerouac, whose novel *On the Road* appeared in 1957, portrayed the juvenile delinquent as a cultural hero. In a breathless, Whitmanesque style, Kerouac penned a *roman à clef*— a thinly disguised autobiographical description of the lives of his friends in New York and San Francisco. As the author sped back and forth across the country, he encountered the cultures of down-and-out Americans, the music of urban blacks, and the macho masculinity of the American working class. And, as Walt Whitman had done before him, Kerouac celebrated the vitality and energy of these people.

Writing in a more academic mode, Edgar Friedenberg, in his book *The Vanishing Adolescent* (1959), described young people as scapegoats for social institutions that had malfunctioned. The adolescent, he wrote, was an individual in conflict with society: No wonder his contempt for a "society which has *no purposes* [his italics] of its own, other than to insure domestic tranquility by suitable medication." Delinquent behavior, he continued, was the understandable response of people treated as a class with few rights or responsibilities. As for crusaders against delinquency, he noted, their lurid overreaction to the behavior of teenagers displayed unhealthy aggression.

By 1961, it was no longer fashionable to worry about wayward youth. Since the publication of Friedenberg's book, much had happened: John Kennedy was elected in a campaign stressing youth and activity, and children born of the baby boom had entered their teens. Exploited by burgeoning media and consumer industry and no longer feared so much as courted and solicited, young people, merely in terms of numbers, came of age socially. As sociologist Kenneth Keniston told a conference assembled in 1961 to discuss the challenge of youth culture: "The Rock'n'roller, the Joe College student, the juvenile delinquent, the beatnik, whatever their important differences, all form part of this general youth culture." By the early 1960s, seventeen-year-olds emerged as the largest single age group in the American population, and their weight and special interests helped to shape society for several years.

Of all the works to explore the demographic and cultural changes in the family—to slit the seamless web of successful marriage—none was so sharp or ruthless in its implications as the nonfiction best-seller *In Cold Blood*, written by Truman Capote in 1966. Stylistically, Capote's work made a significant contribution to the "New Journalism," a new technique pioneered by other writers, such as Norman Mailer and Tom Wolfe, stressing their own participation in the events they experienced or fictionalized. But notice came to Capote because he focused on a brutal and pointless murder. To the author, the Clutter family was the perfect American family—loving, happy, successful, and healthily dependent upon each other. Their murder by two desperate thieves, therefore, became all the more senseless and tragic. Yet, the author's exploration of his own undisguised tenderness and sympathy for the murderers implied values that deeply compromised the traditional family and heterosexual love. For all the tragedy of the situation, Capote seemed to repeat what other contemporary authors were saying: The American family was disappearing. If perhaps not murdered by society, it was doomed by the extreme pressures of modern life and changes in values.

☆   ☆   ☆

Obviously, the American family changed after World War II. It was pulled in several directions simultaneously, and it responded by changing in contradictory ways. As early as 1929, President Hoover's Committee on Recent Social Trends reported trouble: the American family was losing its functions; division was increasing. Yet, immediately after World War II, the family reflected new optimism, and marriage and birthrates rose sharply. Then, just as abruptly, the bottom fell out of the marriage boom in 1957 and 1958, and the index of instability began a rapid increase.

Those who predicted the death of the American family or lamented the passing of the paternal, nuclear family based their judgments upon nostalgia for what had been. That the structure and internal relations of families altered after the war is certain. Divorce by the 1960s rapidly increased, but so did remarriage. Various experimental relationships and living arrangements became commonplace by the 1960s. While many of these contradicted traditional moral axioms, they retained family characteristics. That these alternatives might become permanent was suggested at the American Psychological Association's annual meeting in 1967. Papers presented to the conference formed a symposium on "Alternative Models for the American Family Structure." As the editor of the series remarked, America was still committed to the family, but within this broad allegiance, room existed for experimentation and change, from group marriages to Margaret Mead's suggested "two-step marriage," new living arrangements for elderly people, and serial marriages. The future form of family life would be determined in large measure by the economic and cultural forces that influenced this institution. And none of these was permanent.

4 In the Shadow of the Cold War

The new President in April 1945 was Harry S Truman, a man elevated by ambition, force of personality, and circumstance to a position for which he had little preparation. A small, bespectacled, intellectual boy, Truman grew up in Independence, Missouri. His haunts were neighborhood fields, the First Presbyterian Church on Sundays, and the Independence Public Library during the week. So diligent a reader was he that he had finished all of the books in the library and his family Bible three times by the age of fourteen. His favorite reading matter was history, including Plutarch's *Lives*, the histories of ancient civilizations, and biographies of American presidents. These accounts of the lives of great men confirmed Truman's belief that political leadership means decisive activity. No belief could have better sustained a man who delighted in tough talk and the pugnacity of American politics.

As a boy, Truman's early jobs brought him in contact with farmers, small-town businessmen and speculators, and workers: the variegated and transient population of a state on the eastern reaches of the American frontier. After high school, he hired out to the Santa Fe Railroad as timekeeper, living occasionally in hobo camps along the Missouri River. Shortly afterward, he secured a job at the National Bank of Commerce in Kansas City. By 1906, however, he returned to the family farm, which he operated until the beginning of World War I.

For Truman, like many men of his generation, the war pushed him from one career into another. His stint in the National Guard began before the outbreak of hostilities, but active duty sent him to France. When he returned to Missouri after the war, he was thirty-five, just married, and looking for a new career. Truman first chose haberdashery, but when his clothing shop failed, he agreed to run for local political office. His first victory was as county judge, a position he won by running as a loyal member of the Pendergast machine, which controlled the state Democratic party. Launched on a political career, the only real question was how independent he would be of his dubious supporters.

Truman's service in state politics was competent and honest, but relatively undistinguished. So too was his career as a senator from Missouri. First elected in 1934, he worked hard for most New Deal legislation. A loyal party man representing the political center of the party, in 1944 he was an ideal compromise candidate for the vice-presidency. Both labor and the South, the two largest contending forces in the Democratic party, agreed to him. These very qualities that made him acceptable, however, often worked to his disadvantage: The compromise candidate does not always become the best leader.

In many ways, Truman's presidency was accidental. He became a vice-presidential candidate in 1944, at a time when speculation had it that Roosevelt might not live through another full term. Yet, he was not chosen as a replacement, but rather as a substitute for an unacceptable replacement: Henry Wallace—then Roosevelt's vice-president, but *persona non grata* to the conservative wing of the Democratic party. Truman in 1944 was relatively unknown to the American public, except for his wartime investigations into defense-industry profiteering and inefficiency; he represented loyal but moderate support for the New Deal.

Truman's concept of the presidency combined the necessity of invention with guidance by traditional attitudes toward leadership culled from the biographies of great men and reinforced by his own experiences. To many who observed his career, he exemplified the American myth of success, a modern Horatio Alger, who through pluck and luck went from "window washer, bottle duster, floor scrubber in an Independence, Missouri, drugstore," to President of the United States. Even to Truman, this was a story only half-believed, and in recounting his success, he always displayed a measure of incredulity. As he said the day after Roosevelt's death: "When they told me yesterday what had happened, I felt like the moon, the stars, and the planets had fallen on me."

A shrewd and tenacious political fighter, Truman dramatically changed the tone of presidential leadership. Almost self-consciously the opposite of F.D.R., Truman delighted in making decisions and taking responsibility—even for mistakes. The momentous choices he faced—to drop the atomic bomb on Hiroshima and Nagasaki, for example—simply went with the job,

he felt, and he did not shrink from making them. For this, supporters celebrated him, and critics castigated him. In foreign and
domestic affairs, Truman acted quickly and sometimes rashly. He
brought an element of wit, enthusiasm, and toughness to his task,
perhaps best exemplified by the motto on his desk: "The Buck
Stops Here."

Truman did not discourage the popular view that his tastes and
language represented those of ordinary Americans. Truman
brought straightforwardness, activism, and simple answers to the
increasingly complex questions of the day. He, his wife, and his
daughter symbolized the success of the traditional American family, secure in its values and steadfast, despite the pressures of
postwar society. Affecting gaudy shirts on vacation in Key West,
Florida, the President enjoyed fishing, swimming, poker, and the
rites of the Masonic Lodge, in which he was a leader. When his
daughter Margaret launched a singing career with a marginal
voice, Truman was as protective as any father might be. In December 1950, after a concert at Constitution Hall, one of Washington's leading music critics reported the unpleasant truth about
Margaret's talents. Truman rushed off a retort that later found its
way into the press: "Someday I hope to meet you. When that
happens you'll need a new nose, a lot of beefsteak for black eyes,
and perhaps a supporter below."

Following Roosevelt's death on April 12, 1945, Truman had to
assert his own leadership and yet convince the nation that he
would continue F.D.R.'s policies. Although he paid lip service
to continuity, he did not go out of his way to court Roosevelt's advisers. Sometimes acrimoniously, as in the case of Henry Wallace
and Interior Secretary Harold Ickes, and sometimes quietly,
Roosevelt's key advisers quit or were eased out, and Truman replaced them with his own men. Within a few weeks of taking
office, Truman replaced Attorney General Francis Biddle with
conservative Texas politician Tom C. Clark. Lewis Schwellenbach
replaced Frances Perkins, the only female member of the Cabinet,
as Secretary of Labor. Clinton P. Anderson took over as Secretary
of Agriculture from Claude R. Wickard. Other appointments followed in June: Robert Hannegan to Postmaster General, James F.
Byrnes to Secretary of State, and then in July, Kentucky congressman Fred Vinson to the Treasury. Two of these original appointees,
Clark and Vinson, later received Supreme Court appointments.
Truman's choice of Byrnes as Secretary of State proved an unhap-

President Harry Truman (right) and Secretary of State James F. Byrnes at the bow of the U.S.S. Augusta, *en route to the Big Three meeting with Churchill and Stalin at Potsdam, Germany. (Office of War Information, National Archives)*

py choice. Too independent, and perhaps thinking it should be he sitting in the Oval Office, Byrnes was replaced in early 1947 by General George C. Marshall.

In July 1946, Truman named John Davidson Clark, Leon H. Keyserling, and Edwin G. Nourse to his new Council of Economic Advisers. Keyserling, particularly, became important in setting economic policy. An active New Dealer who had helped draft the National Labor Relations Act of 1935, Keyserling favored programs stimulating economic growth rather than those redistributing wealth. Guided by efficient use of federal instruments of fiscal management, the economy, he hoped, would grow steadily, with minimal inflation. Keyserling's general orientation became the unofficial economic policy of both Truman's and Eisenhower's administrations; prosperity would solve the nation's social problems.

Truman had his worst time with Henry Wallace. A difficult, morally upright man, Wallace well understood that his liberal reputation had cost him the vice-presidential nomination' in 1944. Barely confirmed by the Senate as Secretary of Commerce in 1944, Wallace, nonetheless, used his office as if he had a mandate for leadership. In some sense, he did. In Truman's Cabinet, he represented a large bloc of liberal opinion that was quickly losing its voice in the administration. Particularly outraged by the President's hard line toward the Soviet Union, Wallace first appealed to Truman. In a letter on March 14, 1946, he advised the President to try economic cooperation with the Soviets as a means of avoiding the foreign policy stalemate quickly developing over Eastern Europe. While not conceding American positions, Wallace suggested understanding Russian difficulties and recognizing the "lack of realism in many of their [foreign policy] assumptions and conclusions which stand in the way of peaceful world cooperation."

The President, however, neither changed his policy nor appreciated unsolicited advice from his Secretary of Commerce. When Wallace spoke at Madison Square Garden on September 12, 1946, publicly criticizing American foreign policy, Truman had to act to appease both Secretary Byrnes, who threatened to resign, and the press, which demanded to know who was in charge of the State Department. On September 20, he replaced Wallace at the Commerce Department with Averell Harriman. By appointing one of the architects of United States Cold War policy, Truman signaled his determination to continue confronting the Russians. Thus, the only substantial voice opposing American foreign policy departed from the Cabinet. Wallace later assumed the editorship of the magazine *The New Republic* in order to continue his fight.

Truman's postwar dealings with problems of strikes and inflation revealed a similar natural conservative streak. Although in 1946 the President promised Congress to hold the line on wages and prices, his actions ultimately stimulated price rises and exacerbated labor relations. Not, of course, that it was entirely his own doing. Truman shared Congress's desire to dismantle controls quickly and return initiative to business.

The problems of inflation and a rash of prolonged strikes made development of a consistent policy difficult, but Truman reacted to events as much as he anticipated problems. For the period from V-J Day through 1946, Truman lifted controls, reapplied them, or suggested new ones in his effort to speed the return of private management and free collective bargaining.

Only two days after the end of the war, Truman modified controls over prices, wages, and materials. Then, in September 1945, he suggested a tax cut, which Congress enthusiastically passed in November. Both of these actions warmed the engines of inflation. At the same time, the President announced that the National War Labor Board would cease its activities as final arbiter of wage increases. He hoped that a forthcoming Labor-Management Conference, scheduled for November, would establish informal wage-and-price guidelines. The conference, held in Washington, failed, however, to achieve any real agreement, and Truman's hoped-for industrial statesmanship did not emerge.

Because of looser controls and abrupt changes in hours and overtime which resulted in declining wages, the unions in major industries struck for substantial increases. Well might they have thought this a good moment to flex their muscles. During the war, union membership had increased spectacularly from about 9 million in 1940 to about 14.5 million in 1945, or approximately 36 percent of nonagricultural employees. Membership peaked at a higher point in American history than at any other time, save a brief moment during the Korean War.

Industrial strife boiled over during the fall of 1945 in the oil industry and at General Motors. In all, there were 4,600 work stoppages during that year involving about 5 million workers. The next year continued the industrial wrangling as steelworkers walked off the job in January after industry rejected a wage settlement of 18.5 cents per hour endorsed by the federal government.

In April, the United Mine Workers went out, and in May, Truman seized the railroads to prevent a strike. In all, Truman seized and operated nine industries under powers granted by the War Labor Disputes Act, which remained in effect until June 1946. Although many of these strikes were defensive—to maintain wages and membership gained during the war—the vast industrial turmoil during reconversion created a hostile public attitude toward unions and eventually infuriated Truman. In May, responding to the proposed strike of two railway unions, the President hastily penned a speech denouncing "effete union leaders" and called for vigilante action against them. Fortunately, his adviser Clark Clifford removed most of the offending touches, and Truman kept his political balance.

In approaching price controls, especially on foods, Truman pursued a contradictory policy. Although regulatory acts remained in force six months beyond the war, the President only gave weak support to Chester Bowles, the director of the Office of Price Administration. He also permitted the steel and auto industries to raise prices in order to compensate for wage hikes. And, the President failed to secure legislation extending an effective OPA operation beyond June 30, 1946. Facing a withholding strike by meatpackers and farmers, and despite pleas by homemakers for continued tough controls, Truman permitted the deregulation of food prices. On November 9, after heavy Democratic losses at the polls, Truman lifted remaining price controls. In the resulting inflation, food prices rose almost 30 percent in six months. From 1945 to 1947, retail prices of round steak increased by about 86 percent; bread rose 42 percent; and bacon increased about 89 percent. The general consumer price index rose about 24 percent in these two years, after moving up only 22 percent in the four years from 1941 to 1945.

Truman's inability to provide satisfactory leadership in price policy or calm the angry strikes of the winter of 1945–1946 reinforced a growing conservative trend that influenced the congressional elections of 1946. Only twice between 1945 and 1970—in 1946 and in 1952—did the Republicans capture a majority in either or both branches of Congress. In a sense, both these elections were referenda on the Truman administration, one in its initial stages and one at its close. From another perspective, the elections were less significant. Whether or not Republicans actually dominated, the election of conservatives to Congress had stymied the New Deal since 1938, and frequently blocked Truman. In 1946, many Republican congressmen had promised their constituencies to undo the New Deal, but the only major New Deal legislation ever threatened were the laws that regulated labor unions. Unpopular because of protracted strikes and the butt of an extensive media campaign, labor unions were also reeling from internal struggle. In particular, after a year or so of jockeying for power within the CIO, anti-Communist unionists, led by Walter Reuther, succeeded in convincing Philip Murray, President of the CIO, to support expulsion of Communist-dominated unions from the brotherhood. When this expulsion occurred in 1946, eleven unions with around 1 million members were forced out of the organization. Although this move delighted liberals and conservatives alike, it did not earn much public approval for other union activities. More subtly, this ideological housecleaning signaled a less aggressive posture of industrial unionization. Invited in during the 1930s, when their organizational skills could be put to work in the steel industry, automobile industry, and others, the Communists were accounted a major obstacle by many unionists, who hoped for continued peaceful collective bargaining in recently organized industries.

At first dubious of Truman, despite the friendly attitude of his Secretary of Labor, and put off by his hasty actions during strikes, the AF of L and the CIO were encouraged when he vetoed the Case Bill in June 1946. This bill, introduced by Representative Francis Case, of South Dakota, cut seriously into the power of the unions. Pushed through the House without hearings, the bill would have created a tripartite Federal Mediation Board for strikes involving interstate commerce and a required cooling-off period after notification of a walkout.

But Truman's veto only obstructed the inevitable. In early 1947, the new Republican Congress came to Washington determined to pass some form of restrictive labor legislation. During the first four months of the new Eightieth Congress, members introduced over seventy labor policy bills, most of them directed at setting up public machinery to settle strike disputes. Choosing among competing bills fell largely to House and Senate Labor Committee chairmen, Representative Fred A. Hartley, Jr., of New Jersey, and Senator Robert A. Taft, of Ohio. Taft, in particular, emerged from this legislative turmoil as a national conservative leader, a latter-day David slinging his barbs against the New Deal Goliath. Certainly no friend of unions, Taft did not always fit the conservative mold, and his stands on some social issues, like public housing, and his reluctance to involve the United States in Cold War adventures cast doubt on the purity of his credentials. On the issue of "excessive" union power, however, there was no mistaking the appropriateness of his nickname, "Mr. Republican."

Just as adamant on the other side were the AF of L and the CIO, who wanted no modification whatsoever of the gains made under the New Deal Wagner Act. Dubbing the Taft-Hartley proposal the "Slave Labor Bill," major unions campaigned against its passage. Nonetheless, the Republican congress, aided by southern Democratic conservatives and bolstered by antiunion public opinion and strong pressure from business organizations, pushed through the act in the spring of 1947.

The most important features of the Taft-Hartley Act outlawed the closed shop (whereby to work, an employee had first to join a union), outlawed secondary boycotts and jurisdictional strikes in violation of National Labor Relations Board decisions, outlawed welfare funds except where jointly administered by labor and management, and made unions suable in federal court for violation of contracts. It required unions to file an annual financial report with the Labor Department and their own memberships. Union officials had to sign a non-Communist affidavit annually or lose their rights under the act. Employers and employees could petition for decertification elections, and federal government employees were forbidden to strike. Two final features legalized "right-to-work" state laws, prohibiting compulsory membership in a union shop, and gave the president power to invoke an eighty-day cooling-off period during which labor would be compelled to return to work.

Passed by the Congress on June 9, 1947, the bill went to Truman for his signature; now, the focus of lobbying and pressure politics shifted to the White House. Most of the important administration agencies, like the Council of Economic Advisers, and the President's political advisers recommended a veto. On June 20, Truman sent his reply to Congress: a sharply worded rejection of the law on the grounds that it undid the rights of workers and created massive government interference in union and management activities. That evening, Senator Taft went on radio to rebut the President's reasoning. Congress enthusiastically seconded Taft and voted the next day to override the Presidential veto, 331 to 83 in the House and 68 to 25 in the Senate. Aided by crucial southern votes in both houses, the Republican majority in Congress reversed the most liberal provisions of New Deal labor legislation. Neither side fully anticipated the effects of Taft-Hartley. Advocates of the bill were disappointed when union political activity did not decrease; on the contrary, labor organizations realized their vulnerability and firmed up their alliance with the Democratic party. The new act scarcely affected serious union problems, such as a lack of internal democracy and racketeering. And those who hoped to use the act as the opening wedge to dismantle the New Deal were sorely disappointed. But the legislation did bolster postwar conservatism in major American unions and increased their reluctance to enter serious organizing drives. Through the antiunion shield of right-to-work laws, it encouraged industrialization of the Sunbelt using nonunion labor.

Opponents of the act wrongly anticipated that it meant "slave labor." Nothing of the sort happened. Truman, despite his vociferous opposition, invoked the act several times during his administration. Once they realized they could not repeal the act, established unions learned to live comfortably with most of its features. In fact, the greatest effect of Taft-Hartley was probably political, for Truman's veto message cemented the coalition that helped elect him in 1948.

If Republicans saw Taft-Hartley as a first skirmish in their Armaggedon with the New Deal, Truman and his advisers, particularly Clark Clifford, recognized in the act a pretext to counterattack and to secure Truman's reelection in 1948. To win, the President had to reestablish the coalition that had disintegrated in November 1946. This required considerable skill, for conservative southern congressmen opposed civil rights action that might encourage black Democratic voters. On the liberal side was the Americans for Democratic Action, a group that fought to reestablish liberalism free from the tint of radicalism that had been brushed on the New Deal. Since early 1947, this organization, peopled by illustrious former New Dealers and anti-Communist liberals, had promoted the nomination of General Dwight Eisenhower or Supreme Court Justice William O. Douglas to replace Truman. Further left, a Henry Wallace candidacy threatened to siphon off millions of votes in crucial industrial states.

In late 1946, the Democratic party leadership and presidential advisers met to consider Truman's future. The resulting strategy, outlined in a memo drafted by Clark Clifford in late 1947, analyzed the upcoming election, predicting that the Republicans would nominate Thomas E. Dewey, Governor of New York. Clifford urged Truman to appeal to liberal voters, to court labor and urban constituencies, to create a militant progressive program, and then blame Congress for failing to enact his program. In particular, Truman needed the votes of union members and of black and Jewish Americans.

The President had already moved tentatively in this direction. Following the Republican tidal wave of 1946, he issued Executive Order #9008 creating a Civil Rights Committee headed by Charles E. Wilson, President of General Electric, to propose a general program of civil rights action. Dominated by liberals with ties to labor and organizations like the NAACP, the body was predisposed to recommend firm action on civil rights. In June 1947, Truman personally dramatized his support for civil rights by appearing before the NAACP, where he promised that the federal government would become a "friendly, vigilant defender" of the rights of all Americans.

When the Committee on Civil Rights delivered its report on October 29, 1947, it handed Truman more, perhaps, than he had bargained for. The message demanded equality for all Americans. Besides invoking this respectable platitude, the report suggested concrete measures: self-determination for Washington, D.C. (a largely black city, then ruled by congressional committee), an immediate end to segregation in the armed forces, protective legislation for voters in national primaries (which in the one-party southern states were more important than elections), establishment of a permanent commission on civil rights, a stronger civil rights section in the Justice Department, and an end to restrictive housing covenants and discrimination in hiring and interstate commerce.

The President incorporated some of these suggestions in his civil rights message to Congress on February 2, 1948. When Southerners vehemently opposed such legislation and threatened to bolt the party, Truman beat a strategic retreat into inaction. In March, however, under pressure from the NAACP, other black organizations, and the Committee Against Jim Crow [segregation] in Military Service and Training, which threatened civil disobedience if the army were not integrated, Truman adopted Clark Clifford's strategy. On July 26, 1948, by executive order, he established a review appeal board to oversee federal-hiring discrimination cases and appointed another committee to begin desegregation of the armed services.

In courting Jewish votes, Truman revealed the same pattern of drift followed by decisive preelection action. Large numbers of Jewish voters in key states such as Illinois, New York, Ohio, and New Jersey fervently supported establishment of an independent state of Israel. The United States, they demanded, should endorse this goal. Zionists in the United States pressed the White House for action, but Truman had other factors to consider: the actions of the British and future access to important oil reserves in Arab territories. When order broke down in 1948 because Palestinian Arabs refused to participate in a partition of the region, Truman decided upon recognition of the state of Israel. Israel proclaimed itself an independent state on May 15, and Truman almost immediately proferred United States diplomatic recognition. He extended this diplomatic shield later in the spring when Arabs attacked the new nation. By threatening sanctions, the President secured an uneasy armistice. While these actions did not win Truman the election in 1948, they did help him squeak to victory in key states such as Ohio.

Truman took another step toward victory by calling a special session of Congress on July 16, one day after the Democratic convention. This astute move diverted attention away from the terrible divisions in the Democratic party that the convention had revealed. Unable to influence the choice of a candidate, Democratic liberals, led by Hubert Humphrey, of Minnesota, forced through a tough civil rights plank. Southern Dixiecrats walked out of the party convention and met in Birmingham, Alabama, to form the States' Rights Party. Nominating Governor Strom Thurmond, of South Carolina, for president, the party dedicated itself to one particular right of states—the right to discriminate against black citizens. On the left, the Progressive party nominated Henry Wallace for President. Challenged on both sides, Truman picked his fight with the Republican congress, largely ignored Thurmond, and questioned the loyalty of Henry Wallace. The Republican congress obliged the President. Dubbed the "Turnip Day" special session, it passed almost none of the proposals made by Truman: antiinflationary legislation, comprehensive housing, aid to education, extension of social security, and repeal of the Taft-Hartley

Act. After two weeks, Congress adjourned: Only controls on credit and housing construction legislation had passed. The Republicans had handed Truman a perfect issue, a do-nothing Congress, and a lackluster candidate in Governor Thomas Dewey of New York.

The official campaign began in September—an uphill struggle for Truman. This was, however, his sort of fight. Rolling up his sleeves and delivering rapid punches to the conservative Wall Street lawyer image projected by the Republicans, Truman criss-crossed the nation, stopping in small towns, but also carefully aiming his campaign at big labor centers. In an extravagant populist idiom, Truman lambasted the class-conscious Republicans and promised a revival of the New Deal. If the mantle of Roosevelt hung loosely around his smaller shoulders, many voters failed to notice it. Contrary to the confident predictions of the polls, the President won a small plurality of around 2 million votes and a significant electoral majority. Strom Thurmond received 39 electoral votes, all in the South, and Wallace gained none. More important, a decisive Democratic majority swept into the House and Senate, bringing with it a new generation of liberals; among them, in the Senate, were Hubert Humphrey, Paul Douglas, and Estes Kefauver and, in the House, Eugene McCarthy, Sidney Yates, and Abraham Ribicoff.

With his victory, Truman had revived the New Deal coalition of labor, urban residents, Catholics, farmers, and black voters. He accomplished this by protecting the gains of the 1930s, not the achievements of the 1940s. Truman had secured legislative reorganization in 1946 and unification of the armed forces in 1947, as well as centralization of overseas spying operations in 1947. The Hospital Survey and Construction Act of 1946 passed as well as a Federal Airport Construction Act. But these were not the stuff of liberal reform; indeed, most of Truman's proposals had fallen on deaf congressional ears.

Buoyed by his victory, however, Truman proposed an ambitious social reform program. In a rousing State of the Union message in early 1949, he suggested major innovations in medical care, housing, and farm policy. This "Fair Deal" agenda was designed by administration liberals and direct descendants of the New Deal. At its heart stood a farm program created by the new Secretary of Agriculture, Charles F. Brannan. The Brannan Plan proposed to maintain farm income through direct subsidies to farmers while allowing commodity prices to rise or fall. Enthusiastically greeted by labor and some farmers, the program encountered fatal opposition from Republicans, the powerful Farm Bureau Federation, and southern congressmen, who opposed the limitations placed on cash benefits to large farming operations.

Weak congressional leadership jeopardized other Fair Deal projects: a national health insurance program, repeal of Taft-Hartley, and the creation of a Fair Employment Practices Committee all failed. Only in the areas of Social Security benefits and housing did the President achieve legislative victory. The Social Security amendments of 1950 extended coverage and benefits, and the Housing Act of 1949 provided for construction of 810,000 low-cost housing units and loans and grants to cities for slum clearance.

On another count, the President scored a substantial victory. In April 1950, Senator Robert Kerr, of Oklahoma, introduced a bill exempting natural gas from federal price regulation. Squelched in the House by Speaker Sam Rayburn, of Texas, liberals belatedly mounted opposition in the Senate, but they failed to stop the bill. Urged on by liberals, Truman decided to veto the measure. Likewise, in 1952, Truman successfully blocked the Tidelands Bill, which would have turned over title and control of offshore oil deposits to shoreline states. The effect of this bill would have been to leave private oil companies unregulated by friendly or weak state governments.

During his second term of office, Truman learned one of the most important truisms of American politics: victory at the polls does not always translate into legislative success. A coalition of Southern Democratic conservatives and Republicans stymied liberal legislation. His electoral coalition had neither strength nor coherence enough to achieve new legislative victories. While it may not have been apparent at the time, Truman's tough stands on foreign policy matters and his vociferous antagonism to Communism may have helped explain his surprise victory in 1948. Indeed, Truman benefited from America's desire for security as much as from its need for change in 1948. And most of his attention after 1948 went toward foreign policy.

By 1948 and 1949, the Cold War threatened to engulf the world in military struggle. The borders of China and Eastern Europe became serious trouble spots. Disputes in these areas had been building since the end of the war, and they worsened because the superpowers failed to settle problems raised by the defeat of Germany and Japan. Shifts in power that accompanied the war disrupted traditional relations in Europe and Asia, and neither the United States nor the Soviet Union was willing or able to make compromises that would have stabilized those areas.

In Europe, the contradiction between American and Russian interests loomed dangerously—Germany being the most contentious problem. The Russians believed that only their hegemony over Eastern Europe could prevent future threats from Germany. They had three possible means to achieve such a goal. They could continue the wartime alliance with the United States and agree on a friendly division of Europe into spheres of interest. They could continue military occupation of Eastern Europe. Or, they could transform the societies on their borders into Communist states and integrate them into the Soviet political and economic system.

From the vantage point of Western Europe, the United States had much the same choice: It could guarantee peace by agreement with the Russians, continue to build up military occupation forces, or promote capitalist social and economic organization in friendly nations. While none of these options was ever completely rejected by either side, the exercise of social and economic hegemony became more and more the recourse of both superpowers. Moreover, failure to settle outstanding issues intensified the commitment to rearmament on both sides. When the Russians successfully tested an atomic weapon in 1949, they broke the short-lived United States nuclear monopoly. From then on, a balance of terror reinforced the balance of power.

Truman's first meeting with Stalin at Potsdam in 1945 decided the early course of American-Soviet relations. From hindsight, Truman claimed that he decided two things about the Russians at this conference: They believed that the United States was headed for a postwar depression and therefore needed Russian trade; and they sought control over Eastern Europe. The President bluntly deduced that "Force is the only thing the Russians understand."

Truman and Stalin failed to agree on the position of the German-Polish border or on a peace treaty with Germany. Lack of accord on the future of Germany and Eastern Europe led to a gradual division of Europe into two armed camps. This did not occur immediately; there were even moments when a shift in policy seemed possible, but the general course of events flowed toward confrontation. Germany was almost immediately divided into two, not four zones. This policy of "bizonia," advocated by General Lucius Clay, split the conquered nation into a Russian zone and a joint French-United States-British area. Competition for peripheral areas also increased; countries occupied by Soviet troops gradually reorganized along Communist lines, ending in February 1948 with the Communist coup d'état in Czechoslovakia. Similar pressures and competition also played on the stage of Western Europe. United States involvement in the Greek civil war in 1947 resulted from the exhaustion of the British. In September 1946, a much-contested plebiscite returned King George II to power in Greece. Opposition to his conservative government quickly heated up into armed struggle. By the winter of 1947, Britain, which had been supplying arms to the Greek royal government, could no longer sustain the endeavor. Truman had to decide: either enter the fight in a significant way or risk a victory by Communist-supported insurgents. The President chose the first option and, upon advice from Dean Acheson and Republican Senator Vandenberg, appeared before Congress with a message designed to persuade—and frighten—that body into appropriating aid. Truman's address to Congress on March 12, 1947, worked. In many ways, his speech galvanized anti-Communist opinion as effectively as had Churchill's "Iron Curtain" address a year earlier. By the middle of May, Congress had voted substantial aid. Including both Greece and Turkey under the umbrella of United States power, Truman admitted that these governments were not perfectly democratic. But, he argued, as friends of the United States, they were allied to democracy and the ideals of a free press, a free radio, and personal liberty.

Problems of reconstruction and stability in Western Europe preoccupied policymakers in early 1947. A new plan was sketched first by Dean Acheson and then dramatized by Secretary of State George C. Marshall in a commencement address at Harvard. Secretary Marshall's plan for European aid went to Congress in 1947 and eventually passed in April 1948. The European Recovery Act, or Marshall Plan, provided $17 billion in assistance to Europe. It might not have passed, however, had it not become an obvious Cold War act. Over the summer of 1947 in Paris, Marshall Plan negotiations were held that included the Soviets and their allies. The Russians, however, rejected the strings that the aid program would attach to their economy, and they walked out, forcing Czechoslovakian representatives to follow suit. Assured that Communist nations would not benefit from American aid, Congress more willingly appropriated money for the program.

The deepening economic and political division of Europe eventually solidified into military alliances. In the spring of 1948, the United States moved to create an anti-Soviet European defense pact and an official state of Western Germany. When a new West German currency was introduced inside the western sector of the shared city of Berlin, the Russians responded with a total blockade of traffic via road and railway into the city. Faced with a number of possible responses, Truman chose to airlift supplies to Berlin, and the Russians balked at shooting down American cargo planes. After a number of grim months, the Soviets relented and allowed normal supply routes to operate. But the bad feelings engendered by this confrontation worked their mischief. Congress swallowed its objection to foreign aid and entangling alliances and ratified the North Atlantic Treaty on July 21, 1949, creating a military alliance including the United States, France, Britain, the Benelux countries (Belgium, the Netherlands, and Luxembourg), Canada, Portugal, Denmark, Norway, Italy, and Iceland. Point Four Aid passed on June 5, 1950, extending American aid to friendly Third World countries. By 1951, thirty-three nations had assistance agreements with the United States under the act.

If anything, events in Asia were more unsettled after World War II than in Europe. In Southeast Asia, American policymakers acquiesced in the reintegration of Java into the Dutch empire and Indochina into the French empire. In China, Roosevelt had banked on the survival of Chiang Kai-shek, the corrupt but clever leader of the recognized Nationalist regime. During the war, the Japanese conquered much of China, but Chiang seemed more interested in battling Communist insurgents led by Mao Tse-tung than in engaging the invading armies of the Axis power.

If Roosevelt had unrealistically committed himself to the fortunes of Chiang, Truman had to preside over the consequences of this policy. For almost forty years, the United States had supported a strong, friendly China, but by the late 1940s, this policy was obviously stalemated. Immediately after the war, Truman tried without success to secure a truce between warring Chinese factions, largely because Chiang refused to end his attacks on the Communist insurgents. By the summer of 1946, fighting had broken out over a broad area of China. General George C. Marshall, who had been dispatched to negotiate with Chiang, returned home, convinced that the Chinese leader would never institute reforms or broaden his political base. Truman realized the United States could do little except watch in frustration as the Chinese Nationalists lost the civil war.

In 1948 and 1949, the tide of battle turned, and Chiang's forces rapidly lost control of their strongholds in southern China. Anticipating a defeat, Truman approved publication of a "White Paper" blaming Communist victory in China on the corruption and inefficiency of Chiang. On December 8, 1949, Chiang fled to the Chinese island of Taiwan with the remnants of his army and supporters. At the same time, the State Department rejected tentative feelers from the important Chinese Communist leader Chou En-lai, suggesting that he and other factions in the revolutionary leadership desired friendly relations with the United States.

Korea was a danger spot on a smaller scale. Unable to agree on a joint settlement with the Russians, who occupied the northern half of that nation, the United States allowed the right-wing leader Syngman Rhee to set up a Republic of Korea in 1948 in the south. The Russians countered with the creation of the Democratic People's Republic of Korea under Kim Il Sung. Both major powers then withdrew their troops in 1949, leaving the two small states to confront each other across the thirty-eighth parallel.

These events raised a din of fury from Republican enemies of the Truman administration. Attacking Truman, the New Deal, and "Communists in government," members of the Republican party led by the "China Lobby"—a group of pro-Chiang congressmen— pilloried the Democratic administration. Their special target was Dean Acheson, now Secretary of State. Dean Acheson's remarks to the National Press Club in January 1950 did not help the administration's cause. The Secretary of State noted that the United States defense perimeter did not include Korea or Taiwan.

The Republicans claimed this speech to be an invitation for attack. But when the North Koreans did invade the South in June 1950, no such simpleminded reason could explain their act. Following previous skirmishes and a heated-up propaganda war between both sides, armed hostilities were as much caused by local events as they were by outside encouragement.

The beleaguered Truman administration acted swiftly to prevent its South Korean ally from falling. The President dispatched the 7th Fleet to protect Taiwan from conquest by the Chinese Communists, and, taking advantage of the Soviet boycott of the United Nations, secured a Security Council resolution condemning the invasion and calling for armed resistance. Truman also announced on June 27 that he would take measures to aid French military forces in Indochina attempting to quell a rebellion there. It seemed that confrontation with Communism had arrived at last.

Yet, like everything else in the Cold War, the Korean adventure proved frustrating and indecisive. It quickly became apparent that the U.N. resolution principally meant United States aid to South Korea. Other nations provided only token support. To save Syngman Rhee, Truman dispatched American ground forces to Korea on June 30. By late summer, General Douglas MacArthur, head of the U.N. command, had rebuffed the North Korean armies at Pusan on the southern tip of Korea. Then, on September 15, he launched a counterattack behind enemy lines at Inchon. Within two weeks the tide of battle had turned; United States forces retook Seoul, the capital of South Korea, and Truman permitted MacArthur to cross the border at the thirty-eighth parallel in pursuit of the North Korean armies. Had he been satisfied, the President might have declared an end to the conflict, thus restoring the prewar status quo. But, encouraged by his advisers, committed to reunification, and barely able to restrain MacArthur, Truman allowed the invasion, insisting that non-Korean troops be kept away from the Chinese borders. In October, Truman flew to Midway Island in the Pacific to talk with his headstrong military commander. MacArthur assured him that neither China nor the Russians would intervene.

Although the Indian ambassador to China warned that the Chinese would enter the war if non-Korean troops passed far beyond the thirty-eighth parallel, Truman chose to ignore him. Promising to bring United States troops home by Christmas, MacArthur pushed the retreating North Koreans toward the Yalu River, threatening Chinese bridges and hydroelectric plants. Chinese reaction was swift and surprising. On October 26, Chinese troops intervened, defeating advance United States forces, driving them back toward the thirty-eighth parallel. MacArthur demanded more troops and urged help from Chiang Kai-shek. Truman refused to grant his general's request to escalate the war for fear of widening the conflict into a world conflagration.

By early winter, Truman's commander was still losing ground, but he was sounding all the more like a policymaker. On March 7, 1951, he issued a statement ridiculing Truman's concept of limited war. Two weeks later, the President ordered his general to keep

The Korean War, 1950–1953

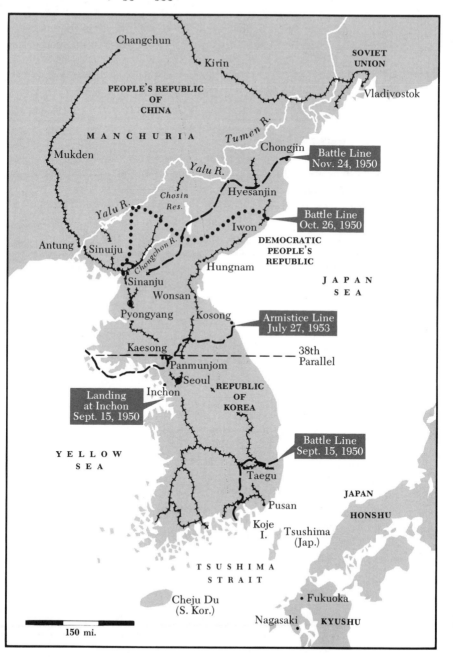

silent on foreign policy matters. But MacArthur persisted, sending off a critical message to Representative Joseph W. Martin, which the Republican released to the press. Faced with insubordination, the President had no choice. He relieved MacArthur of his command on April 11. The disgraced general flew home to the cheers and plaudits of Truman's critics. Yet a political movement never solidified around him or his desire for a wider war, and after a period of glory, MacArthur suffered the fate he predicted would be his: "Old soldiers never die," he told a reverential Congress, "they just fade away."

If the war in Korea caused a constitutional showdown between the President and his military field commander, the backlash from the war and mounting foreign policy failures fed into a domestic crisis that left ugly stress marks on the nation for several decades. Failure to win the unwinnable Cold War or to end the hot war in Korea touched off an ideological cannibalization of the federal government that decimated the ranks of liberals in office. It engendered scapegoating at a crucial turning point in foreign and domestic policy when new and creative thought was most necessary. When the ideological bloodletting known as McCarthyism finally passed, the feverish anti-Communism of the nation subsided, but the problems and reversals of Cold War policy remained like rocks after a receding tide.

Agonizing over statements of American prisoners of war in North Korea supporting their captors, a special report of the U.S. Defense Advisory Commission in 1955 declared: "The battlefield of modern warfare is all inclusive. Today there are no distant front lines, remote no man's lands, far-off rear areas. The home front is but an extension of the fighting front." For many Americans, the Cold War demanded a total, national ideological mobilization. Support in the struggle came from everywhere. Even American comedians Lou Costello and Bud Abbott wrote to the President in early 1953, offering to contribute anti-Communist jokes for Voice of America broadcasts.

President Truman shared the anti-Communist convictions of most of his critics. But, as the American leader during the darkest days of the Cold War, his task was to moderate between extreme opinions and to offer guidance in protecting the rights of citizens to free speech and freedom from intimidation. Once out of office, Truman assessed his record on civil liberties in the most positive terms. Charging the Republicans and Senator McCarthy in particular with outrageous violations of individual rights, he argued in his *Memoirs* that his strongest commitment as president had been to protect freedom of speech.

The truth, however, is more complicated than his partisan declaration. Of course, some members of the Republican party—Congressman Richard Nixon, of California, and Senators McCarthy, of Wisconsin, Karl Mundt, of North Dakota, and William Jenner, of Indiana—used the "Communist" issue to smear opponents. But Republicans were certainly not alone in creating a national obsession with ideological purity. Labor leaders, liberals, Democrats, Republicans, and leading newspapers and journals all contributed to defining rejected ideas as treasonous acts.

It is more accurate to say that Truman used the anti-Communist issue with more discretion than his Republican opponents—but he still used it. In 1946, he established a Temporary Commission on Employee Loyalty. When the commission reported, he accepted their suggestion of a loyalty program for federal employees. On March 22, 1947, the President asked his attorney general to draw up a list of subversive organizations. He established federal departmental loyalty boards and pre- and post-employment security checks. By March 1952, 20,733 employees had been investigated. Over 11,000 were cleared; almost 3,000 initially okayed stood under review; about 2,500 left service on their own accord; and about 400 were dismissed.

Truman also allowed the activities and budget of the FBI to increase, augmenting the power of J. Edgar Hoover and adding more agents to his tightly run private army of crime-stoppers and ideological watchdogs. Congress stepped up its investigations of Communism, with diverse committees conducting as many as eighty-four inquiries between 1945 and 1952. Led by the House Committee on Un-American Activities (HUAC) and the Senate Internal Security Subcommittee, Congress held extensive hearings into the film industry (helping to generate a blacklist of Hollywood writers and stars suspected of leftist sympathies) and the federal government. Very little legislation came from these investigations. Instead, their rather clear purpose was to provide a forum for attacks on liberalism and the New Deal.

Only one piece of legislation dealing with the Communist issue passed during the acrimonious days of the second Truman administration: the Internal Security Act of 1950. An administrative nightmare, the law required the Justice Department to register the names, finances, and memberships of all Communist party and designated front organizations. All of their literature was to be labeled: Communist. Known Communists were denied passports out of or visas into the United States. And provision was made to intern suspected disloyal Americans in time of emergency, much as thousands of Japanese had been placed in camps during World War II. Truman dispatched a vigorous veto message saying that the act would throw away the ideals of "our free society." He added that he already possessed most of the powers granted by the act and had been using them for several years. Nonetheless, Congress overrode the veto, and the act became law.

Truman was right; he had been fighting suspected Communists on several fronts. The loyalty program was in full swing. Several individuals were denied passports (the most famous would be Paul Robeson in 1952), and the federal government indicted and secured the conviction of Communist party leaders under the Smith Act. But nothing defused the Communist issue in Congress. Truman's efforts appeared halfway measures at best—if not downright suspicious—to those who believed that radicals had infiltrated the administration. The perjury trial of Alger Hiss in 1949 and the 1950 espionage trial of Julius and Ethel Rosenberg, accused of passing atomic secrets to the Russians, seemed to confirm the worst accusations about security lapses. In fact, these trials proved the opposite—how little justified were fears of Communists operating at the core of government, passing secrets to the Soviets. Yet, both became a kind of public exorcism of frustration with failures of America's Cold War policies.

Whatever else, Alger Hiss was a stereotypical New Dealer, bright, well educated, well connected, and sometimes carelessly arrogant. Not a real member of F.D.R.'s inner circle, Hiss had run afoul of James Byrnes and of Adolf A. Berle in the State Department during the 1930s, and both of these men developed strong antipathies to him, if not suspicions about his loyalty. After helping to organize the U.N. Conference at San Francisco, Hiss was edged out of the State Department by Truman. In February 1947, with the sponsorship of John Foster Dulles (later Secretary of State under Eisenhower), Hiss became president of the Carnegie Endowment for International Peace.

His retreat from government service, however, did not protect him from attack. Self-confessed Russian agent Whittaker Chambers testified before HUAC, accusing Alger Hiss of passing secret documents to the Russians. "Mr. Hiss," the witness later declared, "represents the concealed enemy against which we are all fighting and I am fighting." Hiss vehemently denied charges that he had passed secret documents to Chambers; indeed, he claimed he did not recognize his accuser. When Chambers repeated his attack on NBC's *Meet the Press*, Hiss sued for libel. Then, on December 3, 1948, Chambers led HUAC investigators to his farm in Maryland, where he produced microfilm copies of the documents in question hidden in a pumpkin patch. This dramatic turnabout led to the indictment and conviction of Hiss on two counts of perjury in 1950.

Although Hiss did not tell the truth on several counts—he did know Chambers, for example—it is not clear to what extent, if any, he had consciously worked for the Russians or what was the value of the documents that he had allegedly passed in the 1930s. But questions of this sort were irrelevant to Republicans, like Richard Nixon, who used the issue to blast the administration for leaks and intrigue. Truman ineptly and irrelevantly counter-charged the Republicans with weakening his struggle against Communism.

The next trial was even more bitter and had grave consequences for the defendants. In 1950, Klaus Fuchs, a nuclear physicist and confessed spy, initiated a chain of revelations leading to Julius Rosenberg and his wife, Ethel. Both Rosenbergs were active Communists; both were children of immigrants; both were Jewish. And, in some ways, all three of these identities stood in the docket in 1950. With some substantial evidence against Julius, the FBI also had Ethel indicted, probably in hopes of making her husband reveal other members of an atomic spy ring. Neither defendant would confess, even after their convictions, even when the government offered clemency if they would name names. On June 19, 1953, the accused were executed at Sing Sing prison. This end, after countless pleas, stays of execution, and interminable waiting, shocked much of the world, but satisfied those who demanded stern measures against Communists. Perhaps not the martyrs pictured by their staunchest defenders, the Rosenbergs were nonetheless the focus of national outrage.

Senator Joseph McCarthy, the junior Republican Senator from Wisconsin, turned this frustration into political capital. Coming from one of the most liberal states in the union, McCarthy nonetheless articulated the fears and suspicions of a part of this constituency. Boosted by such newspapers as the *Chicago Tribune* and conservative elements in the Catholic Church, McCarthy also found approval in the Republican party. Senator Taft, majority leader in the Senate, made McCarthy head of the Government Operations Committee in 1953. From this position, the senator flung down his accusation of Communist infiltration into government.

McCarthy's first visible attacks on Communists in government came in late 1949 with a speech to the Young Republicans, charging infiltration of enemy agents in the State Department. In February 1950, at Wheeling, West Virginia, he accelerated his attack, claiming 205 Communists in the employ of the State Department. On February 20, McCarthy read a revised number of enemy agents—only fifty-seven—into the *Congressional Record*. Working down his list of suspected individuals and illustrative events, McCarthy honed in on the real target of his remarks, Secretary of State Dean Acheson. "This pompous diplomat in striped pants, with a phony British accent," had defended the character of Alger Hiss—and perhaps worse.

Although some observers reacted in disbelief that such wild charges could be believed, they were quickly disabused. McCarthyism, if perhaps not McCarthy himself, was deadly serious. A senate committee dominated by Democrats, called to investigate his charges, exonerated the State Department, but Republican members and McCarthy refused to accept the results. Despite the vigorous opposition of some Republican senators led by Margaret Chase Smith, of Maine, who issued a Declaration of Conscience, the Republican party allowed the Communist issue to become a partisan charge against the Democrats. And Truman, unable or unwilling to see beyond immediate issues, defended his administration in partisan terms. Nonetheless, the Communist issue hurt the Democrats. In the 1950 election, several liberal Congressmen (among them Claude Pepper, the liberal senator from Florida) fell victim to an anti-Communist crusade.

Relations between the administration and Congress after 1950 thickened with acrimony, charges, and countercharges. With the Korean War continuing relentlessly and McCarthy riding high in Washington, Truman's position disintegrated further with the discovery of corruption in his administration involving Attorney General J. Howard McGrath and with suggestions of gangster influence in Democratic-controlled cities uncovered by the Kefauver

Committee investigating organized crime. Compromised by his angry and unconstitutional seizure of the steel industry during a summer strike in 1952 and threatened with another split in the Democratic party, Truman's position looked bleak. Despite his achievements, he was not a popular president, and this unpopularity tarnished the whole Democratic party. Unable to create a coalition around anything but his own reelection, Truman failed in his ambitious Fair Deal. In foreign policy, he pursued aims that led to frustration and then war. The result was a loss of direction and control in government. Perhaps inevitable, it came when the times demanded the subtlest and most innovative political skills, which Truman, unfortunately, did not possess.

5 Cities and Suburbs

In his cellar room at the edge of Harlem, under the glare and warmth of 1,369 electric light bulbs, the "invisible man," the hero of Ralph Ellison's great novel of the same name, shouted his refusal to remain hidden and ignored. "Perhaps that's my greatest social crime," he pondered, "I've overstayed my hibernation, since there's a possibility that even an invisible man has a socially responsible role to play." Ellison's autobiographical novel chronicled one of the great American migrations of the twentieth century: the flood of blacks from the rural South into northern cities like New York City. Searching for jobs, social opportunity, and political freedom, these new urbanites transformed American city life. And, in the 1950s, they demanded recognition and new responsibilities.

Another major migration occurred simultaneously in the 1950s and 1960s, out of and beyond cities like New York City and into the suburbs and the Sunbelt. The escape predominantly of white Americans from high-rise cities to low-density suburbs occurred along a system of roads built under the greatest public-works project ever undertaken in this country. These projects came from the fertile imagination of men like Robert Moses, Park Commissioner and Planning Commissioner of New York City. Operating atop a financial pyramid of toll bridges and roads, Moses invested state funds in a system of highways connecting parks, city, and suburbs into a vast grid of endless motion.

Both Ellison and Moses can be seen as symbols of two divergent populations that participated in the relentless movement that transformed American cities and suburbs after World War II. These two populations helped create a civilization that not only looked different (it could be seen best from the air or photographed through a wide lens), but thought differently about itself. The revolution in urban and suburban life and the drain of population into the South and West extended a process of demographic dispersal already well under way before World War II. America had become a predominantly urban society in the 1920s but simultaneously began to abandon its central cities for the suburbs. The Depression of the 1930s retarded this motion, but it resumed after World War II. By 1974, about three-fourths of the population of the United States lived in 250 standard metropolitan areas (comprising central cities and their satellite suburbs). Thus, urban life had two phases: the dense population of the central cities and the sprawl surrounding them, the one contracting and the other expanding. The declining percentage of population in central cities relative to their suburbs reveals the extent of change. In the greater Baltimore, Maryland, area, the city proper fell from 67.6 percent of total population in 1950 to only 43.7 percent in 1970. In Detroit, during the same period, the decline was slightly steeper, from 61.3 percent to 36 percent. Practically every other American central city experienced the same phenomenon.

This shift is not hard to explain: Population simply followed jobs, housing, shopping opportunities, and roads. The changing economic base that stimulated population dispersal also shifted the tax base and available public services. And, again, these changes affected the demography of cities and suburbs: who lived in them, their race and ethnic origin, family size and income, and age.

Overall, economic activity in the nation's twenty-five largest metropolitan areas increased rapidly after World War II. From 1948 to 1963, employment in manufacturing went up by 16 percent, in trade by 21 percent, in services by 53 percent. But growth was differential; the central cities lost 7 percent of the jobs in the first two categories and increased service employment only by 32 percent. In the suburban areas, however, manufacturing employment went up 61 percent, trade increased 122 percent, and service jobs boomed by 135 percent. In the same metropolitan areas, the central cities lost about 300,000 jobs, while employment increased by almost 4 million in outlying areas. By the end of the 1960s, suburban areas had more manufacturing jobs than the central cities.

Inside the city, the nature of work changed. From 1960 to 1970, 101 central cities lost over 800,000 blue-collar positions, but gained 500,000 white-collar jobs. In surrounding areas, both categories increased, but new white-collar jobs doubled the number of positions in manufacturing. Urban work, in other words, in-

Central Expressway, Dallas, Texas, 1972. Expressways and limited-access highways, often built with federal financing, transformed the appearance of American cities. Growth in Sunbelt boom towns such as Los Angeles, Dallas, and Houston was particularly affected by dependence upon the automobile.   (Bob W. Smith/EPA Documerica)

creasingly became dominated by service, administrative, and information industries rather than manufacturing.

The flow of business outward from the central cities enormously stimulated the suburban housing market, creating the postwar boom in housing starts predicted by business leaders during the war. New housing units in suburbs sprang up at a rate almost three times faster than in central cities. Federal Housing Authority and Veterans Administration loan programs brought new, cheap homes within the reach of millions of Americans who previously had to settle for urban apartment living. As a result, the percentage of Americans who owned their own homes rose by 30 from 1940 to 1970. Property values also reflected this shift in population pressure; from 1960 to 1970, city housing prices increased slightly compared to rapidly increasing values of suburban property. Along with housing went the appurtenances of new suburban life: new schools and roads, shopping centers, religious and recreational facilities.

The outward shift of population shrank the potential fiscal resources of central cities. Measured by retail sales, economic activity in most major cities expanded very little in the ten-year period between 1958 and 1967, while outlying areas shot up in total sales. Typically, in the city of Chicago, sales increased only 5 percent over the ten-year period, while suburban trade went up almost 87 percent. Los Angeles experienced more balanced growth, but even there, within the city limits, sales showed a 22 percent rise compared to 75 percent in suburban areas.

Compared to earlier periods, the economic position of the central cities had greatly deteriorated. In 1932, American cities together collected more tax revenues than either the states or the federal government. In 1959, however, city revenues amounted to only about one-half the total collected by the states and approximated only 15 percent of federal income. This trend was not readily apparent until about 1950, for city financial resources peaked immediately after the war. By the mid-1950s, however, the situation became obvious and serious. Tax revenues shrank as the tax base declined. By 1967, the median income of city dwellers fell to almost $2,000 less than that of suburbanites.

The diminished economic opportunity of the central city reflected the changing racial and class basis of the urban population. The influx of black and poorer Americans into the central cities and the outflow of white, wealthier residents constituted a demographic upheaval that shook every population group loose from traditional residential patterns. After a period of little change during the 1930s, the rural population of the United States resumed its rush into urban areas. From 17.5 percent of the total population in 1945, the rural share diminished to only about 5 percent in 1970. The racial complexion of this exodus proved even more remarkable. From 1960 to 1970, the white population on farms decreased by about 33 percent, but the black population declined by more than 60 percent.

Population of Standard Metropolitan Statistical Areas
(By Region, Size, and Race, 1950 and 1970)

		Inner City	Outside* Central City	Black Pop. as % of Inner City	Black Pop. as % of Suburbs
1950	White	43,001,634	33,248,836		
	Black	6,194,948	1,736,521	12.5%	4.9%
	Other	216,210	102,531		
1970	White	49,430,443	71,148,286		
	Black	13,140,331	3,630,279	20.5%	4.8%
	Other	1,226,169	843,303		

*Suburbs.
Source: Historical Statistics of the United States, Bicentennial Edition, Vol. I, p. 40.

Housing and job segregation filtered this population flow. Up to 1948, the courts enforced restrictive covenants in house sale contracts. Thereafter, the practice continued informally. New suburbs employed restrictions and pricing policies that excluded most black Americans, and occasionally other ethnic or religious minorities. In inner-city areas, whites sometimes turned to violence to prevent integration of their neighborhoods. During the 1950s, house bombings and sometimes riots occurred in such major cities as Chicago, Los Angeles, Dallas, Atlanta, and New York City.

Occasionally, city governments acted to preserve racial and ethnic separation by placing public-housing projects in areas away from white populations, or sometimes they voted not to build them at all. Nonetheless, by the early 1960s, inner-city black ghettos emerged as large centers of social problems. Black city dwellers became more visible in their dependence upon shrinking social services. By 1968, many American city school systems had more than 50 percent black students, with much higher percentages in Washington, Baltimore, Chicago, Detroit, St. Louis, and New Orleans.

☆   ☆   ☆

Compared to the rural poverty of the Deep South left behind, the city represented a vast improvement. Yet, at the same time, the disparities and inequities the new black urbanites suffered became more obvious. Rural unemployment was easier to overlook than urban unemployment. The bonds of custom in small towns disintegrated in the cities of the North. Inadequate schools in rural areas went unnoticed; overcrowded, segregated northern schools became a persistent social problem. Increasing pressure on social services, while the tax base was eroding, exhausted urban resources. The suburbs needed schools, roads, and medical, recreational, and religious facilities, and they got them. The cities found themselves overburdened and overwhelmed.

Cities occupy a paradoxical place in the American imagination. Acknowledged centers of sophistication, commerce, culture, and government, they have the most visibly heterogeneous populations, where ethnic group bumps against ethnic group, where work and daily life mix and filter diverse populations. Yet, many Americans feared urban life because it was so visibly changeable and integrated. For those who wanted to start over, to flee crowded apartments, close neighborhoods, heat, slums, and dirt, the suburbs and the new communities of the Sunbelt exercised a dramatic attraction. As cities, particularly in the North, changed rapidly after World War II, becoming the focus of racial problems and concentrated centers of poverty, they came more and more to symbolize an older America, representative of old problems, not new opportunities.

The population shift out of the industrial North into the Sunbelt responded in part to stimulation provided by the federal government. Powerful southern senators and congressmen, who dominated defense and appropriations committees, secured large defense

Net Migration by Color
1940–1950 and 1950–1960

1940–1950

Region	White	Nonwhite
Northeast	− 173 (− 0.5%)	+ 483 (+34.3%)
North Central	− 948 (− 2.5%)	+ 632 (+42.0%)
South	− 583 (− 1.7%)	−1,597 (−16.0%)
West	+3,181 (+23.8%)	+ 323 (+60.5%)

1950–1960

Region	White	Nonwhite
Northeast	− 206 (− 0.6%)	+ 541 (+26.0%)
North Central	− 679 (− 1.6%)	+ 558 (+23.8%)
South	+ 52 (+ 0.1%)	−1,457 (−14.1%)
West	+3,518 (+18.7%)	+ 332 (+23.6%)

In thousands and percentages.
Source: Statistical Abstract of the United States, *1963, p. 39.*

contracts for industries in their states. As late as the mid-1970s, the pattern of net outflows of federal expenditures remained favorable to the South and West.

In some Southern states, right-to-work laws, legalized by the Taft-Hartley Act, enticed important industries such as shoe manufacturing and textiles into the South. Given available cheap labor, and legally and politically armed against unions, states such as North Carolina, South Carolina, and Texas picked up the remnants of the declining Northeastern clothing industry. Enormous federal sums expended for roads and airports gave these new manufacturing regions greatly improved access to markets.

New industry and transportation pulled population south and west. All regions of the United States gained population from 1940 to 1970, but the West grew twice as fast as the Northeast. The South also increased at a faster pace than either the Northeast or the north central section, signaling a relative decline of the old manufacturing states of the East and Midwest. In political terms, this shift cost older areas votes in the presidential electoral college.

For example, in 1940, New York State cast 47 votes in the electoral college; by 1970, it had only 41. In 1940, California had 25 votes, but in 1970, it increased to 45. California exhibited the most rapid population rise. From the fifth most populous state in 1940, it rose to first place in 1963. About 5 percent of the American population lived within its borders in 1939; by the 1960s, this figure had multiplied to almost 10 percent. After World War II, most of the new population settled in the suburbs, making California one of the most suburbanized regions in the world. Even while rapidly urbanizing in this period, California witnessed a decline in population density in its most crowded areas.

Every poll asking Americans where they would prefer to live and travel invariably finds California as first choice. This is not surprising, for California has been a trend setter in establishing the

Population in Selected Central Cities, 1960–1970
(Changes in per annum white and nonwhite populations)

	White Pop. Change % per Annum	Nonwhite Pop. Change % per Annum
Bridgeport, Conn.	+ .4	+ 5.6
Chicago, Ill.	− 2.0	+ 3.1
Dayton, Ohio	− 1.9	+ 2.6
Detroit, Mich.	− 3.4	+ 3.2
Los Angeles, Calif.	+ .5	+ 4.3
Milwaukee, Wis.	− 1.1	+ 5.3
Montgomery, Ala.	+ .2	− .6
New York, N.Y.	− .9	+ 4.4
St. Louis, Mo.	− 3.7	+ 1.7
San Francisco– Oakland, Calif.	− 1.9	+ 3.4
Washington, D.C.	− 4.9	+ 2.7

Source: Statistical Abstract of the United States, *1975, pp. 887 ff.*

Net Flow of Federal Expenditures Over Taxes by Region (1975)

Region	Net Flow (in millions of dollars)
Northeast	− 762*
Mid-Atlantic	− 10,013
East North Central	− 18,618
West North Central	− 1,456
South Atlantic	+ 4,986
South Central	+ 6,536
Mountain	+ 3,631
Pacific	+ 7,008
Washington, D.C.	+ 8,690

*Per capita diffferentials are even more striking.
Source: National Journal, *June 26, 1976, Government Research Corporation* (quoted in Statistical Abstract of the United States, *1977, p. 257*).

culture of modern work and leisure. As the center of the film and television industries and the backdrop for countless advertising campaigns, California became the stage for realizing the consumer dreams of millions of Americans. Not just the most populous, most suburbanized state in the union, it also strongly influenced national fashions, art, dress, housing, and life-styles.

The most popular situation comedy in television history, *The Beverly Hillbillies* (1962–1972), captured this westward shift and satirized the clash of cultures in California. When the hillbilly Easterners, with country manners and language, confronted the slick, new consumer world of California, the potential for comedy became unlimited. In exaggerated form, this represented the experience of millions of Americans who moved to the Golden State during the same years.

This transformation in demography and culture would not have been possible without the automobile. Throughout the period, the rapid construction of freeways, availability of cheap gasoline, and general affordability of cars transformed the American city and countryside in an unprecedented fashion. Dependence upon the

The Edsel, produced for a few years in the mid-1950s. This experiment by the Ford Motor Company, intended as a new family car that would appeal to the unconscious motivations of buyers, failed to attract a significant number of purchasers.   (Library of Congress)

car changed what people ate and where they ate it; where they lived, worked, and vacationed; what sort of air they breathed; and what their houses, public buildings, and cities looked like. As never before, the health of the economy depended upon the restless and anarchistic energy of the automobile. As one of America's wisest critics, Lewis Mumford, put it, "We have been living in a fool's paradise . . . the brave new, simplified, automatic world of the machine."

Propagandists for the great American road system were anything but hesitant in their assessment of this paradise, however. Bernard De Voto, critic and interpreter of American culture, writing for the Ford Motor Company in 1956, rhapsodized, that "A highway is not only a measure of progress, but a true index of our culture." A complex new system of highways, he said, would unbind "the giant" American nation. Undoubtedly, most Americans agreed with De Voto.

Modern automobile culture existed on an infrastructure of new federal highways and bridges. Following the opening of the limited-access Pennsylvania Turnpike in 1940, New York, Indiana, New Jersey, and Ohio constructed successful toll highways. California constructed an elaborate system of freeways financed by its own tax revenues. Nonetheless, early in the Eisenhower administration, it became clear that neither tollways nor state-financed expressways could relieve the congestion on the nation's highways. As a result, Eisenhower appointed General Lucius Clay in September 1954 to chair a committee to propose a new federal system of interstate roads. Representatives of the Teamsters Union and businessmen associated with the construction and automotive industries joined the resulting National Highway Program Committee. When the group reported in 1955, it outlined a massive building program justified by traffic tie-ups around American cities and by the need for rapid evacuation of urban areas in case of nuclear attack.

As passed in 1956, the Highway Act planned the construction of approximately 41,000 miles of interstate and defense highways, of which 5,000 miles would be urban freeways. The 90 percent federal share of construction costs would come from the Highway Trust Fund, accumulated through taxation on road usage and gasoline. The states were to contribute the other 10 percent of the costs. Original estimates pegged the total cost at $27 billion, although this forecast rose to $50 billion by 1970. In addition to periodic estimates and surveys of the system, the act required public hearings for any federally aided highway bypassing or traversing a city, town, or village

The direct consequences and multiplier effects of this system and other road-building projects undertaken in the 1940s and 1950s greatly intensified America's commitment to a car-centered culture. Automobiles competed successfully with all other forms of transportation, delivering a *coup de grâce* to an already moribund passenger rail system. By 1970, less than 1 percent of intercity passengers traveled by railroad. Automobile registration leaped from 27 million in 1940 to almost 90 million in 1970, more than tripling in thirty years. Of the twenty-fold increase in energy generated over the period, automobile traffic consumed a large share. More people possessed more cars and traveled farther, until by 1970, average car owners went 10,000 miles per year in their automobiles.

The automobile transformed America's living spaces. Los Angeles devoted about 50 percent of its total land area to streets and parking lots, although other cities limited this percentage to around 30. Shopping centers, "freeway industries," such as electronic companies, and housing developments sprang up along urban highways and clustered at the exchanges of beltways. Motor-home sales boomed, and after 1950, large chains of motels dotted the interstate landscape. The new drive-in way of life sharply differentiated urban from suburban living. The uncongested thruways sped cars between cities, national parks, suburbs, and the countryside. They made the United States accessible to its citizens in a way unheard of before World War II. But they also stimulated traffic, speed, and accidents until motor-vehicle deaths became America's fourth leading cause of death through the 1970s. And, over all of America's metropolitan area, a pall of smog accumulated.

Only in the 1960s did significant hesitations about this system begin to surface. Passed under President Kennedy, the Highway Act of 1962 sought to soften the inconvenience of road building by providing displacement aid for families moved out of the path of expressways. It granted power to the Secretary of Commerce to ensure that urban highway projects coincided with local city plans. Citizens groups began successful organization against the proliferation of highways. Residents of New York City, already choking on gasoline pollution, defeated a proposed lower Manhattan expressway. Perhaps the most remarkable confrontation, however, occurred in New Orleans, where the demands of the highway builders clashed with the traditions that gave the city its unique character.

From the motorist's perspective, the worst traffic problem of New Orleans was the Vieux Carré, the old French Quarter and tourist center. Plans to alleviate traffic in the area had long been on the drawing board. In 1946, New York City's planner Robert Moses submitted an "Arterial Plan for New Orleans" to the State Highway Department, featuring an elevated expressway between the Mississippi River and the edge of the Quarter. Several plans and years later, the city decided to construct a Riverfront Expressway. In 1965, the (renamed) Riverfront and Elysian Fields Expressway became I-310, a projected part of the Interstate Highway System. At an estimated cost of $40 million, the roadway would have eliminated through-traffic in the Quarter, but would have erected a towering, noisy barrier between the city and the river. Proponents contended that they could construct lighting and fences to preserve the character of the Quarter, but the prospect of a massive rush of traffic cordoned off by wrought-iron gates satisfied no one who loved the old section. Despite enormous local pressure for the highway, national architecture and preservation groups finally stopped it in 1969, when the Secretary of Commerce exercised his power under the new Highway Act of 1966 to halt any highway project that threatened the destruction of an historic site. The worst excesses of the highway barons were halted.

Yet, automobile traffic profoundly shaped the new urban and suburban landscapes of the postwar period. The universal architecture of billboards and fast-food drive-ins in the suburbs and the massive, opaque glass-and-steel skyscrapers punctuating every American downtown depended on an automobile culture. The modern buildings were devoid of traditional ornaments. The clean, cool lines created by the great architectural firm of Skidmore, Owings and Merrill; the dreary bureaucratic tombs of Washington, D.C.; and the stylish massiveness of the "new brutalism" repeated the same message: function dominated form. Grandiose and overpowering, modern American urban architecture followed the specifications of space, materials, cost, and parking access. It expressed a valid but self-absorbed optimism about the future of American society, and, sometimes, a contempt for its urban or natural surroundings.

One of America's most renowned postwar architects, Ludwig

Mies van der Rohe, once wrote that "Architecture is the real battleground of the spirit." During the 1950s and 1960s, this battleground became the suburban environment. At the cutting edge of American civilization after World War II, the suburban culture set off controversy, for the architecture, social life, and culture that grew up in the suburbs seemed to contradict traditional American ideals of individualism and self-help.

Perhaps the most renowned suburbs were the three Levittowns constructed in New York, New Jersey, and Pennsylvania during the 1940s and 1950s. Mass-produced communities had long been an idea dear to American social planners. During the 1930s, the New Deal built demonstration Greenbelt cities in Maryland, Ohio, and Wisconsin. But the ventures of William Levitt broke new ground, because they illustrated the profitability of sophisticated tract-housing projects when combined with town planning.

During the Depression, Levitt had made a fortune in real estate, and during the war, he gained valuable experience in constructing Navy housing. After 1945, he turned to tract housing. His first Levittown, on Long Island, constructed in 1947, conformed to a relatively traditional subdivision style with schools, churches, and businesses added after residences. His second experiment in planning proved more radical. His firm planned a new town in Bucks County, Pennsylvania, in 1951, with shopping centers at the edge of residential districts. Levitt found, however, in this and the first experiment, that placing social services after housing was completed caused serious problems. His third experiment in Willingboro, New Jersey, organized houses in neighborhoods or superblocks centering around schools and other social services. Land was set aside for religious structures.

Levittown houses were detached but mass-produced. The manufacturer offered several styles: the Cape Cod, the Rancher, and the Colonial. Color variation ensured that every structure looked different. Architectural designs were eclectic—that is, with features mixed without much regard to continuity or purpose. Wishing his houses to be superficially different on the outside, Levitt wanted relative uniformity in his residents. Homeowner manuals warned against erecting unauthorized fences or changing house colors without permission. No washing could be hung outside on weekends, and from April to November, owners promised to cut the lawn once a week. Levitt also used house prices to funnel residents into his community. The New Jersey town offered relatively expensive houses to attract a somewhat higher class of resident. The New York Levittown excluded prospective black buyers with a restrictive covenant that read: "No dwelling shall be used or employed by members of other than the Caucasian race, but the employment and maintenance of other than Caucasian domestic servants shall be permitted." When the courts declared such restrictions unenforceable, Levitt instructed his salespeople not to sell to blacks. Overt discrimination finally ended by court order in 1960.

Levittowns and other new suburbs were no more exclusive than the town and city communities from which their populations came, but their homogeneity showed more visibly through countless picture windows. Residents resembled each other in race and classs, but not in ethnic group and religion. For example, in 1967, the New Jersey Levittown was 47 percent Protestant, 37 percent Catholic, and 14 percent Jewish. Residents tended to be young, with a high percentage married; almost no older people or single people lived in the community. The population enthusiastically supported their churches and civic organizations. Sociological surveys concluded that they had moved to the suburbs because they sought the leisured life, the open space—sometimes the exclusiveness—and the psychological benefits that home ownership bestowed on them.

These were sufficient reasons to persuade many Americans to migrate to the suburbs, but they worried a growing chorus of critics who denounced the social and cultural sterility of suburban living. From novels like John McPartland's *No Down Payment* (1957) to the serious philosophic work of Hannah Arendt, the growing sameness of American society distressed commentators. Widespread belief in the homogeneity of American culture emerged from many factors: the mass media; enlarged federal government participation in the economy; the bureaucratization of American business; political and social conservatism; and McCarthyism. And it seemed most rampant in the conformist life-style of the suburbs.

Exposés exaggerated and sensationalized the faults of suburbia. Paper-thin walls, barbecues, all-night dancing-and-drinking parties, and wife- and husband-swapping became clichés in satiric novels of the suburbs. Popular journals and sociological essays discussed the "suburban captivity of the churches," the relentless organizing of clubs and kaffeeklatsches, the identity changes of

Democrats into Republicans, vengeful and frustrated suburban mothers, tacky houses, flocks of bored children, and fathers whose only real function was home repair.

Even serious works sometimes shared this hyperbole. The most astute analyses of suburban life came from two sociologists, David Riesman and William Whyte, Jr. Riesman entitled his analysis of modern American life *The Lonely Crowd* (1950), a title as suggestive and powerful as the argument of his book. Declaring the existence of a new mass form of society, he sketched a progression of character changes he thought typified traditional societies, "inner-directed" societies (the Victorian Age), and "other-directed" societies (the 1950s). The great transformation of the modern age, he proclaimed, replaced inner- with other-directedness. "Inhibited," "self-willed," "aggressive," "aggrandizing," "creative," and "destructive" were words he used to describe the inner-directed man, a person who listened to his conscience and followed a self-constructed gyroscope to direct his life. His personality perfectly suited the heyday of finance capitalism and the rapid growth of population in the late nineteenth century.

For Riesman, modern consumer capitalism demanded a revision in personality structure to conform to the demands of bureaucracy and efficiency. In this type of personality, human motivation moved out of the conscience to reside in the peer group. To please others, to conform to superficial niceties, to be congenial and easy to get along with—that is, to be shallow—these were the demands of a society whose principal activity had turned from work as production to work as the manipulation of people. Inner-direction sought success; other-direction pursued security.

Looking back on his work a few years after he published it, Riesman said he had been much misunderstood and misinterpreted. He did not intend to argue the superiority of inner-direction (as so many readers seemed to think) nor did he mean to imply that such personalities, as he sketched them, really ever existed; they were convenient sociological straw men. He and his fellow researchers, he claimed, were not "conservatives harking back to a rugged individualism." Yet, for all his protests and disclaimers, Riesman's interpreters and critics rightly sensed the overtones of criticism. He did seem to prefer the inner-directed Victorian.

The ambiguity of Riesman's work did not characterize William Whyte, Jr.'s *Organization Man*, published in 1956. This brilliant and caustic attack on the ethics of peer group culture is decidedly conservative. Building on Riesman's insights, Whyte examined modern corporate work and the new corporate suburb Park Forest, Illinois. In the background of this critique lay a cherished memory from his own first days in business. As a young salesman in training, he entered Vicks Chemical Company's School of Applied Merchandising. There, in the rough-and-tumble world of production and selling, he learned aggressiveness and independence. It was a test for the survival of the fittest, and he survived. Modern rites of passage into business, however, had nothing of the ruthless honesty of such old-fashioned competition. The man who joined the modern corporation passed not through the jaws of competition, but over bureaucratic hurdles of personality tests. These entrance examinations, administered in leading corporations, identified the requirements of a modern business career. These included conformity, getting along with a group, approval from others, and further personality skills. Especially outrageous, Whyte argued, was the role of social science, which worked hand in glove with employers seeking to enforce this code.

Just as bureaucracy seduced the ethos of the workplace, conformity had conquered the suburb. Rootless, but with an insatiable desire to belong, the organization man and his wife behaved at home as if in training for corporate jobs. Suburban education taught "sociability" to their children. The norms of the neighborhood substituted for individual taste. Across the United States, Whyte found, from "the courts of Park Forest, the patios of Park Merced in San Francisco, Philadelphia's Drexelbrook, the New Levittown, Pennsylvania—there is an unmistakable similarity in the way of life."

Both Riesman and Whyte described the most menacing form of mass society, but sociologist Vance Packard, in his bestselling book *The Hidden Persuaders* (1957), tried to explain how that new society had emerged. In doing so, he exonerated the American public and blamed the manipulations of advertisers. Motivational researchers in the 1930s and 1940s had taught advertisers that consumers acted from nonrational motivations. They bought images of an idealized self when they purchased clothing; they acted to quell insecurities or to affect a high status, but they almost never selected a product for its real qualities. Packard argued that advertisers exploited this new knowledge and created a world of symbols in which food, cigarettes, clothing, and automobiles defined success and happiness. His most striking example came from the Chrysler Corporation. Dr. Ernest Dichter, a motivational researcher, convinced the corporation to redesign its automobiles. His study, "Mistress Versus Wife," argued that men were drawn to auto showrooms by convertibles, which they unconsciously associated with possessing a mistress. But they purchased a four-door sedan—or wife. To combine these two urges, Dichter suggested a union of the images, the four-door hardtop—a product that became a best-seller for years.

Packard's most serious point warned about the perils of motivational research in politics. Politicians could use psychological manipulation to sell shopworn and obsolete ideas. While this public relations approach to politics was still relatively rare in the early 1950s, a few politicians, most notably Richard Nixon, had begun to realize the potential of a practice that became widespread by the 1970s.

Riesman, Whyte, and Packard raised fears about the direction of mass culture; they worried about its tendency to commercialize and vulgarize. Their readers, already nurtured on lurid images from George Orwell's *1984*, published in 1949, imagined that they saw the same tendencies in McCarthyism and the drab sameness of life in the "Little Boxes" of Marin County, satirized in Malvina Reynold's song of 1963. But, suburbia was not the cultural desert or the malevolent blight that many critics claimed. Much like the city dwellers who had been their forefathers, suburbanites neither became instant vulgarians nor switched to the Republican party nor joined vapid, optimistic social religions. Instead, the suburbs illustrated and sometimes exaggerated already existing racial and class distinctions in American society. If some critics worried about suburbia, a great many other Americans regarded the city with deep suspicion.

In the early part of the century, millions of immigrants had taken up residence in the centers of industrialism and commercialism, where they became the subject of countless reform movements. After World War II the cities became the focus of America's racial problems. City governments, therefore, welcomed new tools of urban renewal granted them by the Taft-Ellender-Wagner Housing Act of 1949. The act aimed to ensure "a decent home and a suitable living environment for every American family." Specifically, it granted cities the power of eminent domain to condemn blighted areas and gave them federal funds to raze buildings there. These cleared properties could then be sold at a lower price to developers for construction of new housing or offices. With slum-clearance laws in force in about twenty-five states already, this legislation dictated a more coherent and homogeneous approach to urban renewal.

Another provision of the 1949 act expanded federal loans and subsidies for local low-rent public housing. The number of units constructed in any one year remained flexible, between 50,000 and 200,000, so that the president could employ the money in a countercyclical fashion. Public-housing rents, furthermore, were pegged at 20 percent below similar private units to eliminate competition with profit-making rental properties. Subsequent modifications of the program in the Housing Act of 1954 emphasized rehabilitation of neighborhoods and provided federal grants for comprehensive city planning.

Although this program promoted some public housing (much of it initially in the form of skyscrapers), it also displaced thousands of urban residents and subsidized the private reclamation of commercial areas. Relocation proved costly and difficult, so that urban renewal in some cities merely moved poor people from one section of the city to another, without improving their housing opportunities. Increasingly, poor, black urbanites occupied public projects, thus intensifying city ghettoization. While thousands of citizens moved into better housing, much of this new construction quickly deteriorated because of poor management, spotty upkeep, and abuse by residents.

Opposition to renewal projects gathered quickly. Antagonists protested the wholesale destruction of neighborhoods and architectural treasures. Writers, such as Jane Jacobs in her *Death and Life of Great American Cities* (1961), condemned slum clearance, calling it a profit-making shift of the poor from one section of the city to another, without dealing with the problems that created or increased urban blight. Martin Anderson's *The Federal Bulldozer*, published in 1964, blamed Washington for much of the destruction of cities. In response to such criticisms, the 1961 Housing Act—and the Demonstration Cities programs carried out later under President Johnson—modified slum clearance and required more comprehensive planning. But, even these improvements and growing willingness of city governments to hear out citizen opposition to renewal projects did not begin to solve the problems of slums, segregation, and the economic decline of the central cities. Slum residents had neither the political nor economic power to assert control over local governments more generally attuned to property values than to urban sociology.

Local governments reacted slowly to housing problems and city blight, in part because the victims of urban decay were generally poor and black. Traditional American attitudes toward the poor assumed that this population lacked the means to adjust to a complex industrial society. The Victorian Age had talked of an absence of willpower, immorality, and alcoholism as the causes of poverty. Post–World War II observers tended to emphasize shortcomings in education, inadequate health care, and segregation. No one in the 1950s denied that inequality could intensify poverty, but a new and widely held theory explained the behavior of urban blacks in terms of cultural deprivation. As Ralph Ellison wrote, even a sympathetic critic, like Gunnar Myrdal, defined black culture as a product of "social pathology." According to this theory, the American Negro was nothing but a shadow of white America.

This notion of cultural deprivation became a full-blown sociological theory by the 1960s, partly in response to the slow motion of urban reform. Borrowing the concept "the culture of poverty" from the anthropologist Oscar Lewis, writers such as Nathan Glazer and Daniel Moynihan felt they detected a similar culture in America's urban slums. In the isolated and degrading atmosphere of the ghetto, they argued, black culture operated to prevent successful integration of its residents into the rest of the society. This emphasis upon isolation and the disjointed culture of urban slums merged into a larger debate about the nature of American culture: Was it one rich and variegated culture or two separate ones? This attitude, based upon comparison of black Americans with immigrant ethnic groups that had previously flowed into the cities, focused upon economic mobility.

On another level, however, Americans increasingly recognized black culture as a major component in mainstream culture—from the important novels of Ellison and James Baldwin to the popular arts. The black ghettos of postwar society increasingly set trends in American mass culture. The identities of black and white culture have never been strictly segregated; even in the early nineteenth century, under the slave system, powerful interchanges flowed both ways. Nonetheless, black Americans, particularly in music, developed separate variants of songs, orchestrations, and rhythms that periodically merged into and refreshed the larger surrounding culture, splitting off again in new directions.

In the 1950s, the impact of black music repeated old patterns

Chuck Berry. One of the early rock stars. Berry was a virtuoso guitarist and composer who wrote such famous hits as "Maybelline." His career was marked by heights of success and wealth as well as scandal and jail.   (UPI)

The beginnings of rock-'n'-roll.

Pat Boone. In the mid-1950s, Pat Boone took songs written by black artists and cut his own recordings of them. These modified and "sanitized" versions helped popularize rock-'n'-roll in the white community. Boone's career was a model of teen-age propriety. In 1959 he was voted "Father of the Year."   (UPI)

but established new relationships. During the 1920s, white musicians in places like Chicago heard the astounding sounds and virtuosity of black jazz players, and they adopted and transformed that sound for white audiences. Throughout the period and into the 1930s, jazz and the blues existed at two levels, in the black community, where "race records" featured popular black artists like Bessie Smith, and in performances and recordings made by white jazz players for white audiences. George Gershwin and Darius Milhaud, the French composer, adapted the jazz idiom to classical music because its sounds and rhythms seemed uniquely modern and urban.

While jazz arrangements and sounds influenced every element of American music, the position of black artists remained ambiguous. Many black players and composers performed at exclusive, white nightclubs; sometimes they scored and played music for Hollywood films; but, in general, they did not receive full credit or reward for their efforts. For example, the great black composer Duke Ellington performed a Carnegie Hall concert in January 1943, but not before white jazz players, like Benny Goodman, had already appeared there.

In the 1940s and early 1950s, the introduction of rhythm and blues, a new urban music that also emerged largely in the black community, repeated the same patterns. White audiences became aware of this new danceable beat when disc jockey Alan Freed (who took the name Moondog) played it on the radio in Cleveland in 1951. In 1954, Freed moved his show to New York City. By then a number of popular black groups had emerged. White artists like Pat Boone began to cut sanitized "cover records" of the same songs to capitalize on their success. Other cover groups, like the "Crew Cuts," appeared. Their versions of rhythm and blues and a further evolution—rock and roll—quickly made the top-ten yearly sellers.

The explosion of rock and roll was also visual: the film *Blackboard Jungle*, released in 1955, used Bill Haley's rendition of "Rock Around the Clock" as background to a story of high school juvenile delinquency. This association with delinquency, sexuality, violence, and alienation made the film and the music more inflammatory. Teenage audiences leaped into the aisles to dance to Haley's music, and newspapers all over the country reported riots, fights, and vandalism incited by the movie.

By the middle 1950s, Chuck Berry, one of the most versatile

black artists, and Elvis Presley, the "white man who had the Negro sound and the Negro feel," emerged as leaders in popular music. Working first for Sun Records in Memphis, Tennessee, Presley became a new kind of recording star, who openly exploited the sexuality and rebelliousness associated with this music. His music also added a strong ingredient of country-and-western sound. By the end of the 1950s, rock and roll had transformed popular music. The radio-TV series, the *Hit Parade*, born in the heyday of big bands, died in 1959. This ultimate in "cover" performances could not reproduce the excitement, rhythm, and sexual thrust of the new music. Dick Clark's *American Bandstand*, from Philadelphia, replaced it as the showcase of popular music. Much more attuned to the teenage audience, it emphasized dancing and original recording artists. By 1957, the show was seen nationally on television. Perhaps most significant of all, black artists who wrote, played, and recorded popular music for a national audience began to emerge as celebrities. As the popularity of cover records declined, these artists established their own reputations and fortunes. The new urban popular culture had firmly established itself.

Adverse reaction to rock and roll came partly from its association with delinquency and juvenile misbehavior and partly from its reputation as black music. In return, rock artists gleefully satirized middle-class norms. The lyrics of Chuck Berry's "Roll Over Beethoven" (1956) illustrate the defiance and humor of this new music:

> Well, I'm gonna write a little letter, gonna mail
> it to my local D.J.
> Yes, it's a jumpin' little record I want my
> jockey to play
> Roll over Beethoven, I gotta hear it again
> today
> You know my temp'rature's risin' and the juke
> box blowin' a fuse
> My heart's beatin' rhythm and my soul keeps
> a singin' the blues
> Roll over Beethoven and tell Tchaikovsky
> the news.[1]

Parents' groups, law enforcers, churches, and newspapers rarely saw the humor. Major American newspapers, such as the *New York Daily News*, throughout the 1950s predicted the imminent and hoped-for demise of rock and roll. Angry parents blamed the music for an outbreak of misbehavior at home, and some newspapers even printed stories claiming that popular music was an integrationist plot organized by the NAACP.

In 1959, public outrage against rock and roll reached Congress, and the House Committee on Interstate and Foreign Commerce held hearings to investigate "payola" (lucrative arrangements between disc jockeys and record companies). Although Alan Freed, one of the principal witnesses, was never convicted of accepting bribes, his career was ruined. The committee's assumption was clear: Rock and roll was too vulgar and degrading to be popular; audiences had been "misled as to the popularity of the records played." Committee members even attacked Dick Clark for slighting crooners Bing Crosby and Perry Como.

The impact of this new music represented something rather different, however. This burst of energy from America's black ghettos illustrates the changing nature of American culture. The transformation of inner cities into degrading slums did not speak the whole truth about the urban experience of the 1940s and 1950s. Crime, violence, juvenile delinquency, and cultural impoverishment did not constitute the sole result of this experience. Ralph Ellison was right about his invisibility: It was time to become visible. Not just in culture, but in all elements of life, black Americans demanded integration into the mainstream. In the years of the Eisenhower administration, the rest of society began to grant reluctant recognition to these demands.

6 Republican Era

Author and playwright Thornton Wilder dubbed the 1950s the "Silent Generation" in an epithet accusing Americans of smugness and inaction. To *New York Post* columnist Murray Kempton, America came "of Middle Age" between 1950 and 1962. Both characterizations protested the bland politics of these years, and both blamed the central political figure of the era: Dwight David Eisenhower. To many observers, Eisenhower's middle-of-the-road Republican presidency represented a distasteful compromise in an era of recurring dramatic possibilities. It defined a policy born out of the cautious conservatism of the suburbs and the security-minded politics of old-fashioned morality.

Eisenhower's age (he was sixty-two when he took office) and appearance suggested that the reins of government had slipped into the control of the older generation. Eisenhower, the oldest man until Ronald Reagan to be elected president, served an American population that, in spite of the baby boom, had the oldest median age in the twentieth century. To *The New York Times*, Ike resembled "everybody's grandfather." A far friendlier evaluation came from Republican Senator Everett Dirksen, of Illinois, who in eulogizing Eisenhower, construed his conservatism differently: "Perhaps there are times when a Nation needs brilliance in diplomacy, skill in administration, in-depth background in legislative needs," he admitted. "But there are also times when a Nation needs an abiding father with the wholeness approach of a national leader. . . ."

Eisenhower conservatism frustrated both Democratic liberals and right-wing Republicans, but it pleased an enormous majority of the American electorate who gave the former general two resounding victories despite the electoral unpopularity of his own party. Expectations for the new Republican administration differed widely. A few Republican party ideologues hoped the new president would break the icy truce with the Russians and initiate hot pursuit of Communism. Some voters hoped that in clearing up "the mess in Washington," the Republicans meant purging liberal insiders who had supported New Deal reforms and the Russian-American alliance of World War II. But an overwhelming majority probably supported him for opposite reasons: He promised to end the war in Korea, and he assured Americans he would consolidate, not reverse, the reforms of the 1930s.

For the eight years of his administration, Eisenhower pursued compromise, failing to consolidate his viewpoint in the Republican party. After his departure as president, the moderate, eastern Republicanism he represented wilted quickly in the heat of Sunbelt conservatism. Unexpectedly called to preside over the first small retreats of Jim Crow and segregation, his cautious enforcement of the *Brown* v. *Board of Education* desegregation decision of 1954 pleased almost no one. His defense budget conservatism and his blustery but inconclusive foreign policy roused criticism from all sides. Yet, in this time of immoderate choices, Eisenhower proved to be precisely what most Americans wanted.

Dwight Eisenhower was born on October 14, 1890, in Denison, Texas, and grew up in Abilene, Kansas. His family had a long ancestry, but uncertain standing in the small pioneer plains village. Led by Jacob Eisenhower, a minister and leader in the Protestant sect of the Lykens Valley River Brethren, the Eisenhowers had made their way to Kansas in 1878 from Delaware. Unlike the rest of his family, Dwight's father, David, tried his hand at engineering school. At Lane University, he met and married Ida Stover, of Virginia. But neither engineering nor merchandising, which he took up briefly, could support his growing family. By 1890, David was working on the railroad.

Despite the visible poverty of Dwight's family—in his fourth-grade class picture, he is the only boy wearing farm overalls—Dwight's childhood was generally a happy one. Ignoring his mother's professed pacifism, young Dwight earned a reputation as a skillful fighter and the nickname "Little Ike." Later recollections pictured his family days as warm, loving, and tinged with strong religious faith. His father constructed an immense chart of biblical history, on which the children could see the historical chronology of the Bible in 10 feet by 6 feet hieroglyphics.

Ike was not a studious boy, although he enjoyed history and the action of classic battles. His real interests focused on the playing field, and in high school he became an accomplished athlete. Still, he scored well on the United States Military Academy's competitive exams, and in 1911 he received an appointment to the academy. Handsome, athletic, with a mischievous grin and sandy blond hair, Eisenhower arrived at West Point to join the very special society that embraced his life for the next forty-one years. As a plebe football star, Eisenhower suffered a knee injury that forever ended his athletic career. Known as a maverick and prankster, he earned poor marks in discipline and graduated with a moderate standing in his class. He had not been an obvious success.

Out of school and serving with the infantry in San Antonio, Texas, however, Eisenhower began a rapid, careful ascent through army ranks. While in Texas, he met and married Mamie Geneva Doud, a wealthy and popular young beauty. By 1917, when World War I finally engulfed the United States, Ike had become a skillful organizer with important friends to advise him with his career. After the war, Eisenhower moved steadily upward, joining the Army General Staff in 1925 and attending Command School. At the same time, he wrote a military guidebook of American battlefields of World War I, without visiting Europe.

Congenial and with impressive competence in organizing and leadership, Eisenhower was dispatched to England to head American forces in the European theater during World War II. Work with troublesome French and British allies proved difficult, but Eisenhower emerged as a popular, politically skilled head of the victorious Allied armies on the western front. Long wartime absences from Washington and his wife, Mamie, took their toll on his marriage. Rumors of an affair with his driver, Kay Summersby, spread to Washington. If Ike was tempted to put personal happiness before duty, he quickly gave up dreams of a permanent liaison with Summersby. He had been in the army too long. Rejoining Mamie in Washington after the war, he planted his feet firmly on the track that led eventually to the presidency.

Appointed Chief of Staff in Washington after 1945, Eisenhower, like two other generals, had a political future. The others were George Marshall, later the controversial Secretary of State under Truman, and Douglas MacArthur. Eisenhower admired Marshall, but he frequently referred to MacArthur as a "baby" in his diary. Both political parties courted Eisenhower as a presidential candidate. In 1947 and 1948, the Democrats made overtures to him, and the Republicans nominated him in 1952. From 1948 to 1952, Eisenhower bided his time, accepting an offer from Columbia to become president of that university. An improbable choice, Eisenhower remarked, "I told them they were talking to the wrong Eisenhower," indicating that his brother, Milton, a well-known educator and government consultant, would have been a better candidate. No doubt, he was right. He was unpopular with Columbia's liberal faculty and ran his office through a general staff. Fund-raising proved to be an unpleasant chore. Yet, this academic interlude did nothing to diminish his political prospects. He pushed no policy or party, and even when he rejoined the Army to command NATO forces in late 1950, he avoided close identification with the Truman administration.

Without apparent political debts to pay, Eisenhower was a perfect presidential prospect. In April 1952, he announced his candidacy for the Republican nomination. Nonetheless, Ike had serious opposition. After the electoral disaster of 1948, the Republican conservative wing, led by Senator Robert Taft, of Ohio, made a strong bid to control the party. Solid among state organizations, Taft seemed to promise what many regulars wanted: defeat of the Democrats, a hard-line foreign policy, and an end to social reform.

Robert Alphonso Taft, son of the late President William Howard Taft, was born and bred to Republican party politics. Yale-educated and a Cincinnati lawyer, Taft emerged in the late 1930s a leading critic of the New Deal and an opponent of the liberal-labor coalition that underwrote the Democratic party. An enigmatic, distant man, Taft inspired staunch loyalty from Republicans who opposed the social reform and wartime alliances of the Roosevelt and Truman administrations. Republican right-wing adherents hoped he would reverse the liberal and internationalist policies of twenty years of Democratic rule.

While his candidacy sat well with party regulars in 1952 and was greeted with rapturous accolades by conservative newspapers like the *Chicago Tribune*, Taft's career was strewn with inconsistencies that frightened potential followers. His toleration of Joseph McCarthy and his use of the Communist-in-government issue eliminated some support. Generally committed to unilateralism in foreign policy, he struck curious and sometimes inconsistent positions. As Eisenhower remarked of him once: "In some things I found him extraordinarily leftish." He opposed NATO, the Marshall Plan, the Truman Doctrine, and the International Monetary Fund as needless foreign entanglements. Yet, deferring to the bipartisan policy of the Republican party, he voted for these policies in the Senate. An intelligent critic of postwar internationalism, who

Dwight D. Eisenhower.   *(National Archives)*

doubted the wisdom of much Cold War policy, he sometimes found himself supporting measures that violated his principles.

Taft's power at the Republican convention in Chicago during early July ran down the Midwestern backbone of the party into the shadow Republican organization of the South. Many of his supporters were driven by the accumulated bitterness of twenty years of frustration, focused on Dewey's narrow defeat in 1948. Senator Dirksen, of Illinois, vented this anger during a crucial credentials floor fight, when he pointed to Dewey, standing in the midst of the New York delegation and shouted: "We followed you before and you took us down the road to defeat." Dirksen and the Taft forces, however, were brushed aside by the Eisenhower band-wagon, which picked up disputed delegates in Texas, Georgia, and Louisiana. Even warm support from keynote speaker Douglas MacArthur could not prevent Taft's defeat. The Eastern wing, led by Dewey and Henry Cabot Lodge, had triumphed. But party leaders tendered the vice-presidency as a compromise. Both factions agreed on Richard Nixon, senator from California. Nixon was a shrewd and fateful choice. With a reputation inside the Republican party as an opportunist, Nixon was a tough fighter—a California McCarthy—and thoroughly acceptable to party conservatives. But Nixon had also ingratiated himself with Easterners such as Dewey. The match was ideal: a presidential nominee who seemed above politics, a vigorous vice-presidential candidate, and a party platform narrowly based on Republican conservatism. A three-month Republican crusade against traitors "in high places," against Communism, Corruption, and Korea, began, led by a man who abhorred ideologies and political brawls.

The Democrats had to choose between improbabilities in 1952. President Truman considered a third term, but after a disastrous showing in early primaries, he turned from front-runner to king-maker. Senator Estes Kefauver, of Tennessee, widely known for his Senate investigations into organized crime in 1950 and 1951, entered the race, but Kefauver's investigators had discovered embarrassing ties between Democratic city bosses and the under-world, and the party organization blocked the senator. Despite early victories in primaries, Kefauver's candidacy gradually sank as that of Governor Adlai Stevenson, of Illinois, rose.

Stevenson had long-standing ties to Democratic politics. His grandfather had been a congressman and then vice-president in 1892 during the Cleveland administration. After an Eastern education at Choate, Princeton, and Harvard, Adlai returned to the Midwest to work as a journalist and a lawyer. During World War II, he joined the office of the Secretary of the Navy. Sent to San Francisco as an adviser to the American delegation to the United Nations Conference in 1945, he continued as adviser to the American delegation to the U.N. in 1946 and 1947. Serious politics began in 1948 when he won the governorship of Illinois. His four years in office were competent, but uneventful.

By temperament a witty and urbane man, Stevenson was a political moderate and a strong anti-Communist. Yet circumstances made him a lightning rod for liberalism; he both attracted and dispersed hopes for vigorous reform. His elegant speeches and affirmation of the New Deal invited scurrilous attacks heaped on him by conservative newspaper columnists, giving him a reputation he did not entirely deserve. But, he was a candidate Truman could support, and he was acceptable to the liberal wing of the party and the South.

To win in 1952, the Republicans merely needed to last out the campaign without committing serious gaffs. Stevenson had the unhappy task of running for and against the Truman administration. The best theme the Democrats could muster was "You never had it so good," an unfortunate slogan that newspaper cartoonists gleefully satirized. Stevenson tried to establish political breathing room by moving his headquarters to Springfield, Illinois, but Truman insisted on entering the campaign anyway, undercutting the candidate's independence with a last-minute, whistle-stop defense of his administration in October.

Within the Republican party, Eisenhower had to make peace with Taft and then defend his lead in opinion polls. His presidency, he announced in Boise, Idaho, in August, would seek the "middle road." By this course, he hoped to steer between liberal Democrats and the conservative wing of his own party. Embracing the activist Republican heritage of Lincoln and Theodore Roosevelt, he defended federal intervention into the economy to preserve the market economy. He promised to maintain the "solid floor that keeps all of us from falling into a pit of disaster." He would not campaign against the welfare state.

In foreign policy, conservatives had more to praise. Eisenhower agreed with their firm opposition to Communism and he accused the Truman administration of errors and appeasement. The slurs and broad charges of McCarthy and Senator William Jenner, of

This cartoon appeared on the front page of the Chicago Tribune *on August 6, 1952.
During the election campaign of 1952, a majority of American newspapers supported
the Republican ticket, urging a change in political party leadership for the first time
in twenty years. The Tribune was among the most active and vociferous critics of
Democratic rule.* (Reprinted courtesy of the Chicago Tribune. *All rights reserved.)*

Indiana were, however, another matter. Unwilling to voice his distaste for these men, Eisenhower backed into endorsing their candidacies. This accommodation cost Eisenhower personally, initially preventing him from defending his old friend, General George Marshall, of charges of being soft on Communism. Condemned by anti-Communist crusader McCarthy for "surrendering" China to the Communists, the general was ridiculed and smeared during a campaign that charged the Democrats with "twenty years of treason." Eisenhower's bargain with anti-Communist activists in his party on the vice-presidency risked his election for a short time. On September 18, the *New York Post* uncovered a secret $18,000 slush fund provided by wealthy California businessmen to Richard Nixon, catching the Republican apostle of ideological purity with political grime on his face. Several newspapers in the Eisenhower camp, like the *Washington Post* and the Republican *New York Herald Tribune*, called on the Californian to quit. Eisenhower remained ominously silent, signaling Nixon to clear himself.

On September 23, the Republican vice-presidential candidate explained his finances to a national radio and television audience. In the most famous political speech of the decade, Nixon mixed mumbled humility with belligerent innuendo. Using the irresistible intimacy of television, he portrayed himself as the victim of a smear. He acknowledged the existence of the fund used to pay office expenses, but claimed that he personally had received nothing. In a long, pensive introduction, he counted the roads to corruption he might have taken: to put his wife on the payroll ("She's a wonderful stenographer"), to sell his influence, or to exploit family riches—if he had them. Then, in embarrassing detail, he outlined the family finances. He was satisfied with his success; unlike mink-clad Democrats, his wife, Pat, accepted her "respectable cloth coat." He had received a gift—a dog named Checkers, beloved by his children—but there was nothing wrong with this. He would keep the dog.

The speech was both disingenuous and prophetic. The candidate never squarely faced the meaning of the slush fund. More peculiarly, in an uncensored moment, he thought out loud about some of the very forms of corruption he later pursued in his own presidency. But, the performance was a masterful stroke of public relations. Favorable telegrams poured into the national Republican headquarters, and a similar sort of fund for Stevenson surfaced. Nixon secured his position but undercut his relationship with Eisenhower. From that moment on, Nixon fruitlessly sought what he could never acquire: the consistent friendship and support of the general.

Despite a comfortable lead in the polls, the Republican campaign only caught fire on October 24, when Eisenhower suddenly announced in Detroit that he would visit Korea. Vague as it was, this promise suggested that the candidate would seek a quick peace to the seemingly interminable war. This announcement raised the odds even more against Stevenson. He could neither restore the Roosevelt coalition with fire-and-brimstone New Deal rhetoric nor divorce himself from the unpopular Truman administration. Even so, the November results were surprising. Eisenhower swept 34 million votes to only 27 million for Stevenson. More striking, the Republican mustered considerable strength in the South, taking Texas, Virginia, Tennessee, and Oklahoma. Elsewhere, the ticket slashed into the urban-ethnic coalition of the Democrats. The congressional Republicans fared less well, squeaking by in the House with a majority of ten and in the Senate only with Vice-President Nixon voting to break a deadlock.

The president-elect began immediately to summon his Cabinet and his staff, and quietly fulfilled his principal campaign pledge. Together with General Omar N. Bradley and future Cabinet members Herbert Brownell (Attorney General) and Charles E. Wilson (Defense), he slipped away under tight security to visit Korea for several days in November. Conferring there with American generals and Korean Premier Syngman Rhee, he emerged with no new policy, but he had kept his pledge.

Unlike subsequent presidents, Eisenhower relied heavily upon the advice of his Cabinet. Secretary of the Treasury George Humphrey, a conservative industrialist from Cleveland, emerged as his closest adviser. Secretary of State was John Foster Dulles, a personal friend and an experienced diplomat. Ezra Taft Benson, a Taft supporter, became Secretary of Agriculture. Dewey's supporter, Herbert Brownell, was appointed Attorney General. In 1953, when Congress created the Department of Health, Education, and Welfare, Eisenhower selected Oveta Culp Hobby, former commander of the Women's Army Corps, as Secretary. Martin Durkin, head of the Plumbers Union, became Secretary of Labor, a post he shortly relinquished to James Mitchell, a vice-president of Bloomingdale's department stores. The Cabinet carefully balanced the ideological wings of the Republican party and represented

Election of 1952

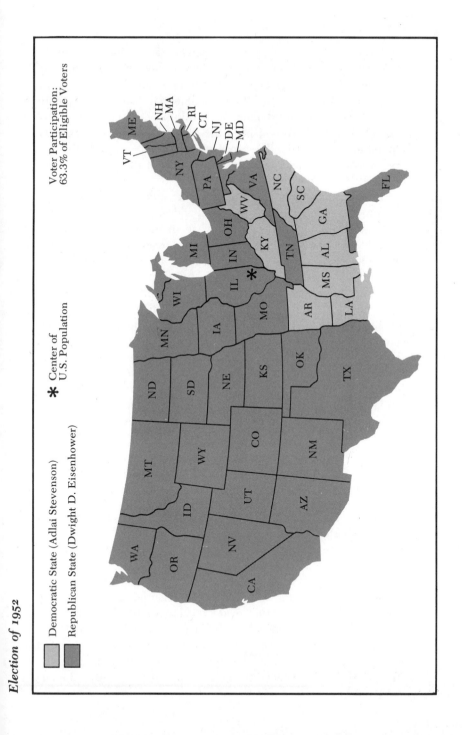

Democratic State (Adlai Stevenson)

Republican State (Dwight D. Eisenhower)

★ Center of
U.S. Population

Voter Participation:
63.3% of Eligible Voters

established wealth and economic power. This was certainly no departure from tradition, but Eisenhower chose his appointments from large commercial or manufacturing establishments. Except for Dulles, none belonged to the influential group of corporate lawyers that had advised Truman. In addition to the Cabinet, Ike appointed Allen Dulles to head the Central Intelligence Agency. Operating in tandem, the two Dulles brothers commanded the open diplomacy and clandestine operations of the American government.

Eisenhower's appointments appeared to underscore his commitment to the status quo. His inaugural address of January 20, 1953, was a platitudinous example of what theologian Will Herberg named "civic religion." Eisenhower had even penned his own prayer for the occasion. Two weeks later, he and his wife joined the National Presbyterian Church as full communicant members. In public, he acted as a spiritual leader, using the presidency as the ceremonial chief of staff of the Republic. Eisenhower was careful not to detract from his public image as a man above party, committed to traditional values of honesty, integrity, family, and simplicity in office. In part, too, the new president recognized the pervasive sentiment against strong, activist leaders. He was the first man to serve under the new Twenty-second Amendment to the Constitution, ratified in 1951, which limited all presidents following Harry Truman to not more than two terms.

There was, however, another side to Eisenhower—intelligent and sensitive to the burdens of leadership. In a diary entry early in the summer of 1953, the President privately ruminated about the difficult job he had undertaken. So far, his administration was immobile: the Korean War and Senator McCarthy still dominated the news. The United States, he worried, faced an unresolved crisis, a shortage of wisdom and common sense. "Daily I am impressed by the shortsightedness bordering upon tragic stupidity of many," he wrote, "who fancy themselves to be the greatest believers in and supporters of capitalism." Class struggle and revolution would never touch the United States, he assured himself. Yet, the extremes of selfishness that made revolutions possible existed in the United States. Americans, he hoped, would commit themselves to long-term goals, not short-term profits. The United States must promote equitable trade and industrialization in the "free world" and protect its access to raw materials. But, to sur-

During a visit to Korea in November 1953, Vice President Richard Nixon stands at attention while the national anthem is played. (*U.S. Army Photograph*)

vive, the nation also had to dedicate itself to a religious faith of unselfishness and cooperation.

In public pronouncements defining middle-of-the-road Republicanism, Eisenhower steered a course between political extremes. Obviously shocked by the proposals of some liberals, he also recognized challenges from his own party's conservatives. He firmly committed his administration to a balanced federal budget, with a small and efficient military establishment relying upon nuclear weapons. The danger, he told a news conference in 1953, lay in creating a militarized society: "We don't want to become a garrison state. We want to remain free."

The immediate background of these remarks was probably the administration's still-born "Operation Candor." Set up in April, a group of advisers prepared background material for a major address on atomic warfare. Several unacceptable drafts later, the President abandoned his proposal to speak frankly to Americans about "the age of peril." Such strong language and frightening prospects, he decided, would shove the nation toward the militarized psychology he opposed.

Up to his farewell address, in which he eloquently warned of excessive Cold War zeal, Eisenhower opposed the creation of a large military establishment. Nonetheless, his toleration of Republican extremists tugged him in another direction. The breaking point was Senator McCarthy. Ike had to encourage him or destroy him. The Wisconsin senator seemed to set up this extreme choice himself.

McCarthy and Eisenhower had already skirmished over the reputation of the President's friend George Marshall. In 1951, Marshall had been the subject of a poisonous book by McCarthy called *America's Retreat from Victory*. Distasteful as it was, Eisenhower supported McCarthy in 1952, even while he tried to rescue Marshall's reputation. And, after the election, compromise with the right continued to be Eisenhower's policy. Indeed, he allowed John Foster Dulles to hire former FBI agent and current McCarthy supporter Scott McLeod to investigate security risks in the State Department.

Still, McCarthy refused to relent. Driven by an insatiable urge for publicity and encouraged by conservative followers, the Wisconsin senator lambasted the federal government from his position on the Senate Government Operations Committee. During the summer of 1953, McCarthy and his aides, Roy Cohn and David Schine, investigated overseas State Department libraries, finding works by philosopher John Dewey, historian Henry Steele Commager, critic Bernard De Voto, and poet W. H. Auden, whom they declared to be unacceptable politically. With this in mind, Eisenhower denounced "book burners" on June 14, 1953, at a Dartmouth College graduation ceremony. Almost immediately, however, he backtracked, assuring reporters that he didn't propose free speech for Communists.

The President cut off this confrontation for several reasons. In part, he feared McCarthy's popularity. Even his own advisers disagreed over how to handle the anti-Communist crusader. Moreover, the Republicans controlled the Senate by only one vote. Up to a point, Eisenhower agreed with McCarthy. He resolutely believed in the guilt of Julius and Ethel Rosenberg and refused to pardon them or commute their sentences, allowing them to die in the electric chair on June 13, 1953. Later in the year, on the basis of rumor, Eisenhower blocked J. Robert Oppenheimer, a distinguished nuclear scientist, from access to classified research materials. Charges that Oppenheimer was a security risk, because of his wife's politics and some earlier associations, played a role in this affair, but the scientist's most serious misstep was opposition to building the hydrogen bomb. He had, after all, received security clearance during World War II, when he worked on the atomic bomb.

Although Eisenhower clearly understood the dangers of excessive anti-Communism, he resisted action until the antired tide began to break on the outer banks of his own administration. In early 1954, Senator McCarthy began his fateful television investigation of the United States Army. The ensuing Army-McCarthy hearings, beginning on April 22, focused first on an Army dentist accused of subversive beliefs, but quickly deepened into a challenge to the top brass of the military establishment. Understandably, the President recognized this as a veiled attack on his own career.

When it finally occurred, McCarthy's demise was a public suicide. His bluster, bad manners, and heavy sarcasm beamed daily into American living rooms, deeply embarrassing the Senate. And, McCarthy was outwitted by Army lawyer Joseph Welch. Unable to intimidate witnesses and confused about the purposes of his pursuit, the Senator was first brutish and finally boring, his decline mercilessly exposed by television cameras. In August, the Senate appointed a committee to study censure charges. Safely after mid-term congressional elections, the chamber, in December, voted to condemn him. McCarthy sank slowly and unceremoniously from public sight, condemned by rumor and innuendo, dying on May 2, 1957. Some of the excesses of anti-Communism also passed into obscurity with him, but neither the Congress nor the administration admitted the origins of McCarthyism in a national—and their own—obsession with ferreting out subversive ideas. As if to confirm this impression, in 1954 Congress passed, and the President signed, the Communist Control Act, requiring the American Communist party to register as the agency of a "hostile foreign power."

Eisenhower emerged stronger from his two-year maneuver with McCarthy, but he also established his independence from the Republican right in foreign policy. This was no easy task, for the Republican platform of 1952 contained a ringing denunciation of Truman's policy of containment. Moreover, Secretary of State Dulles advocated the "liberation" of Eastern European countries from Soviet hegemony and the roll back of the "Iron Curtain." Dulles's memorable slogans drew upon his evangelical belief in the American economic and political system. In practical terms, Dulles suggested that a rejuvenated Germany and Japan could create the western and eastern poles of a tight net of collective-security pacts to ring the Soviet-Chinese worlds. However, if this sounded like the confrontation demanded by some extremists, it was not. When opportunity came to undo Communist gains in Eastern Europe, Dulles refused to act. In mid-June 1953, Soviet armed forces repressed East German workers, who rioted against the Walter Ulbricht regime. The United States did little more than deplore the action. The policy of "liberation" proved to be rhetorically aggressive, but, in fact, it was another version of containment.

Eisenhower's containment policy became clearer in Korean peace negotiations, although at the same time, the State Department fired George Kennan, the author of the doctrine. Eisenhower renewed talks at Panmunjom with the People's Republics of North Korea and China. The repatriation of thousands of captured Communist prisoners of war proved to be a major snag. Many told their captors they refused to return home. Working quietly, Dulles passed word to the Chinese and Koreans that the United States would lift all restrictions on the weapons of war—meaning the atomic bomb—if satisfactory progress toward a settlement did not occur. By June 8, 1953, both sides agreed on a tentative agreement, but South Korean President Rhee objected and tried to scuttle the accord by releasing 27,000 POWs, most of whom disappeared into the South Korean population. Nonetheless, the agreement held, and Rhee had to back down. On July 26, 1953, Eisenhower announced an armistice. The costly three-year struggle ended without any resolution of the issues: the map of Korea looked very much as it had in 1950, divided between two hostile forces.

Clearing the boards of the Korean War freed Dulles and Eisenhower to implement their foreign policy. Their general strategy was to protect and extend world-wide United States interests through "massive deterrence"—the threat to use atomic weaponry—a policy of maximum effect and minimum cost. Coupled to this were collective-security alliances. Powerful nations, organized into groups such as NATO, hopefully could prevent limited aggression from becoming permanent gain. Massive deterrence, announced by Dulles in a speech on January 12, 1954, made possible a small federal budget while exploiting American nuclear weapons superiority. To avoid open intervention, the Central Intelligence Agency (CIA), headed by Allen Dulles, intervened surreptitiously in situations that required deception and minimal force.

The administration's shadow foreign policy apparatus sometimes worked against the interests of its open diplomacy. The Central Intelligence Agency evolved from World War II intelligence operations. The National Security Act of July 26, 1947, defined the basic structure of this new agency. Provisions of the law organized intelligence operations into one body, which reported to the National Security Council (made up of the President, Vice-President, Secretaries of State and Defense, the Director of the CIA, the Chairman of the Joint Chiefs of Staff, and the Assistant to the President for National Security Affairs). Exempted from public scrutiny of budgeting, purchases, hiring, and funding by the Central Intelligence Agency Act of 1949, the body escaped public accounting and control. During the Eisenhower administration, it sometimes pursued clandestine operations that undercut the stated foreign policy of the government. Under Allen Dulles, the operation expanded beyond traditional espionage in a great many foreign nations, operating inside the United States as well.

In one instance, the agency's operations touched the private interests of the Dulles brothers, although this fact probably had little to do with their behavior. In 1952, President Jacobo Arbenz

Guzmán, of Guatemala, expropriated United Fruit Company properties in his nation, and the company demanded a steep compensation. With rumors of rebellion circulating in 1954, the small
country turned to the Communist bloc for arms and political support. John Foster Dulles (whose law firm, Sullivan and Cromwell,
had United Fruit Company accounts) and Allen Dulles (who once
sat on the board of directors of the company) met with the President and Latin American experts. Allen Dulles convinced
Eisenhower to approve a clandestine operation against Arbenz
Guzmán. With this go-ahead, a secret army quickly prepared for
an invasion. When it landed in June, it quickly overcame the
Arbenz Guzmán forces. The newly installed President Castillo restored United Fruit properties and eliminated his political opposition. To bolster the new government, the United States sent in
large amounts of economic aid.

Nowhere were CIA operations more extensive or important than
in Southeast Asia. Having struggled for eight years after World
War II to regain their colonial position in Indochina, the French,
in 1954, were exhausted. Worse, they committed a military blun-
der of enormous proportions. Early in the year, they gathered a
large army at the fort of Dien Bien Phu, hoping to attract and then
destroy their opponents. Instead, they found themselves surrounded by a larger army of Viet Minh insurgents. Led by Ho Chi
Minh, this movement had sought independence for Vietnam since
the early 1940s; now victory was close. After a fifty-five-day
assault, the French surrendered. During this time, Dulles and
Eisenhower weighed several responses. Already providing most of
the military supplies to the French, the administration hinted at
direct intervention, but met an outcry of displeasure. Air Force
Chief of Staff Nathan Twining suggested using small atomic bombs
around the fortress, but Eisenhower rejected this as well as conventional air strikes. Fear of involvement in another Asian war tied
the hands of the President. On April 7, 1954, Eisenhower expressed his frustration with the situation when he enunciated a
new theory, "what you would call the 'falling domino' principle":
when one state falls to Communism, it will cause neighboring
states to fall. Any thoughts of direct involvement evaporated after
Pierre Mendès-France, the new French premier, negotiated a
peace agreement with the Viet Minh in late July. According to the
treaty signed in Geneva, Switzerland, Vietnam would be divided
temporarily into two administrative units, in the north and south,

until elections reunified the nation. The Viet Minh, Great Britain, France, the Soviet Union, and the People's Republic of China initialed the accords, but the United States refused. Unable to prevent the fall of the French, the Eisenhower administration worked to deprive the Viet Minh of the fruits of victory. In September, the United States convened a conference in Manila to create the Southeast Asia Treaty Organization. Consisting of Great Britain, France, Australia, New Zealand, Thailand, Pakistan, and the Philippines, this defense organization was designed to prevent further decay of European and American influence in Southeast Asia. Inside Vietnam, the United States quietly replaced the French. Supporting Ngo Dinh Diem, who had close ties to the CIA, the administration bypassed the French in the south. Bolstered by American military and economic aid, Diem rose to prime minister. Holding a referendum, he stripped the French-supported emperor of Vietnam of his last pretense to power. Then, operating on the fiction that South Vietnam was a permanent nation-state, he consolidated his rule. At the same time, the CIA, operating inside various cover organizations, like the United States Information Service, worked secretly to improve South Vietnamese administration and to pacify the countryside. When Diem refused to hold scheduled reunification elections, the United States agreed with his position. Eisenhower himself predicted that Ho Chi Minh would have won a national election.

Unable to do anything but hold the line in Southeast Asia, the Eisenhower administration confronted a new crisis in September 1954. The People's Republic of China suddenly began shelling offshore islands still held by the Chiang Kai-shek forces. Ultimately indefensible and probably of little importance, Quemoy, Matsu, and Tachen nonetheless became symbols of resistance to Communism. The United States responded with a mutual-defense treaty with the Nationalist government. In the Formosa Resolution, passed by the Senate in early 1955, the President received unspecified powers to protect Formosa and the Pescadores Islands between Formosa and the coast of China. This assignment of war powers by Congress allowed the President more latitude in initiating action in Asia, a power that some critics believed could lead to adventurism in this unstable part of the world.

In Europe, Eisenhower and Dulles tried to firm up alliances around Communist power centers. Success hinged upon a revitalized and rearmed Germany. While the United States could agree with the Soviet Union, in 1955, to neutralize the former Axis ally Austria, no such accord was possible in Germany. Eisenhower insisted upon a free Germany reunited by elections in all of the occupied zones. The resulting nation should then, he determined, be entitled to sign defense pacts and enter alliances of its own choosing. If the Russians refused, as they most certainly would, then Western Germany should be integrated into NATO.

Although Germany remained an unresolvable point of contention, the United States and the U.S.S.R. paid considerable attention to disarmament. The enormous cost of nuclear weaponry and upgraded conventional armaments threatened to distort Eisenhower's parsimonious "New Look" military budget. For the Russians, rebuilding wartime damage, while supporting a sophisticated military establishment, constituted a terrible burden.

Eisenhower first elaborated his disarmament policy in December 1953, in an address to the United Nations on peaceful uses of atomic energy. He proposed a United Nations stockpile of atomic materials and controlled destruction of atomic weaponry. The Russians responded by calling for complete and unconditional banning of all nuclear weapons. As it unfolded, the argument between the two sides revived positions first raised around the Baruch Plan of 1946. The United States insisted on controlled disarmament and unlimited inspections to monitor compliance. The Russians demanded total disarmament and no inspections. In the spring of 1955, however, the Soviets amended this stand to agree to surveillance and a more limited, four-phase schedule of disarmament. The United States postponed its reply until July, when Eisenhower had a planned conference with Russian leaders, Prime Minister Edgar Faure, of France, and Anthony Eden, of Britain, in Geneva.

The Geneva Conference marked a turning point in foreign affairs. More optimistic about negotiating with the Russians than Secretary of State Dulles, Ike remained adamant on reunification of Germany and its integration into NATO. The Russians were just as firm in opposing anything but the permanent neutralization of their former enemy. On disarmament, Eisenhower made a public bid on July 21, addressing delegates to the convention. His "Open Skies" proposal, prepared several months in advance, suggested opening both the Soviet Union and the United States to air inspection. Both nations would exchange military blueprints and other information. A possible step toward mutual understanding, the

Open Skies proposal did not represent a significant disarmament plan. Moreover, it would have favored the United States more than the Russians. Although no substantial agreement occurred, the American press spoke of the "spirit of Geneva." By this, they meant the possibility of more cordial relationships. Perhaps this was an exaggeration, but the United States and the Russians had at least determined to accept the status quo. The United States had become more interested in negotiating on such issues as disarmament, and, in turn, the Soviets recognized they could do little to prevent the independence and western orientation of West Germany.

Eisenhower's moderate success in softening the Cold War with the Soviet Union matched his modest achievements at home. The President's view of office differed considerably from the activism of his predecessors. The administration operations followed a military model, with chief of the White House staff, Sherman Adams, in command. Eisenhower's goals were also different; he hoped to reduce expenditures and balance the federal budget, yet he promised to preserve popular social legislation and expand capital projects in transportation. Obviously, he needed the close cooperation of Congress. A slim Republican majority in 1953 and 1954 made this possible, but after the Democratic sweep of the mid-year elections in 1954, Eisenhower's task became more difficult. Never again did the administration have a friendly Congress, although Eisenhower worked successfully with Democratic party leaders, such as Lyndon Johnson. Nonetheless, in the last years of his administration, the President found himself locked in a struggle against new social legislation and large proposals for defense spending generated by congressional Democrats.

Despite problems with Congress, Ike achieved moderate success in budget-balancing. Federal receipts exceeded expenses in 1956, 1957, and 1960. Deficits in 1954 and 1958 were insignificant. Moderate imbalances appeared in 1953 (Truman's budget) and 1955. Only in 1959, during the severe slump, did imbalance become serious. This general fiscal conservatism, coupled with relatively stable international prices for raw materials and a favorable United States trade position, helped control inflation. Measured by the wholesale price index, yearly inflation during the Eisenhower administration hovered around 1 percent.

In farm policy, Eisenhower agreed with Secretary of Agriculture Ezra Taft Benson that federal crop price supports should be lower.

New Deal and Fair Deal policy set high commodity prices by calling for federal purchases of surplus grains and produce. In the Truman administration, the federal government established a 90 percent parity, or price supports to guarantee 90 percent of the earning power of agricultural products keyed to the 1910–1914 period. To maintain high prices, the government purchased vast quantities of grain, tobacco, and cotton. Benson persuaded Congress, in 1954, to lower parity to 70 percent on most commodities except tobacco. While this created more price fluctuation, it did little to solve the problem of high farm productivity and low prices. Nor did it help reverse the decline of the family farm.

If farm policy seemed a step toward orthodox free enterprise, Eisenhower took several strides in the opposite direction of the welfare state. In 1954, he signed a bill adding millions of self-employed workers to the Social Security system. He supported a higher minimum wage and new public-housing programs. Two large capital programs heavily involved federal financing. On May 13, 1954, he signed a bill to construct a St. Lawrence Seaway, joining the Great Lakes to ocean shipping through the mouth of the St. Lawrence River. The vast public-works project to build an interstate system of limited-access highways, which passed in 1956, further established Eisenhower as a president who had a Republican vision of the welfare state.

Eisenhower's most serious domestic problems were partly a consequence of his appointment of Earl Warren (formerly attorney general and governor of California) to the Supreme Court. Almost immediately after his confirmation as Chief Justice in 1953, Warren faced a decision on five segregation cases pending before the Court. The five cases challenged state and District of Columbia practices of school segregation. NAACP lawyers, led by Thurgood Marshall, argued that the old doctrine of "separate but equal" constituted inevitable discrimination. The practice of separation, they continued, established a psychology of inferiority independent of the physical condition of the schools. Conscious of the enormous step they proposed to take, the Court justices required a unanimous and forceful decision. Warren's installation as Chief Justice made this possible. On May 17, 1954, the Court declared school segregation unconstitutional in *Brown* v. *Board of Education of Topeka, Kansas*. Accepting Marshall's psychological argument, it ordered desegregation in 1955 "with all deliberate speed."

Eisenhower regarded this decision with initial ambiguity and then hostility. He had allowed the Attorney General to file in support of the NAACP, but, according to Warren, he personally implied that the Court should be lenient with school segregationists. After its announcement, Eisenhower refused to speak in defense of the decision. Thereafter, relations between the President and his Chief Justice cooled. In the remaining six years of his tenure, Eisenhower never proposed implementing the Warren decision, nor did he defend the Court from outrageous attacks mounted by members of his own party. First the John Birch Society, a right-wing fringe group, attacked the Chief Justice. Then, after the *Watkins* v. *U.S.* decision in 1957, defending the Constitutional rights of persons accused of subversive beliefs, even members of the American Bar Association bitterly attacked Warren. Ike remained silent.

Criticism of the Court's desegregation decision accused the judicial branch of making decisions with wide legislative and executive implications. The Court was overstepping tradition to act as legislator and executor of controversial policies. To a degree, this reaction was accurate, although abundant precedents for Court activism exist in its long history. On the other hand, the Supreme Court had acted to defend the civil rights of black citizens that had remained flagrantly unenforced since the Civil War. Controversial though it was, the desegregation decision set irreversible forces into motion that eventually destroyed legal segregation in America.

By the summer of 1955, Eisenhower's moderate Republicanism was well established. Away from the din of partisan politics, the middle way he chose depended entirely upon his own leadership and popularity. But suddenly this proved to be fragile. On September 24, in Denver, Colorado, the President suffered a serious heart attack. His illness required complete bed rest for several days. Although he recovered speedily, he was struck with ileitis, which required corrective intestinal surgery, during the spring of 1956. Neither of these illnesses permanently disabled the President, but they did rouse talk about Vice-President Nixon's role and the possibility that he would have to step into the presidency. During the summer of 1956, although Ike's renomination was assured, party members discussed removing Nixon from the ticket. Much to the Vice-President's dismay, Eisenhower remained mute, although when the replacement movement fizzled, the President warmly endorsed Nixon.

As a campaign orientation in 1956, the President tried to impress his philosophy of modern Republicanism on the party. With Eisenhower's official endorsement, Arthur Larsen discussed modern Republicanism in a campaign book, A Republican Looks at His Party. The author argued that on fundamental national issues, "we have greater agreement than ever before in our history." This new consensus, he argued, synthesized two contradictory political tendencies: the conservative Republicanism of 1896 and the radical liberalism of 1936. The pivotal election of 1956, he proclaimed, would reaffirm the basic moderation of most Americans, who wanted to avoid the Scylla of liberal projects to redistribute income and the Charybdis of conservative unregulated competition. The new Republicanism, he hoped, would attract millions of voters. It did—at least for the presidential ticket. But, the Republicans continued to be a minority party in the Congress.

The ticket of Eisenhower and Nixon perfectly suited the inertia of the mid-1950s; the Democrats, with few new ideas, called again upon Stevenson. Stevenson departed from custom to allow the convention to select a vice-presidential candidate, but to some observers, this seemed a cavalier act of nonchalance. The delegates at the convention in Chicago did not enhance the ticket when they selected Estes Kefauver, one of the most liberal senators and a man repugnant to much of the party establishment. Stevenson and Kefauver tried to define real issues and differentiate clearly between the two tickets, but they failed to convince the electorate. Stevenson's discussion of nuclear fallout from testing fell on deaf ears. Even his last-minute warning about the health of the President backfired. Eisenhower and Nixon captured 57 percent of the vote, with 457 electoral votes to 73 for the Democrats. In the South, the Democrats won only Alabama, Arkansas, Georgia, Mississippi, Missouri, North Carolina, and South Carolina; the once-dependable South now split its votes. Nonetheless, in the Senate and House of Representatives, the Democrats increased their majorities. If modern Republicanism expressed the desire of Americans for a national consensus and unified purpose, the congressional elections revealed a desire for change and continued reform. This paradoxical voting pattern of the American electorate remained characteristic of every subsequent contest through the 1970s, thereby allowing a shrinking Republican party to contest the presidency successfully despite overwhelming Democratic party registration.

As in 1952, foreign policy issues were decisive in this election. Despite Secretary Dulles's 1955 threat to go "to the brink" of war with the Russians, events prior to the election evoked caution. In October 1956, Hungarians, caught up by the impulse of de-Stalinization sweeping Eastern Europe, rose against the repressive, Soviet-backed regime in their country and installed Imre Nagy as premier. At first, Nagy extended political and economic freedoms, which the Russians tolerated, but when he declared his nation's withdrawal from the Warsaw Pact, the Soviet Army acted quickly. On October 30, Russian tanks and troops streamed into Budapest, arrested Nagy, and crushed further opposition, installing a new government headed by János Kádar. From the beginning, Dulles and Eisenhower indicated that they would not intervene. Despite broadcasts of encouragement by CIA-sponsored Radio Free Europe, no American help materialized.

Just a few days later, the United States found itself allied to the Soviet Union against France, Britain, and Israel. Over the summer of 1956, relations between Egypt and the Western powers deteriorated. The new revolutionary regime of Gamal Abdel Nasser applied for United States loans and expertise to build a huge power and irrigation facility at Aswan. John Foster Dulles, however, finally rejected the project, and Nassar turned to the Soviet Union for help. To finance his industrial and military projects, Nasser nationalized the Suez Canal, built by the British and the French. Dulles hoped to pressure Nasser into some compromise, but the British and French demanded immediate retaliation. When Israel attacked Egyptian forces on October 29 in the Sinai Desert, the French and British used the flare-up as a pretext to intervene. On November 5, Anglo-French troops landed at Port Said. At this point, the Russians insisted on immediate withdrawal, threatening to send volunteers to aid their new Egyptian ally. Dulles and Eisenhower abandoned England and France, voting with the U.S.S.R. for a U.N. Security Council cease-fire resolution. Facing an impossible alliance of two superpowers, the French and British withdrew, thus ending their last grand imperial adventure.

☆   ☆   ☆

Dwight Eisenhower's second presidential term was unique in American history, because he was the first president who by Constitutional amendment could not serve more than two terms.

Nonetheless, he continued to pursue the goals of modern Republicanism, a balanced budget, and increased peace initiatives with the Soviet Union. Despite his distaste for the *Brown* decision, Ike moved cautiously toward limited integration goals. In 1955, he appointed Frederic Morrow, the first black American on the presidential staff. More important, he actively supported a civil rights voting bill in Congress. The act languished until August 1957, when Lyndon Johnson, the majority leader in the Senate, cajoled his fellow Southerners into allowing passage of the bill. Somewhat watered down, the act created the Civil Rights Commission and the Civil Rights Division of the Justice Department. It also strengthened voting rights. Most important, the law represented the first positive civil rights act since the end of Reconstruction.

Unwilling to speak in favor of school integration, the President found that events in 1957 compelled him to enforce it with military power. The stage for the nation's first great confrontation over integration was set in 1955 when the school board of Little Rock, Arkansas, submitted a plan for gradual desegregation to the courts. Most of the elected officials in the city supported the proposal, but Governor Orval Faubus suddenly intervened to prevent its implementation. The courts insisted, however, and the schools planned desegregation for September 3, 1957, at the opening of a new school year. Governor Faubus acted to stop integration. Calling up the Arkansas National Guard, he ordered troops to prevent black children from entering Little Rock Central High School.

The Governor's action turned a local incident into a challenge to national power, forcing the President to act. Meeting with Faubus on September 17, Eisenhower thought he had obtained assurances that the Governor would moderate his stand. But, he was wrong. On September 20, after a federal injunction forced Faubus to allow integration of the school, he withdrew his troops. At the same time, he warned black parents to keep their children away from school. These inflammatory remarks turned a bad situation worse, and when the school attempted to open on September 23, angry mobs of whites rioted. Little Rock's mayor, Woodrow Wilson Mann, appealed to the President for help. Finally, on September 24, Eisenhower dispatched troops to the riot-torn city, appealing at the same time on national radio and TV for calm. His actions were a small, reluctant step forward, and the walls of southern school segregation did not crumble for another decade.

The year 1958 represented the nadir of Eisenhower's presidency. Earlier, in 1957, the economy began to slip into serious recession. The downturn lasted until 1958, with industrial production remaining sluggish until the middle of the year. Unemployment rose from slightly more than 4 percent to around 7 percent in 1958. Recession stretched the length of unemployment so that 30 percent of those out of work were without a job for more than fifteen weeks. As in any recession, nonwhite workers were hardest hit, with official statistics recording almost 13 percent seeking work.

Deepening recession and unemployment stimulated demands for a Keynesian solution, a tax cut, and public-works projects. Eisenhower instinctively opposed both proposals, although the cabinet discussed a tax cut in May 1968. In April, the President signed the Emergency Housing Bill, designed to pump money into federal programs, like the Veterans Administration house mortgage program. In general, however, Republican policy was to sit out the slowdown.

Scandal close to the heart of the administration rocked the party just before the congressional elections of 1958. On June 16, a House Legislative Oversight Committee accused Sherman Adams, the President's chief of staff, of maintaining an illegal business relationship with textile manufacturer Bernard Goldfine. In exchange for intervening with the Federal Trade Commission in his interest, Goldfine had given gifts to Adams and paid some of his hotel bills. Adams denied the charges. Even after the committee exonerated him, Adams was a liability to the President. Something of a martinet, Adams' unpopularity with Congress made his departure inevitable. Reluctantly, Ike accepted his resignation on September 22. Then, on November 26, Eisenhower suffered a mild stroke, one more grim event in this difficult year. Although he quickly recovered, the permanent effects of hesitant speech thereafter marred his news conferences and speeches.

To the Republican party, the elections of 1958 were a disaster. Distance between the President and the party was never greater. The Democrats increased their congressional majority significantly; in the House, they held 283 seats to 153, and in the Senate, they gained 64 to 34 for the Republicans. Such lopsided results signified more than frustration at the economic downturn or scandal in the administration. They proved the failure of modern Republicanism to inspire either the party or the public.

One of the hardest-fought issues of the congressional campaign focused on America's defenses. Eisenhower's New Look military budget was conservative and cautious, susceptible to attack from Democrats who proposed extraordinary largesse with public money for missiles and bombers. In 1955 and 1956, leading Democrats had belabored a "bomber gap," a fictitious Russian lead in nuclear weapons delivery systems. The issue was relaunched after October 4, 1957, when the Russians successfully tested their first *Sputnik* space satellite. Lacking a parallel success, the United States suddenly discovered its vulnerability despite its ring of bomber bases circling the Soviet Union.

Senate Democrats directed charges of waste, inefficiency, and poor planning at the administration. To calm fears, Eisenhower went on television, November 7, to defend American science and his defense policies. During his speech, he announced the appointment of James Killian, President of MIT, as assistant for science and technology. Yet, on the same day, the President received more bad news. An advisory committee, headed by H. Rowan Gaither, Jr., of the Rand Corporation and later of the Ford Foundation, delivered its report on American defenses to the National Security Council. While the President and his cabinet could accept some of its conclusions, they firmly rejected others, like the call for a massive civil defense program. Because of the implicit criticism of his policies, Eisenhower decided not to publish the report. Nonetheless, bits and pieces of the report leaked to the press; more than ever, it appeared that the United States had fallen behind in the arms race. Eisenhower still refused to release the document, invoking the executive privilege of his office. He did, however, finally agree to allow the members of Lyndon Johnson's Subcommittee on Preparedness to examine it in secret session.

As Dr. Killian later explained, Eisenhower's reluctance to increase defense spending came from his desire to negotiate seriously with the Russians. But there was another reason why the President was confident but unrevealing in his assessment of Russian defenses: He knew about, but could not release, information gathered by secret U-2 overflights, demonstrating Soviet military weaknesses. Caught in this position, the President was understandably troubled by the extensive advertising campaign conducted by arms manufacturers. In the end, he did authorize more defense funds. In 1958, National Science Foundation grants (some used in military research) rose to $50 million, and then to $136 million in 1959. On September 2, 1958, he signed the National Defense Education Act, providing about $1 billion in loans and scholarships for students in math, languages, and the sciences. In early 1958, Killian's Science Advisory Committee suggested consolidation of space research and operations. The result was the National Aeronautics and Space Administration (NASA), created on July 29, 1958.

Early in 1958—and none too soon for national prestige—the United States achieved several space successes: the launching of *Explorer I* on January 31 and the successful test of Atlas ICBM systems. While quieting some fears about Russian weaponry, these achievements did not eliminate the defense issue in the 1960 election. Claiming a "missile gap," the Democrats blamed Eisenhower's relatively low defense budget for alleged Russian superiority. In the long run, however, the greatest impact of *Sputnik* and its aftermath was probably on American education. Funds flowing into mathematics, sciences, language training, and engineering mounted rapidly as educators successfully convinced the public that there was also an "education gap."

Cut loose from any real future in his party, after 1958, Eisenhower tried to make his personal mark in history through foreign policy initiatives. But his strategy lacked clarity. He pursued a contradictory policy that found him edging toward closer relations with Nikita Khrushchev, the new premier of the U.S.S.R., only to be undercut by the secret activities of the CIA that he had approved. The area of nuclear testing did seem potentially one for agreement, however. Russian and American tests were belching huge quantities of radioactive material into the atmosphere, and scientists and the public worried increasingly about the effects.

Three days after he took office in March 1958, Premier Khrushchev announced suspension of open-air testing and urged the United States to follow his lead. In late August, Eisenhower promised to terminate American open-air testing once the current series ended. Early in November, the Russians resumed with a short series of test devices, but the United States continued its moratorium, and the Russians again suspended tests. Informal actions, however, did not lead to a permanent agreement, and in 1961, the Soviets resumed testing, followed by the United States in early 1962.

With the exception of flare-ups in the Middle East (the United

States landed troops in Lebanon in the summer of 1958) and continued acrimony over Quemoy and Matsu, the United States and the U.S.S.R. cautiously moved toward substantial negotiations in 1959. Like so much else in the Cold War, this relaxation of tension began in hostility. In March 1958, Khrushchev demanded normalization of the city of Berlin. By this, he meant a treaty to turn over access to West Berlin to his East Berlin allies. The result would be *de facto* recognition of East Germany, a possibility Eisenhower resolutely refused to consider. Khrushchev stiffened his demands by setting May 27, 1959, as a deadline for acceptance of his plan.

When spring of 1959 approached, the deadline slipped by as Eisenhower and the Russian premier embarked on a more concentrated phase of personal diplomacy. Eisenhower invited the Russian leader to visit the United States in September, and Khrushchev reciprocated with an invitation for 1960. Even this phase of relations began on a sharp note. In late July, Vice-President Nixon guided Khrushchev through an American exhibition in Moscow, during which the two leaders engaged in a running debate about the relative merits of American and Soviet societies. Because Nixon and Khrushchev stood arguing in front of stoves and refrigerators, American newspapers dubbed this the "kitchen debate." The Russian sharply denounced America's obsession with consumerism and homemaking. Nixon retorted: "I think that this attitude toward women is universal. What we want to do is make easier the life of our housewives." Khrushchev replied that Russian women were different.

Beneath his critical exterior, however, Khrushchev was ambivalent about America's consumer society. He rejected the gadgetry and materialism but promised to build more and better consumer items for Russian citizens. This attitude of awe and criticism also characterized Khrushchev's tour of the United States, beginning on September 15, 1959. For ten days, the Russian party, including Mrs. Khrushchev, followed an itinerary through American cities, California's Disneyland, and a farm in Iowa. Immense security problems and scattered incidents along the way did not detract from the success of the tour. Final negotiations at Camp David, Maryland—Eisenhower's retreat in the Catoctin Mountains—brought a postponement of the East German peace treaty. The two leaders also set plans for a spring summit meeting of the Big Four powers.

Shortly before Christmas, Eisenhower embarked on his own goodwill tour, visiting eleven countries in Asia, Europe, and Africa. By including India and Afghanistan, in addition to NATO countries, the President signaled a new attitude in American foreign policy toward neutral countries. This change was easier, in part, because John Foster Dulles retired as Secretary of State in early 1959, but it was also a logical extension of Ike's domestic policy of placing himself above the disputes and wrangling of politics.

Just as this policy seemed to open up prospects for peace, the President suddenly became mired in the unseemly business of espionage. Long eager to open the skies over the U.S.S.R.—with or without Russian approval—Eisenhower had authorized secret aerial surveillance of the Soviet Union. Utilizing the U-2 aircraft, which flew above the normal Russian missile range, these flights returned useful photographic reconnaissance materials. Of course, the Soviets knew about them, but could do nothing—that is, until shortly before the scheduled Paris summit in the spring of 1960, when they downed one of the spy planes. Official United States explanations at first claimed that a weather plane had strayed into Soviet air space. When Khrushchev produced the pilot and spy equipment, captured 300 miles inside the Soviet Union, its purpose became apparent. Rejecting the chance to blame subordinates, Eisenhower accepted personal responsibility for the overflights on May 9. In doing so, he probably doomed the summit meeting scheduled for one week later. When Khrushchev arrived at Paris, he seemed determined to explode the meeting, demanding a personal apology from the President. Failing to get it, he withdrew his invitation to Eisenhower to visit the Soviet Union.

Ninety miles from home, Eisenhower agreed to another CIA intervention that turned to fiasco. In early 1959, Fidel Castro led a successful revolution against the ruthless, but pro-American dictator of Cuba, Fulgenico Batista. During the 1940s and 1950s, Batista had transformed Cuba into a vacation and gambling center linked to the American underworld. Given its close proximity and single-crop agriculture (sugar), the island nation, outside the hotels of Havana and seaside resorts, continued to be an impoverished colony of the United States. Castro determined to change this. Beginning in the summer of 1959, the Cuban revolution deepened. Castro's government expropriated American industrial and agricultural property. When the Cubans signed a trade pact with the Soviet Union in the spring of 1960, Eisenhower agreed to a CIA plan to train and land rebels, hoping for a quick repeat of earlier intervention in Santo Domingo. Using open diplomacy, the Eisenhower administration tried to convince the Organization of American States to isolate Cuba, but the larger, more independent Latin American nations refused. With only a few months left to his administration, Eisenhower put the invasion off, leaving its timing and responsibility to his successor.

☆   ☆   ☆

To the very end of his term, Eisenhower remained popular with the American electorate. For Republicans this presented a problem: Was popularity transferable? Vice-President Nixon hoped it was, and he eagerly courted Ike's support for the nomination. But the President was less than encouraging. Indeed, shortly after Nixon won the Republican presidential nomination, reporters asked Eisenhower what Nixon had contributed to his administration. "If you give me a week, I might think of one," responded the President. "I don't remember." Subsequent warm endorsements did not reverse the impression that Ike hesitated to pass his mantle on to Nixon.

Eisenhower's most significant policy statement came in retrospect, as if to assess the lessons he had learned in office. On January 17, 1961, he delivered his farewell address, warning Americans to beware of the growing military-industrial complex. "This potential for the disastrous rise of misplaced power exists and will persist," he declared. Arms manufacturers and their clients in defense and the military constituted a powerful interest group that threatened American democracy. A secondary and equally ominous nexus of federally sponsored scientific research threatened to choke off intellectual freedom. "The prospect of domination of the nation's scholars," he said, "is gravely to be regarded."

Eisenhower's words went largely unheeded during the next few years, except by Americans already convinced of their truth, and he did nothing to follow them up. Like much else in his administration, his best sentiments received no second; no motion followed. Whatever Eisenhower understood about the perils of excessive defense spending, based on his anger at the huckstering merchants of arms, never got translated into policy. Some of his best initiatives in foreign relations were undercut by the latitude he allowed to Allen Dulles. Domestically, Eisenhower played the same role. Unwilling to take a stand against McCarthy, he prolonged the agony of anti-Communism. His refusal to promote the Supreme Court decision on school segregation doubtlessly intensified later struggles. He did act with restraint and intelligence in a world that demanded thoughtfulness. But, even to his warmest supporters, Eisenhower's years seemed to be an interlude, a respite from the normal turbulent tides of American politics. And, after eight years of his presidency, the nation and the world seemed as much as ever precariously balanced between the forces of destruction and the energies of creativity.

7 The Automatic Society

In his memorable farewell address of early 1961, Dwight Eisenhower evoked the image of American society squeezed in the grasp of a technocratic and military elite. His warning about the military-industrial complex beamed a spotlight on a debate about the direction of social and economic change growing since World War II. For a decade, sociologists, economists, and historians had puzzled over an apparent quantum leap in the development of American capitalism. Americans often appeared unsure about these changes. Sometimes, they seemed to prefer the simple homilies of Dwight Eisenhower or looked back to Harry Truman's blunt, homespun ideals. At other times, they preferred the rhetoric of technology, development, and growth. Applications of scientific, informational, and managerial innovations seemed to occur faster than society could smoothly absorb them. Stress points erupted around the impact of automation, the uses of new energy sources, the effects of information tools, like computers and television, and new corporate forms of economic organization. These issues became the focus of imagination and worry over the nature of modern society.

Concern about the deployment of technological ingenuity, ranging from nuclear energy to the smallest calculator chip, did not preoccupy just intellectuals and politicians. Even in the popular culture of the day, particularly science fiction, which enjoyed an immense boom in the 1950s, the same issues appeared in costume dramas removed to other planets and other times. But the preoccupations of popular culture were as timely and immediate as the tracts of sociologists and economists. How could modern men and women control the forces unleashed by modern industrialism? they all asked. What was the future of industrial society?

In 1950, Isaac Asimov, a widely respected science popularizer and science fiction author, published a remarkable book called *I*,

Robot. This collection of incidents dramatizes the problems of controlling robots, but its real subject is modern technology. Asimov's three "Laws of Robotics," printed as a foreword to the stories, define the relationship between humans and the machines they create. Robots are programmed not to injure humans. They have to obey humans, unless such actions bring harm. And, they are to protect their own existence, unless it means destruction to human beings. As the reader soon discovers, these laws are riddled with exceptions and contradictions. Asimov appears to be saying that these axioms, designed to guide advanced industrial technology, are inappropriate. They break down, because, in reality, no rules governing technology can anticipate human choices. This message is ironically underscored in the last story. An electronics expert called in to fix the central world computer, which has been sending signals to slow down the earth's industrial output, discovers that this programmed retreat is purposeful. Machines have taken over for the good of the human race and turned back the economic clock to a more primitive time.

This pessimistic but characteristic view of the automated society challenged optimistic, popular futurology, exemplified by a pamphlet on automation published in 1954 by the National Association of Manufacturers. Defending technology as the door to a "golden tomorrow," the NAM called automation a magical key to creativity. "Guided by electronics, powered by atomic energy, geared to the smooth, effortless workings of automation, the magic carpet of our free economy heads for distant and undreamed of horizons. Just going along for the ride will be the biggest thrill on earth," proclaimed the pamphlet.

In these incautious predictions and countless variations on the same theme, Americans celebrated the present and anticipated future successes of technological ingenuity. Stimulating their speculations were three great economic changes in the era: rapid technological advance, a revolution in the workplace, and consolidation of corporate structures. Several unique features in the period sharpened these changes. From the end of World War II until 1966 or 1967, American workers increased their productivity by a healthy percentage. Industry took advantage of low-priced and plentiful energy sources in the form of coal, natural gas, and oil. The period after the war was marked by sustained growth and high employment. Despite recessions in 1948–1949, 1953–1954, 1957–1958, 1960–1961, and 1973–1975, the traditional twenty-year

A *1950s conception of automation. At this Ford engine plant in Cleveland, Ohio, several functions, such as machining aluminum pistons, were carried out automatically. Pistons were transferred by conveyor belts to machines for processing.* (National Archives)

cycles of boom and bust leveled off into smaller peaks and troughs. In this era, America rose to unprecedented political, economic, and military predominance in the world. Exploiting this power, American enterprise penetrated and captured foreign markets and made huge overseas investments. By the late 1960s, the transformation of technology, the organization of work, and corporate consolidation had spread, creating a new economic order in much of the rest of the world. The American system was very much a world system.

The postwar technological revolution depended upon a massive application of energy to production, the discovery and use of new materials and manufacturing processes, and a burst of inventiveness in the field of communications. Together, these factors increased the productivity of workers, transforming factory and office and spurring the consolidation of industry. They also put the potential for destructiveness—as well as for creativity—at the fingertips of political and military leaders.

Production increases in the United States after 1945 depended upon substituting cheap fossil energy for human labor. From 1947 to 1975, output per hour of labor increased by almost 120 percent, while output per standard unit of energy increased by only about 23 percent. This disparity underscores the fact that the efficiency gained came through the application of more energy to production: in effect, electricity-, gas-, and oil-consuming machines replaced workers. At the same time, the efficiency of energy production remained relatively smaller. The consumption of gasoline by automobiles (a major consumer product and the chief means of transportation of the period), illustrates this fact. From 1945 into the 1970s, the efficiency of automobiles in moving passengers remained almost constant, indicating that technological improvements in the industry generally went into design and production, not performance. For all motor vehicles running on petroleum products, the average fuel efficiency per mile actually declined slightly between 1945 and 1970.

In the same period, energy necessary to generate a kilowatt of electrical power decreased by only about 33 percent. Thus, efficiencies in coal, oil, and natural gas generators accounted for only a part of the vast increase in electrical power produced by the United States from 1945 to 1970. Most of the increase came from burning greater amounts of fossil fuels and building new plants. Until the early 1970s, when sudden increases in the prices of oil and natural gas spurred a substantial inflationary spiral, this dependence on cheap fuels had no serious side effects apart from environmental degradation.

Immediately after the war, the United States led the world in development of new materials and ingenious uses of aluminum, plastics, and a long list of alloys and rare metals. More efficient machine tools revolutionized the basic manufacture of autos and steel, although by the end of the period, the United States lagged behind Japan and Germany in the application of advanced processes to steel production. In agriculture, mechanization, in the shape of new harvesting machines and larger tractors; and chemistry, in the guise of better fertilizers and sprays; and new strains of plants and animals increased output dramatically. From 1947 to 1966, total work hours in the United States spent in agriculture fell from 19.2 percent to only 7.5 percent. But output per acre increased by 33 percent. Moreover, the vertical integration of much agriculture into production, processing, and marketing units, or agribusinesses, revolutionized the nature of farming.

American inventiveness measured the dominance of the United States in technology. From 1955 to 1973, American scientists and workers developed over half the world's significant inventions, although this rate declined somewhat after 1974. Inventions transformed whole industries. For example, in 1952, a new Ford plant in Cleveland, with automatic machine-drilling capacities, could turn out 154 engine blocks per hour using only 41 men, whereas formerly it required 117 workers.

Particularly in communications—the transmission, storage, and manipulation of information—the new technology impinged on public consciousness. Television and computers symbolized the new ability to distribute and store information. Television had existed prior to 1945 as a potential, but after the war, the technology of transmitting pictures advanced rapidly. From a mere 6,000 receivers produced in 1945, the new television industry built 7 million sets in 1950, maintaining high production until saturation of the market and foreign competition reduced domestic production in the late 1960s. This new industry called upon scores of innovations and new processes, from transistors to printed circuits. Improvements also allowed color transmission, while videotape and other developments in filming technique increased the mobility and speed of camera work. In a single generation, 99 percent of American homes acquired this electronic window to the world.

The industrial impact of computers was even greater, although home use of these instruments only began at the end of the period. The earliest computer technology emerged from the efforts of IBM (International Business Machines) and other companies to develop code-breaking machines and to ease war-related problems, such as measuring ballistics trajectories. One of the largest machines inspired by wartime demands was the ENIAC machine (Electronic Numerical Integrator and Calculator), installed at Aberdeen Proving Ground in Maryland in 1947. An enormous, energy-hungry conglomeration of 18,000 vacuum tubes and 70,000 resisters, it covered 1,500 square feet of space. After the 1940s, IBM and Sperry Rand (which hired Douglas MacArthur as board chairman in the mid-1950s), competed for a growing market in computing machines.

The federal government provided much of the impetus for the computer industry. In 1951, Washington used three machines to compute the 1950 census returns. By 1966, the federal government had almost 2,500 computers in use; at the same time, 226 insurance companies were employing 700 electric computers. In 1966, over 30,000 computers were on-line in every facet of American industry and commerce. Improvements in size and capacity and lower costs were remarkable. By the late 1970s, a five-dollar micro-processor had twice the capacity of the enormous and expensive machines constructed at the end of World War II, making it possible to automate an incredible range of home and industrial activities formerly done by human memory and computation.

The capacity to store and evaluate information meant that computers attached to feedback sensors could monitor practically any form of industrial process. Programmed to react to production errors or slippages, the computer system could issue instructions to reverse a malfunction. In 1956, such computers controlling industrial production had been tested only in a few spots, such as automobile plants, but by 1960, the chemical and petroleum industries and electric, steel, cement, and paper producers had all begun to adopt computers. In the late 1960s, tentative experiment had become accepted practice.

Advances in communications technology, together with the spur of competition with the Soviet Union, fulfilled ancient aspirations and enabled the United States to complete the Apollo moon-exploration series in the late 1960s and early 1970s. In July 1969, the *Apollo II* spaceship circling the moon launched a smaller craft

Neil Armstrong, the first moon walker, photographed his fellow astronaut Edwin Aldrin on the lunar surface, July 20, 1969.   (UPI)

that touched down on the moon's surface. Astronaut Neil Armstrong emerged and, then, Edwin Aldrin—the first men to walk on the moon. This striking success, coming after President Kennedy's proposal of a crash effort in May 1961, reaffirmed America's faith in its technological leadership. It also created a media event minutely recorded by television, down to the carefully chosen, impersonal words of Armstrong when he touched the surface of the moon: "That's one small step for man, one great leap for mankind." Monitored and planned to the point where crew members were more passengers than explorers, the moon probe represented a triumph of mechanical ingenuity. Nonetheless, the very high costs—NASA spent about $33 billion on various projects from 1961 to 1969—ruled out more distant, manned flights after 1972.

☆　　　　　　　☆　　　　　　　☆

Scientific advance also generated weapons of enormous power and intimations of destruction. In 1964, Stanley Kubrick produced *Dr. Strangelove*, an outrageous film satirizing the American military establishment, the reliance on atomic bombs, and the fail-safe computer technology possible in nuclear warfare, a predicament he would dramatize again in 1968 in *2001: A Space Odyssey*. Ku-

Fastest-growing Industries, 1950 to 1966

| Ammunition |
| Cathode-ray Picture Tubes |
| Semiconductors |
| Computing and Related Machines |
| Guns, Howitzers, and Mortars |
| Tufted Carpets and Rugs |
| Small Arms, 30 mm. and under |
| Electronic Components |
| Primary Nonferrous Metals |
| Optical Instruments and Lenses |

Source: *U.S. Department of Commerce*, Chemicals, Petroleum, and Rubber and Plastics Products (*1969*), *p. 9.*

brick saw human beings trapped by the destructive power of the technology they had created. Having discovered this power, Americans seemed bent upon employing it. Kubrick's fascinating films focused on the somber side of technology during the 1950s and 1960s: its power to destroy.

Evidenced by the ten fastest-growing industries from 1950 to 1966, the technology of annihilation developed as rapidly as the products of consumption. After World War II, the American arms industry continued to be a principal element in the economy. Its importance can be measured by the large percentage of American exports deriving from military production—as high as 20 percent in 1953. Thereafter, percentages declined, but their share remained significant. Defense spending and military production absorbed a major share of federal funds. Money earmarked for defense, excluding Atomic Energy Commission and space expenditures, accounted for a huge proportion of research and development appropriations.

Total defense appropriations, again excluding space research, declined sharply as a percentage of the national budget immediately after the war, but then spurted upward because of the Korean

Federal Funds for Research and Development, 1947 to 1970

Year	Total ($ millions)	Defense ($ millions)	Percentage for Defense
1947	619.5	469.3	76%
1950	972.6	599.7	62
1953	3,106.0	2,577.2	83
1956	2,988.2	2,267.6	76
1959	6,693.5	5,161.6	77
1962	10,289.9	6,722.9	65
1965	14,614.3	6,796.5	47
1968	15,921.4	7,709.3	48
1970	15,340.3	7,360.4	48

Source: Historical Statistics of the United States, *Bicentennial Edition,* Vol. II, p. 966.

conflict, remaining high until the end of the Vietnam War in 1973. During the 1950s, defense drained the federal budget of as much as 65 percent of its revenues; between 1952 and 1959, it constituted more than 50 percent of the total budget, although this figure fell to only 23.3 percent in 1978. This extraordinary commitment rapidly accelerated the destructive capacity of the American army, navy, and air force. Productivity in destructive capacity increased exponentially with the mammoth firepower of atomic and hydrogen bombs.

The United States and the Soviet Union (after 1949) designed nuclear weapons whose power dwarfed the explosions of Hiroshima and Nagasaki. By 1961, the Soviet Union had tested an H-bomb with 3,000 times the power of the first primitive weapons dropped on Japan. In the early 1970s, Russian and American intercontinental ballistic missiles could deliver this explosive power with great accuracy and by remote control. By then, three other nations had broken into the nuclear cartel: France, Great Britain, and the People's Republic of China.

The rapid proliferation of weapons demanded a new attitude toward military strategy. Despite limited agreement by the United States and the Soviet Union in 1963 to cease open-air testing, disarmament remained elusive. The atomic race had a logic of its own, limited by available resources and technology, not by common sense. Having the ability to destroy each other several times over, the two superpowers reached a parity of terror in the late 1960s, each one glaring at the other over a stockpile of unusable doomsday weapons.

The pursuit of security through nuclear terror made weapons development a priority and the potential use of weapons a matter of policy. A few groups, such as the Committee for a Sane Nuclear Policy, founded in 1957, questioned this commitment, calling for limited disarmament and an end to nuclear testing. They raised serious questions about the effects of radioactivity released in tests. Their criticism, however, had little effect. Even government scientists in the Atomic Energy Commission, who understood some of the potential danger, refused to warn residents living near test sites in the West.

Politicians and government scientists could quiet public discussion of atomic warfare, but they did not satisfy deep public suspicions about nuclear fallout. Instead, these fears were diverted into a fantasy culture in popular magazine stories and science fiction

"I could see the bones in my hand like an X-ray," said Paul Cooper, a soldier stationed a short distance from an atomic test like this one, which occurred at Camp Desert Rock, Nevada, on August 7, 1957.   (U.S. Army Photograph)

films portraying atomic Armageddon. In January 1952, the editor of *Galaxy Science Fiction* magazine noted that over 90 percent of the recent stories submitted to his journal discussed atomic or bacteriological warfare, devolution, or mutant children. Beginning in the early 1950s and extending into the 1960s, science fiction films presented the effects of nuclear fallout in scores of ways—none of them positive. Some of these movies were clumsy horror films, but the best gave substance to problems that politicians avoided. Produced primarily in the United States and Japan, their appearance probably also released unarticulated public guilt and horror at the American atomic bomb blasts at Hiroshima and Nagasaki. The most frightening of all was *Them*, produced in 1954, depicting the power of radioactivity to produce genetic changes. The movie's monsters were giant ants. The success of this film and other films like it unleashed a Hollywood menagerie of destructive insects and animals on American cities and small towns—creatures who avenged humanity's discovery of atomic secrets.

Other versions of the atomic horror film urged world cooperation and the control of nuclear technology, as in *The Day the Earth Stood Still* (1951). In the film, a galaxy representative, Klaatu, and his powerful robot visit earth to demand that nations stop nuclear testing. Unheeded by all but a family that befriends him, he is assassinated, and his robot begins to destroy the earth. Only intervention by those who believed him stops the robot, who then resurrects his master. In this adapted parable of Christ's sacrifice and resurrection, the message is clear: Stop testing or destroy the world and face God's wrath. On the whole, however, these movies rarely confronted the real issue: the immediate danger of nuclear warfare, perpetrated not by spacemen or preposterous monsters, but by real people. Of the few that attempted to be realistic, *On the Beach*, produced in 1959, bleakly depicted the last days of the human race.

Public discussion of survival in a nuclear war finally surfaced in the bomb-shelter controversy of the late 1950s. To construct shelters suggested that they would be used. The American public, after debating the issue for several years, rejected plans for underground bunkers. In effect, Americans preferred to ignore the possibility of life after nuclear warfare than to prepare for it.

Public understanding of the probable impact of atomic warfare emerged slowly in the late 1940s and early 1950s. A Boy Scout "Family Be Prepared Plan," of 1951, issued instructions far more

appropriate to World War II air raids than to nuclear warfare. The
Scouts advised families to stockpile food and keep doors and windows shut during an actual atomic blast. In a companion manual,
the Scouts promised to provide messenger services for civil defense authorities. During the mid-1950s the newly created Civil
Defense Administration devised more sophisticated warning systems, like Conelrad on AM radio. Val Peterson, the federal Civil
Defense Administrator, promoted an evacuation program as the
only effective means to escape atomic blasts. But, while the federal
government did adopt a partial evacuation program (the 1956
Highway Act promised roads to make evacuation possible), most
major evacuation routes in the East and Midwest led toward other
threatened cities. Adoption of a limited national shelter policy for
federal buildings in 1958 acknowledged the impossibility of effective evacuation.

Indecisiveness in federal civil defense policy came from public
ignorance about the effects of radiation, from the assumption that
early warning and subsequent evacuation were possible, and from
President Eisenhower's opposition to an extensive shelter program. Government public relations events, such as "Operation
Cue," an atomic test blast of 1955, covered by radio and television,
confused Americans about radiation effects. Two hundred associations and companies contributed consumer items to the blast area
to test their durability. Television commentators, volunteers, and
trade association members, like Arthur F. Landstreet, the president of Hotel King Cotton in Memphis, Tennessee, crouched in
"Position Baker," a trench cut only 10,500 feet from "ground zero."
As Landstreet wrote afterwards, "Everyone is happy now and
those who were privileged to participate in Baker feel that they
were among the selected few."

Effective pressure to build shelters began after the Russians
launched Sputnik, for the powerful rocket that lifted the world's
first satellite into orbit could also deliver bombs to American
cities. Experts realized the futility of early-warning systems in an
age of intercontinental missiles. Eisenhower reacted to pressure
by reorganizing the civil defense bureaucracy in 1958, but he did
little more than centralize this function in the executive branch.
Rejecting suggestions in the Gaither Report for a crash shelter
program, he pushed a voluntary program of federal "stimulation,
leadership, guidance, and example." But, without funding, this
program accounted for very few shelters by the end of 1960. There

Nelson Rockefeller posed inside a prototype bomb shelter to publicize the civil defense program he promoted while governor of New York. (Walter Sanders/LIFE Magazine, © Time, Inc.)

were other points of resistance too. Even in states like New York, where Governor Nelson Rockefeller pushed for an extensive program, the state legislature balked at such huge new appropriations. Important opposition to shelters came from the military establishment, which was divided on weapons systems. For example, General Curtis LeMay, of the Air Force, criticized an expensive shelter program, fearing it would undermine support for the Air Force program of "counterforce," designed to knock out enemy missiles before they could be launched. A large civil defense budget would starve such projected weapons systems of funding.

Strong support for shelter construction did develop in strategic political sectors, however. The AF of L-CIO strongly endorsed a program, undoubtedly because of potential jobs. Organizations, such as the American Medical Association, approved it. In 1962, the American Institute of Architects held a national competition for the best blast-proof school building, awarding its first prize of $15,000 in December of that year. The most effective lobbying came from the new Kennedy administration, which supported larger arms budgets and a more aggressive foreign policy. Twice, Kennedy asked Congress for large increases in the civil defense budget. In May 1961, he requested tripling the budget but received only $86 million, or about half the sum appropriated in 1960 under Eisenhower. In July, he asked for $207.6 million more to designate shelters in public buildings. Despite strong opposition in the Senate from Wayne Morse, of Oregon, Stephen Young, of Ohio, and Ernest Gruening, of Alaska, the appropriation passed.

The administration tried again in 1963 for new shelter appropriations, but Congress remained reluctant to appropriate large sums for civil defense. By this time, the administration itself had split over how to convince the American people to support such a program. Of the $695 million requested, only $113 million survived congressional budget-cutting; Quite clearly the issue had died.

Civil defense failed because most Americans refused to accept its necessity. As the shelter debate heated up, many citizens expressed horror at the statements of civil defense advocates. Despite extensive positive coverage in the press and on radio and television, few could be convinced that shelters were safe or desirable. Even the works of Herman Kahn, the Rand Corporation's expert on nuclear warfare, did more harm than good to the argument. Kahn's book *On Thermonuclear War*, published in 1960, tried to persuade Americans that limited casualties of 10 or 20 million people were reasonable. Of course, "tragedy" would increase, but "the increase would not preclude normal and happy lives for the majority of survivors and their descendants," he concluded. To many who read his books, this seemed a monstrous prospect.

As the public argument over shelters continued, moral and ethical issues became clearer and absurdities abounded. For example, in September 1961, *Life* magazine ran a cover picture of a fallout suit, although no such protective covering existed. Newspapers reported that a wealthy horse lover built an elaborate fallout shelter for her champion horses. Reports from Nevada claimed that citizens of that sparsely settled state were prepared to shoot Californians fleeing populated cities in the event of nuclear warfare. Probably the most controversial sentiment came from the Reverend L. C. McHugh in his article, "Ethics at the Shelter Doorway," published in September 1961 in *America*, the Catholic magazine. Reverend McHugh justified armed self-defense against neighbors: "I doubt that any Catholic moralist," he wrote, "would condemn the man who used available violence to repel panicky aggressors plying crowbars at the shelter door. . . ." On the contrary, many Americans, including other Catholic moralists, did condemn such extreme behavior. In fact, recognition that nuclear war would destroy the fabric of ethics and society explained the passive resistance of most Americans to the shelter proposals of the 1960s.

☆   ☆   ☆

Americans in the 1950s and 1960s worried almost as much about the creative prospects of great technological change as they did about the destructive powers of nuclear warfare. Abundance was not without its perils. A. J. Hayes, president of the International Association of Machinists, stated this point forcefully: "Automation presents the United States—and eventually every country—with a threat and a challenge second only to the possibility of the hydrogen bomb." The force of technology, symbolized by automation, challenged traditional thinking about economics, the organization of work, and leisure.

In the 1950s and 1960s, labor unionists, politicians, scientists, corporate executives, sociologists, and religious leaders debated the contemporary problems of automation, as well as its benefits and difficulties in the future. As a concept, automation symbolized the possibilities of a revolution in work and social relations. Yet, words like "automation" and "cybernation" were frequently employed during these years with a degree of confusion. As originally defined in 1946, "automation" had at least two different meanings. Used by D. S. Harder, a Ford Company executive, it meant the automatic handling and transfer of parts between successive stages in production—in effect, a more complicated assembly line. But when the management consultant John Diebold wrote his report for Harvard University, "Making the Automatic Factory a Reality," he used "automation" to designate machine tools that could carry out a variety of processes in one place. During the 1950s, the term expanded, taking on new overtones because of the strides in computer technology. By the 1960s, "automation" also meant a factory in which machines replaced human labor and supervisory intelligence.

As the term "automation" stretched to fit new possibilities, mathematician Norbert Wiener coined a new term, "cybernetics." Wiener used "cybernetics" to suggest the relationship of computer technology to production. "Cybernetics" referred to the feedback and information-processing capacities of modern computers and machines. Information gathered by sensory monitors enabled a computer to maintain a manufacturing process according to a predetermined program of instruction. To Wiener, however, the implications of "cybernetics" went far beyond the computer-controlled factory. When he discovered that computers could "learn" to defeat their programmers at checkers, he wondered if decision-making computers could ever be controlled. Attached to a fail-safe atomic defense system, for example, a computer might "win a nominal victory on points at the cost of every interest we have at heart, even that of national survival."

For labor unions, "automation" meant bread-and-butter issues. Early experiments in automation, particularly in the auto industry, and the enthusiasm of management for technologies that replaced workers convinced many labor unions that automation would be turned against them. In 1955, the first fully automated engine factory machine tools drilled, bored, and constructed without constant human surveillance. Walter Reuther, the head of the United Auto Workers, proclaimed this new technology to constitute "the second Industrial Revolution." Reuther's fears about automation emerged in a dialogue that he repeated after inspecting acres of machines at the Ford engine plant in Cleveland. His management guide prodded him: "Well, you won't be able to collect dues from all these automated machines." Reuther replied: "You know, that is not what is bothering me. What is bothering me is, how are you going to sell cars to all of these machines?"

As a union leader, Reuther focused the automation debate on jobs, work rules, and wages. Trade union advances in controlling the workplace during World War II and afterwards had been impressive, and labor leaders were not prepared to sacrifice these gains. In his thinking, Reuther reflected the experience of bitter organizational struggles during the Depression of the 1930s. He calculated that industrial progress, if not properly anticipated, might cause dislocations as serious as the economic downturn after 1929. The economy would have to be tuned to absorb the rising productivity of American workers. As he told the Joint Congressional Committee on the Economic Report in 1955, rather than current rises of 3 to 4 percent, automation might push productivity increases to 5 or 6 percent a year. This immense jump in output threatened a severe underconsumption of goods and services if wages did not also rise rapidly.

☆   ☆   ☆

Mechanization—if not automation—rapidly altered American labor after World War II. It disrupted established patterns of work, intensifying alienation, unemployment, and problems of retraining. The largest single private employer in the United States in 1954, and one of the leaders in automation, was the Bell Telephone conglomerate, with 600,000 operating employees. In this industry, automation of communications equipment appeared early, and wholesale replacement of human operators began in the late 1940s. Joseph Beirne, president of the Communications Workers of America, reported that "the real drama of automation" was its effect on skilled operators. Transferred to new, unfamiliar forms of work, many women broke down emotionally or lost confidence. Although Beirne conceded the company's right to improve technology and even to eliminate workers, he wanted changes to be carried out in an orderly and open fashion, with union participation.

As it has always done, mechanical innovation disrupted established work patterns, dislocating workers and creating what economists called "technological" or "frictional" unemployment. Simply put, it meant unemployment caused by inadequate education and training. Automation procedures in manufacturing industries, coupled with intensive investment and development in consumer production and services, diminished blue-collar employment while increasing white-collar jobs. This effect only increased labor union fears about automation, for they correctly saw their organizational base among manual workers and the unskilled shrinking. In the period from 1945 to 1970, jobs in manufacturing and construction increased only about 35 percent, while available positions in government and the retail, finance, and insurance sectors rose by more than 200 percent. During the same years, trade union membership increased slowly, so that in 1970, the percentage of workers in unions remained only about what it had been in 1946.

New opportunities for white-collar employees and upgraded minimal skills put pressure on colleges, universities, and junior colleges to train what some economists called a new "white-collar proletariat." The average years spent in educational institutions during these years reflected the impact of automation and demands for more extensive training. In 1952, the median year of education of an adult American was 10.9 years; in 1975, it had risen to 12.6 years.

While junior colleges and vocational institutions accommodated more students, elite universities transformed themselves into research centers for the development of further technological innovations. In 1959, Clark Kerr, head of the University of California, suggested naming the modern university a "multiversity," proposing that modern institutions of higher learning become knowledge factories devoted to training engineers, scientists, doctors, and social scientists for service in an advanced technological society.

Management considered the rapid growth of white-collar work and the upgrading of skills a perfectly natural and gradual progression in American capitalism. Testifying before Congress and writing articles for business periodicals, management representatives explained that automation had only good effects. The adaptation of automatic processes, an executive of the Ford Motor Company told Congress in 1955, "will be an evolutionary and not a revolutionary process." It would only gradually shift employment from unskilled, backward production to new growing industries.

In certain industries, automation brought new approaches to

collective bargaining. During the 1960s, a few unions, such as the Electrical Workers in New York, secured a twenty-hour work-week, although many of these workers spent their spare moments in overtime. George Meany, head of the AF of L-CIO, occasionally pressed employers to shorten the workweek to thirty-five hours in order to spread available work. But, despite scattered protests, many unions, including Reuther's UAW, negotiated productivity agreements with corporations during the 1950s and 1960s, trading jobs for higher wages. An example of this development was the 1959 Armour pact with two meatpacking unions. Part of the contract designated a company "Automation Fund" of $500,000. Using this money, an "Automation Committee" composed of labor, management, and neutral observers studied technological displacement and suggested experimental remedies.

Another 1959 agreement, the "Kaiser Steelworkers Long Range Sharing Plan," emerged from the long and costly steel strike of that year. The program promised to pass on a portion of profits gained from increased productivity. If an employee lost a job due to automation, the company promised to place him in a reserve labor pool and pay his average hourly earnings for at least a year. The UAW, in particular, proposed a shorter workweek and guaranteed annual salaries for workers instead of weekly wages, but only in the construction trades did the shorter week become the rule. And none of the automation agreements seriously challenged management prerogatives to apply advanced technology to work.

As in other areas, the federal government acted as referee in the automation debate. The Employment Act of 1946 committed the federal government to pursue full employment for the nation's laboring population. Beginning in the mid-1950s, Congress aired the problems of automation in extensive, frequent hearings. Operating through the Joint Economic Committee and a special advisory group, the executive branch developed policy toward problems raised by automation. The report of President Kennedy's Advisory Committee on Labor-Management Policy in 1962 created guidelines for federal policy. Proclaiming automation a necessity and a benefit, the committee proposed concerted government and business action to eliminate "structural unemployment." Congressional advice on automation seconded this approach. Senator Joseph Clark's 1964 report, "Toward Full Employment," praised automation and suggested that retraining and other programs would help

American workers adjust to the new industrial reality. Accepting what was essentially management's position on automation, Washington rejected labor's call for a shorter workweek. Under Kennedy and subsequently under Johnson, the federal government instituted extensive retraining programs.

Kennedy took a strong interest in technological unemployment because of the sharp recession of 1960 and 1961, which focused attention on rising long-term unemployment. Two acts in the first years of his administration established Kennedy's policy of cautious guidance in economic matters. The government, he pledged, would not interfere with the deployment of new technology; it would concentrate on aiding workers already adversely affected by automation. The Area Redevelopment Act, of 1961, for example, committed the government to seek means to prevent older industrial areas from declining. The Manpower Development and Training Act of 1962 bolstered this program. In this comprehensive bill, Congress authorized establishment of the President's "Manpower Report" to investigate and report on the causes of current unemployment and to predict future employment needs. The core of the program established training programs for workers laid off by "automation and technological changes and other types of persistent unemployment." When funded in August 1962, this legislation provided money, administered by the Labor Department and HEW, for scores of retraining programs. Hardcore unemployed heads of households were eligible for admission to programs that lasted up to fifty-two weeks.

As temporary measures, these programs did not end the automation debate. In July 1963, President Kennedy established a commission to examine the broad social and economic effects of automation. Earlier in the year, the American Foundation on Automation and Employment held an all-day conference at the Waldorf-Astoria Hotel in New York, cochaired by industry and labor representatives. Other conferences sponsored by the International Labor Organization, in London and Geneva, underscored the international dimensions of the discussion. Although one staff member of the House Subcommittee on Unemployment and the Impact of Automation proposed a GI bill of rights for the unemployed, the federal government committed itself to less drastic measures to soften the impact of automation. From 1963 to 1965, Congress added retraining provisions to economic legislation, including the Vocational Education Act of 1963 and the Economic

Opportunity Act of 1964. This commitment remained through the 1970s.

No one could deny that technological innovation and automation exposed serious economic problems. But, neither the worst fears nor the most optimistic predictions materialized. The workweek remained at about forty hours. Worker productivity did not rise as Walter Reuther calculated; instead, after 1967, it fell sharply. Automated production did speed changes in the workplace; it undoubtedly pushed jobless rates up, until the federal government had to redefine the meaning of unemployment. But the dream— and the nightmare—of cybernation remained a distant vision.

☆   ☆   ☆

While labor, management, and government regarded automation as a problem about jobs and profits, much of the popular discussion worried that technological advance increased leisure for workers. How would the working classes spend their spare time once automation shortened the workweek to twenty-five hours?— sociologists and popular magazine articles wondered—although a shorter workweek for most employees was not an immediate possibility.

Apprehension about increased leisure emerged from fears that the work ethic might disappear. Once assumed to be a powerful instinct that generated pride in accomplishment and labor, the work ethic, some observers feared, had been usurped by the desire to consume and spend. Since the beginning of industrialization, Americans had questioned whether repetitious labor tasks would strengthen or weaken an employee's devotion to hard work and individual accomplishment. Automation simply posed this same question more intensively: If work ceased to be the central preoccupation of the population, would consumerism take its place? Even union leaders worried. In 1952, Mark Starr, educational director of the International Ladies Garment Workers Union, declared: "Our problem today is leisure for the mass."

David Riesman, who wrote extensively on the sociology and psychology of the modern industrial world, summarized this popular view of automation as calamitous. Even the *Saturday Evening Post* made this the subject of a story in 1958. The plot of "A Holiday for Howie" followed the hero's reaction to a new four-day week. Unable to fill up his new leisure with anything constructive,

Howie discovered happiness by finding a part-time job to fill the empty space in his week. Exchanging leisure for more work was certainly a stopgap measure, but it probably reflected a dominant public view. A Gallup poll, in 1957, found little public enthusiasm for a shorter workweek. Another poll taken in the same year reflected the persistence of older ways of thinking about work. Most parents, the survey discovered, felt that children, especially, needed work to occupy their spare time; too much leisure meant delinquency. Suspicion that leisure would demoralize workers and youth was a complicated and sometimes patronizing attitude that reflected vague fears of social disorder, brought on by rapid changes in the workplace and in social life.

On the other hand, prolongation of schooling and the decline in the centrality of work added to the enthusiasm for permissive child-rearing after World War II. Even the U.S. Children's Bureau disseminated pamphlets stressing the "fun morality" in child-rearing, advising parents to allow children to pursue pleasure and amusement rather than duty. Modern parenting seemed more a schooling in interpersonal relationships and consumer skills than a traditional preparation for a life of hard work, savings, and sacrifice. Advertisers underscored this tendency by aiming their efforts increasingly at children and adolescents in the 1950s and 1960s.

If adolescence seemed an ambiguous, possibly dangerous, period of leisure time, retirement, at the other end of the work life, became an even more pronounced problem during this period. With increased longevity during the twentieth century, the average individual's work life increased by almost a decade. In 1900, the normal work expectancy of a laborer was about thirty-two years; in 1950, it rose to almost forty-two years. Nonetheless, an increasing percentage of Americans lived several years beyond retirement. At the same time, the federal government encouraged early retirement through lower eligibility for Social Security payments as one means of controlling unemployment. Inevitably, whatever else elderly Americans suffered—poor health care, inadequate retirement benefits, and small pensions—boredom and inactivity also posed a major threat to the "Golden Years."

For other Americans, leisure time represented opportunity, not just problems. Slightly shorter working hours for men and increased life expectancy changed the average proportion of time spent in and out of work. In 1950, the average man generally spent

Around the world, Coca-Cola came to symbolize the importance of leisure and the achievement of a high standard of living in the United States. (NYPL Picture Collection)

63 percent of his years working and 37 percent of his time outside work. In 1975, this changed to 60 percent in work and 40 percent outside. In the same period, due to their rapid entry into the labor force, women spent an increasing proportion of their lives on the job. Such changes in the use of time revolutionized American leisured activities. The "Do-It-Yourself" fad in the 1950s and the rapid expansion of home hobbies reflected increased spare time, as well as wider home ownership and the desire of many Americans to practice the manual skills learned during World War II in the army or defense industries.

American sports activities also evolved rapidly in this period. Participation in and attendance at sporting events changed markedly after the war. Traditional spectator sports like baseball declined, while horseracing and professional football and basketball gained. Technological improvements in television, new suburban stadiums, and rule changes transformed both football and basketball. At the same time, participation sports like bowling, boating, riflery—and toward the end of the period—camping, skiing, bicycling, and jogging attracted millions of new adherents.

The social importance of spectator sports made them a primary target for racial and, later, sexual integration. In 1947, the Brooklyn Dodgers breached baseball color bars by hiring Jackie Robinson as the first black major league player. Sports writers had long agitated for desegregation of national sports, but club owners refused, until Branch Rickey of the Dodgers broke ranks. Rickey selected Robinson for his experiment because of this player's undeniable talent and his ability to take the jibes and insults of fans, other players, and the press. As Rickey told him, "You can't fight back, boy. That's going to be the hardest part of all. No matter what happens, *you can't fight back.*"

In 1950, the first black players entered pro basketball. By 1970, black Americans accounted for 25 percent of all pro baseball players, 32 percent of football, and 55 percent of basketball. Integration of women into spectator sports occurred on a much smaller scale and later. Under guidelines established by HEW, major university systems that received federal funding began to move more funds into athletic programs for women, but progress in this field remained limited.

Because the nation paid so much attention to sports, its heroes increasingly became national celebrities. More than ever, heroes achieved renown for their hard play, not their diligent work or inventiveness. After 1968, the United States acquired in Richard Nixon a president who self-consciously invoked the sanctity of sports language and heroes whenever he encountered a difficult situation; he refused to punt when he was cornered. The old work ideals of competition and achievement still existed; they had simply moved over to the sports arena.

☆　　　　　　　☆　　　　　　　☆

The unfaltering expansion of technology and communications convinced many Americans that society had entered a new phase of development shaped by transmitted images and information-access rather than burdensome hard work and self-sacrifice. The identification with sports heroes was just one phase of this larger revolution caused by information technology. Of those who sought to measure this development, the Canadian writer Marshall McLuhan most successfully popularized the theory that modern communications had transformed life. In several books, *The Gutenberg Galaxy* (1962) and *Understanding Media* (1964), he outraged and prodded Americans into considering the effects of the communications revolution. McLuhan argued that no medium of information (print or television, for example) could be value-free. Each deeply altered a society's perception of the world. Print created one world; radio and movies generated another; and television inspired a third. "If the formative power in the media are the media themselves," he wrote, they deserve the full attention of modern intellectuals.

McLuhan's most perceptive speculation focused on television, a medium that, he claimed, had extended the perceptions of its viewers, transforming their psychologies by making the distant world an immediate experience. This "nowness" precipitated a new attitude toward the world for a generation that viewed reality through the mechanical eyes of television. Some of the programming of modern television appeared to validate this idea. From Walter Cronkite's *You Are There* series (1954 to 1957), which placed a TV cameraman and interviewer on the scene of reenacted historic events, like the martyrdom of Joan of Arc and the Boston Tea Party, to the nightly saga of the war in Vietnam during the 1960s, a generation and a society experienced television as if it were a sixth sense, added to their ability to hear, smell, taste, feel, and see the world around them.

Television—the irresistible eye—seemed also to work another

kind of revolution. McLuhan's concept of the "global village" implied an inevitable unity of diverse experiences and a breakdown of the distinctions between private lives and public exposure. Television relentlessly surrounded the viewer with the intimate experiences of others. It beamed visions of luxury into poverty-stricken urban ghettos. It exposed the private lives of those who made news. It reduced politics to a relationship dependent upon pollsters and image makers, who helped to decide the shape and content of campaigns. And, it selected instant reality from the blur of contemporary history, giving it the plausibility of publicity.

☆   ☆   ☆

As McLuhan suggested, the postwar changes in the economy, in technology, work, and leisure occurred in the context of a revolution in communications and in organization. Larger organizations, performing a multitude of tasks, required new forms and uses of information. In turn, computers, television, and other information technology facilitated the growth of organization and bureaucracy in business and government. This spiral of invention and growth reshaped the United States' economy. Eric Johnston, former president of the American Chamber of Commerce, described the new scale of organization in 1957: "We have entered a period of accelerating bigness in all aspects of American life. We have big business, big labor, big farming and big government." Was this, he wondered, the beginning of an age of "socialized capitalism"? The tendency toward great organized blocks of economic power, described by Johnston, occurred most notably in corporate consolidations. While government expansion and economic regulation increased rapidly after World War II, private organizations also greatly expanded their size and power, as if both were engaged in a bureaucratic arms race.

Large American corporations adopted planning and operations research procedures during and immediately after World War II, although they vigorously opposed federal government planning in the economic field. Spurred by the Ford and Carnegie foundations, management training schools revised their curricula during the 1950s to offer extensive courses in administration. Corporations, as they grew, adopted elaborate internal information-transfer systems.

The increasing size and scale of corporate consolidation, accompanied by mounting bureaucratic complexity, was nothing new; in the late nineteenth century, partly by default and partly by design, primary industrial producers in rail transport, steel, and oil rapidly consolidated. In the resulting corporations, management committees tended to replace pioneering entrepreneurs. To writers of the 1930s, this consolidation and the separation of management from owners of stocks suggested a new form of capitalism in which long-range interests, not short-range profits, had the highest priority.

After World War II, corporate consolidation and reorganization proliferated—resulting in two extremely visible types of mergers. One was the conglomerate; the other was the multinational corporation. Some business organizations combined both types of operation; for example, in its American operations, International Telephone and Telegraph owned a conglomeration of other companies, many of them entirely unrelated to the communications industry. These included Avis Rent-a-Car, Aetna Finance, Continental Baking, the Sheraton Hotel Corporation, Levitt and Sons Construction, the Hartford Fire Insurance Company, and others. An example of the multinational corporation is General Motors, with plants in Germany producing automobiles for sale within the European Common Market.

Corporate consolidation in the postwar period reached a peak in 1968 with 4,462 mergers. By 1968, the 500 largest American corporations (most of them conglomerates and multinationals) accounted for 64 percent of total industrial sales in the United States. Between 1955 and 1971, the economic activity of these same companies increased at a rate about 1 percent faster annually than the total United States gross national product, indicating their growing dominance in the economy. At the same time, the public share of economic activity also increased, so that by 1969, federal, state, and local governments generated about 23 percent of all economic activity. Between them, the largest corporations and the public sector dominated the American economy.

Operations of multinational corporations abroad expanded so rapidly during the 1960s, that by the mid-1970s, the output of United States-owned companies abroad constituted the third largest productive capacity in the world, trailing only United States domestic output and the output of the Soviet Union. During the same time, American investment abroad rose rapidly to $78 billion in 1970, with two-thirds placed in Japan and Western Europe and one-third in the underdeveloped countries. This enormous outflow of capital went primarily to build new plants and productive facilities, which then competed with local European and Japanese firms. Increasingly, this American-owned foreign production returned home in the form of imports that competed with domestic industry in the United States. Some foreign countries, notably France during the early 1960s, vigorously protested this invasion of American capital. By the late 1960s, American trade unions also raised their voices to oppose foreign investment. The AF of L-CIO, for example, estimated that between 1966 and 1971, investments in cheap labor areas had erased 900,000 American jobs.

Corporate consolidation during the 1950s and 1960s was only the most visible phase of the growing managerial sophistication of American business. Inside corporations, increasing size dictated bureaucratization, the division of tasks by function, and the rise of a corporate mentality that often preferred the stability of government regulation to the risks of a free-market economy. As price competition declined, businesses increasingly adopted what some economists called "administered prices." These were set by major corporations that did not lower prices when demand fell. Instead, they increasingly passed their costs—and, sometimes, inefficiencies—on to the consumer.

The new business people this system spawned were very much subjects of discussion during the 1950s and 1960s. Economist John Kenneth Galbraith wrote perhaps the most influential works on the new ethic of the "executive suite." Beginning with his *Affluent Society* (1958) and extending through the *New Industrial State* (1967), Galbraith charmed many readers who disagreed, nonetheless, with his conclusions. Designating the new corporate economy a "technostructure," he argued that corporate managers were motivated to seek security for themselves and their corporations, not to maximize profits. According to the economist, the bureaucratic committees that administered prices and planned production paid little heed to the dictates of traditional economic thinking. In the name of stability, they supported immense military production, financed and underwritten by the federal government. For them, economic success depended upon controlled markets, prices, and access to raw materials. And, through advertising, they attempted to shape the market and consumer behavior. Their enormous power and anonymity sheltered them from public scrutiny and control. To Galbraith, they constituted a new ruling class.

While some of Galbraith's conclusions have been resolutely opposed by other economists, his concern for the size, scale, and inaccessibility of American business organization became a public concern by the late 1960s. Some conglomerates and multinational corporations had incomes larger than the budgets of all but the richest industrial nations. By the 1970s, this unchecked potential power became a significant political issue.

To other observers, this scale of success demonstrated a fortuitous turn in the history of capitalism. The postwar transformation of the economy and the prosperity of the 1950s convinced economist Walt Whitman Rostow that the United States had outrun the traditional problems of capitalism, crossing over into a mature industrial society. In this stage of development, possibilities of consumption, not the "imperatives of scarcity," marked the new economy. Sociologist Daniel Bell described this new society from a different angle. He stressed the absence of ideologies and rigid social classes from American politics. However, both men came to the same conclusion: The United States had achieved an abundance, social cohesion, and political equality only imagined by nineteenth-century utopian thinkers and revolutionaries like Karl Marx.

☆ ☆ ☆

American prosperity from 1945 until the mid-1970s constituted a success story unmatched by other industrial societies. An endless bounty of goods flowed out of manufacturing establishments into the homes of Americans, who purchased them with an apparently limitless supply of consumer credit. Led by spending for automobiles, short-term consumer indebtedness multiplied twenty-two times between 1945 and 1970. From a society in 1940, in which farm animals generated more horsepower than airplanes, the United States swept into an era of abundance, power, and productivity, but the social distribution of this plenty remained unequally divided.

While more equitable than in many other societies, including some Western industrial countries, the American distribution of income remained basically unchanged after World War II.

*Percentage of Money Income Received by Each 5th of Families and Individuals**

	1947	1957	1967	1975
lowest 5th	5.1%	5.0%	5.5%	5.4%
second 5th	11.8	12.6	12.4	11.8
middle 5th	16.7	18.1	17.9	17.6
fourth 5th	23.2	23.7	23.9	24.1
highest 5th	43.3	40.5	40.4	41.1
top 5%	17.5	15.8	15.2	15.5

*Figures rounded.
Source: Barry R. Chiswick and June A. O'Neill, Human Resources and Income Distribution (New York: Norton, 1977), p. 6.

A multitude of taxes and federal and state payments for welfare and other financial assistance changed this percentage only slightly in the favor of the lowest 5th, although the goods and services delivered to poorer families often dramatically changed their quality of life. Even after taxes, the distribution of income remained fundamentally lopsided in favor of the wealthiest Americans. Recurrent unemployment and job and wage discrimination forced a disproportionate number of blacks, other minorities, and women into these bottom categories, exacerbating racial and class and sex distinctions. When the focus of politics changed from celebration in the 1950s to confrontation in the 1960s, these problems emerged with a force that demanded immediate attention. The contrasts of wealth and poverty made the possibility of abundance for everyone a compelling political issue.

8 The Limits of Liberal Politics: Part I

If any single word captures the tone of the administrations of John Fitzgerald Kennedy and Lyndon Baines Johnson, it is the ambiguous term "idealism." Despite remarkable differences of style, intellect, political skill, and manners, Kennedy and Johnson shared the rhetoric of crisis idealism, shaping the events of which they spoke with an almost missionary fervor. While some of this was political rhetoric and not seriously intended, both presidents conceived of their commitments as high moral purposes. They pursued domestic and foreign programs with zeal, promising to cross "New Frontiers" or build "Great Societies." They aroused, but ultimately could not control, a wave of political idealism that flowed into the civil rights movement, into groups opposing the war in Vietnam, and finally, into opposition to liberalism itself. By 1968, at the Democratic convention in Chicago, an older generation of tired and compromised leaders discovered a younger generation demonstrating in the streets for nothing so much as a chance to revitalize and extend the traditions that had nourished them. Instead of being welcomed in, thousands of young demonstrators were confronted by Mayor Daley's police brigades. During the long night of riot that followed, the extraordinary idealism of 1960 died in a ritual of shadow and light played out before millions of Americans, as the demonstrators chanted: "The whole world is watching."

☆   ☆   ☆

For the first time, much of the nation watched the inauguration of a new President on television. This gala event, in early 1961, celebrated the personality and intellectual tastes of the new President. Washington filled temporarily with artists, writers, and performers, who received prominent seats in the reviewing stands. The glittering inaugural ball and the solemn and stylish formal dress made this a memorable pageant of fashion and power, carefully recorded and transmitted through television. The Capitol resounded with Kennedy's promise to make it a cultural center, not just the bureaucratic capital of the nation.

The young President's speech, read in the clear, ringing voice that marked his style, somberly announced a new, crusading foreign policy. Kennedy honed a long campaign against Eisenhower's policies of moderation and conservatism and a repeated call to get America moving again to a single issue that afternoon of January 20, 1961. His administration, he proclaimed, would accept the call to defend "freedom in its hours of maximum danger." This challenge was welcome; the young President pledged the lives of all Americans in the struggle "to assure the survival and the success of liberty. This much we pledge—and more." Yet, standing at his side in the cold winter wind of Washington, Eisenhower, the elderly ex-President must have wondered: Was this not the enthusiasm he had warned against in preparing his farewell address? Where would it lead?

John Kennedy began his race to the White House two giant steps ahead; he inherited great wealth and had a father with power in the Democratic party. Joseph Kennedy, John's father, was the son of an Irish-Catholic political boss in east Boston. Making his way through Harvard and ignoring the snubs of his Protestant classmates, Joe Kennedy showed shrewd financial judgment. Purchasing valuable Florida land after the speculation boom collapsed in the mid-1920s, investing money in Hollywood film productions, and then moving his stockholdings into real estate shortly before the 1929 crash, he became one of America's wealthiest men during the 1930s and an important contributor to the Democratic party. His reward came in an appointment to the Securities and Exchange Commission, created to oversee the stock market in 1934. By 1938, he received appointment as ambassador to Great Britain, although he had to resign in 1940, when his off-the-cuff remarks criticizing Roosevelt's foreign policy found their way into print. Stung by this experience, he became a bitter foe of the liberal wing of the Democratic party.

To some extent John Fitzgerald Kennedy inherited his father's prejudice against liberals. Although he counted on their support in political campaigns, he was not always at ease with them. Kennedy's approach was active, not contemplative; witty, not reflective. The author of two books, *Why England Slept* and *Profiles in*

Courage, he was not an intellectual. He admired action and courage, but became impatient with hesitancy and circumspection. A voracious reader with excellent recall, the new President recognized accomplishments in the arts and letters, but, in politics, he determined to surround himself with "pragmatic liberals" like himself.

From the outset, ambition, charm, and especially an intense commitment to family made Kennedy's career an unusual one. Family was at once the source of his strengths and his weaknesses. From his Irish Catholic background he inherited a sense of social responsibility. Yet the immigrant background was distorted by his father into a desperate desire to succeed and excel. And like his father, he regarded sexual conquests as a right. After Choate Preparatory School for boys, Princeton, and then Harvard, from which he graduated *cum laude,* Kennedy joined the navy in 1941. Already he was something of a celebrity: His senior thesis was published as the bestselling book *Why England Slept.* Given command of P T boat 109, during an operation in the Solomon Islands, in 1943, his ship was rammed and sunk by a Japanese destroyer. Although he had hurt his back in the fracas, he pulled an injured sailor three miles through the dark waters and then got word out to rescuers. For this act, he received a Purple Heart; he had proven himself as heroic as his boyhood heroes: Talleyrand, John C. Calhoun, and Lincoln.

Elected to Congress from Massachusetts in 1946, 1948, and 1950, he entered the Senate in 1952 and was reelected by a landslide in 1958. Unlike Johnson, Kennedy did not ingratiate himself with the inner circles of House and Senate leadership. In fact, he earned a reputation for independence, when, for example, he attacked Truman for not spending enough on defense. Labor leaders suspected the zealous efforts of Kennedy and his brother Robert to indict Teamster leader Dave Beck and subsequently Jimmy Hoffa. Although he lacked a power base in Congress and a distinguished legislative record, Kennedy was a national political celebrity by the mid-1950s. Attention came partly from his marriage to socially prominent and fashionable Jacqueline Lee Bouvier in 1953. In part, it came from his brave bout with a back illness that threatened his life in 1954. In part, too, it came from his bestselling book *Profiles in Courage,* written while he was recuperating.

The courage Kennedy praised most in his book was the willingness of men like President John Quincy Adams to sacrifice political position to principle. Yet, his own courage did not run in this direction; it had more to do with physical risks and military confrontations. Given several chances during the early 1950s to condemn Senator McCarthy, Kennedy refused to do so. When the Senate voted condemnation in 1954, Kennedy was too ill to participate, but even then he refused to take a public stand against the Wisconsin senator, perhaps out of deference to his father's friendship with McCarthy. This reluctance earned him the suspicion and hostility of important Democratic party liberals like Eleanor Roosevelt, who considered opposition to McCarthy to be the litmus test of political credibility.

Almost the vice-presidential nominee in 1956, Kennedy became a presidential contender in the next four years. In 1960, he was a leading candidate. His strategy centered on beating his strongest opponent, Senator Hubert Humphrey, of Minnesota, in preferential primaries when Humphrey might be expected to win. On April 5, in Wisconsin, Kennedy took six of ten districts and then won a large plurality in West Virginia in May. This second victory was decisive, for it defused the issue of Kennedy's Catholic faith. By winning in a rural, Protestant state like West Virginia, he demonstrated to hesitant Democratic party leaders that Americans could elect a Catholic president. With a well-heeled media blitz and personal appearances, Kennedy bumped Humphrey out of the race.

Other contenders played a more cautious game. Lyndon Johnson, relying on his power base in the Senate, hoped that the front-runners would knock each other out, forcing the party to choose him. And, Adlai Stevenson, still supported by a coterie of liberal Democrats, waited in the wings for his third successive nomination. However, the Kennedy machine did not falter, and, with the weight of primary victories, crushed its opponents at the Los Angeles convention. Only Lyndon Johnson salvaged anything: the Vice-Presidential nomination.

Governor Nelson Rockefeller, of New York, and Vice-President Nixon sparred for first place on the Republican ticket. A grandson of John D. Rockefeller, the architect of the Standard Oil monopoly, Nelson inherited fortune and family notoriety. Devoting himself to public service, Rockefeller pushed liberal projects in the 1940s and 1950s in the State Department, and later as head of Eisenhower's committee on administration reorganization. One result of his work was the new department of HEW. On military spending, he advocated expansion, pushing civil defense measures and larger defense budgets. Warning of increased Soviet power, he used a report prepared for him by Professor Henry A. Kissinger (later National Security Adviser and Secretary of State under Nixon and Ford) as the basis of his campaign in 1960. Perhaps his combination of liberal federal programs and large defense budgets better suited him to the Democratic party, but his chief failing in 1960 was an indecisive and fuzzy campaign. This continued to be Rockefeller's fate throughout the 1960s: a sometimes almost successful candidate who couldn't quite commit himself. Richard Nixon, on the other hand, was nothing if not committed to the cause of his own political advancement.

Nixon's rise through American politics is like the plot of a Horatio Alger tale of success and gives a vivid accounting of the costs of such success. Furthermore, his background contrasts sharply with both Kennedy's and Rockefeller's. Born into a modest Quaker family in California, Nixon worked his way through Whittier College and then graduated from Duke Law School. After short service in the Office of Price Administration during World War II, he joined the navy. Elected to Congress in 1946 and 1948, he won a Senate seat in 1950 after a bitter campaign against Helen Gahagan Douglas in which he questioned her loyalty. Detested by liberals, Nixon was the youngest and the brightest of the congressmen to exploit the anti-Communist issue. Although serving in the late 1940s on the House Un-American Activities Committee, where he doggedly pursued Alger Hiss, his anti-Communist tactics were more opportunism than anything else. During this same period, he ingratiated himself with the more liberal, Eastern wing of the Republican party, earning the vice-presidential nomination in 1952.

In 1960, Nixon's surest power base appeared to be in the Republican conservative wing, but he focused his campaign on his experience and closeness to Eisenhower. The elderly Eisenhower, rumored to be privately hostile and sometimes cruel to his Vice-President, could not shake off the tenacious grip of this ardent public admirer.

The 1960 presidential campaign was a spectacle of bravado, matching the tough rhetoric of Nixon, trumpeting his ability to deal with the Russians, against the equally stern rhetoric of Kennedy, who criticized a "missile gap" and demanded firm measures to prevent erosion of America's world position. Forced to defend a modest foreign policy and facing a deepening recession, Nixon still might have won, had he asked Eisenhower for active support earlier in the campaign. As it was, Nixon's poor performance in the

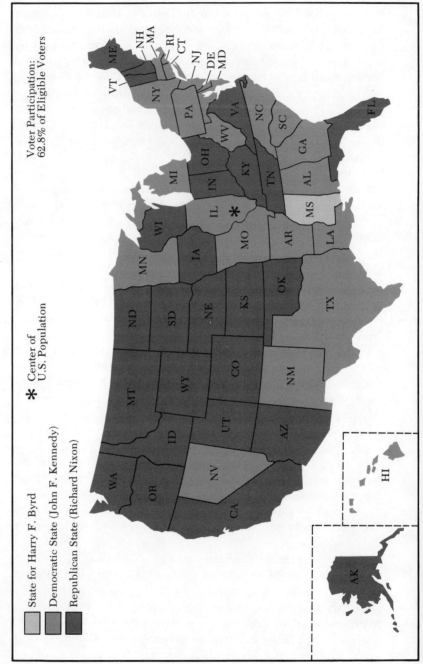

Election of 1960

* Center of
  U.S. Population

Voter Participation:
62.8% of Eligible Voters

State for Harry F. Byrd

Democratic State (John F. Kennedy)

Republican State (Richard Nixon)

first of four televised debates with Kennedy crippled his effort. Kennedy emerged looking and sounding a leader next to Nixon, whose forced gestures revealed nervousness and insecurity, not the experience and maturity that he claimed as his advantage.

Kennedy had other advantages. He could criticize Eisenhower's slow-motion action on civil rights and could promise to get America moving again. As he put it in his Labor Day speech in Cadillac Square, Detroit, he would lead America toward a New Frontier. Voters perceived Kennedy to be a flexible, open-minded, and tough liberal committed to the basic, shared premises of American idealism. Defusing most negative reaction to his Catholicism, Kennedy benefited from a solid vote from Catholics.

Kennedy's assumption of power reaffirmed the basic continuity of Democratic administrations. Familiar faces from the Truman administration returned to government, but Kennedy also appointed a new generation of lawyers, academics, and corporate executives, whom reporter David Halberstam called "the best and the brightest." Several of these advisers, including historian Arthur Schlesinger, Jr., speech writer Theodore Sorensen, and economist John Kenneth Galbraith, already belonged in the Kennedy entourage. Others, such as Robert McNamara, appointed to head the Defense Department, and Dean Rusk, appointed to head the State Department, joined the administration after the election. Some, such as Douglas Dillon, head of Treasury, had been Republicans. The President named labor lawyer Arthur Goldberg as Labor Secretary. Luther Hodges, of North Carolina, went to the Commerce Department. The Attorney General was the President's brother, Robert Kennedy. To his Council of Economic Advisers, Kennedy appointed several outstanding academics, led by Walter Heller. McGeorge Bundy occupied the key post of National Security Adviser. Taken together, this was a group of intelligent and competent advisers, with well-deserved reputations for accomplishment and managerial skills. Embellished by several well-known intellectuals, Kennedy's advisers were dominated by skilled managers like McNamara.

The new President's foreign policy emphasis in his inaugural speech indicated the initial direction of his administration. For him, American determination had to be tested against Communism. Above all, the United States required a more flexible strategy in the Cold War. Eisenhower's massive deterrence policy, Kennedy felt, had been paying too little attention to revolutions in the Third World. Nikita Krushchev's tough speech on January 6, 1961, supporting "wars of liberation," only confirmed Kennedy's belief that American policy should focus on underdeveloped nations.

The new President also felt confident that he understood revolutions in Latin America, Africa, and Asia. Having read the works of important contemporary guerilla warriors, such as Che Guevara, of Cuba, and Mao Tse-tung, of China, he believed that anticolonial revolutions could be guided into the American camp if the United States would bolster liberal middle-class and local reform groups. The romantic appeal of antiguerilla tactics and individual heroism also appealed to the President, who was an unabashed admirer of the dashing secret agent James Bond, hero of Ian Fleming's adventure novels. Failing limited intervention, the United States could send economic aid and military advisers to struggling anti-Communist regimes. Willing to confront the Russians with nuclear warfare, should they alter the status quo in East-West spheres of interest, the President was optimistic about success.

In the three years of his administration, Kennedy had ample opportunity to test his strategy, as twenty-seven countries in Africa and Asia achieved independence. Perhaps the most innovative policy developed toward these new nations was the Peace Corps, announced on March 1, 1961. Directed by Kennedy's brother-in-law, Sargent Shriver, the agency sent hundreds of (mostly young) Americans abroad to help educate and lend expertise to new Third World nations. Although the Peace Corps was never a top priority of policy, its combination of idealism, voluntarism, and technical assistance represented some of the most creative thinking of the Kennedy administration, providing a prototype for subsequent programs initiated under President Johnson.

Unfinished business from the Eisenhower administration, however, became the first public test of Kennedy's approach to revolutions in the underdeveloped world. Eisenhower briefed the President-elect on CIA plans to invade Cuba and overthrow Castro. Kennedy decided to continue preparations; here was a chance to test his theories about counterinsurgency and flexible, limited force. The new President carefully kept American troops, ships, and aircraft out of the operation, but he could not prevent news of the impending invasion from spilling into the press. For those who cared to read about it, the coming action was described in rich detail in *The New York Times* and the *Nation* magazine.

With Kennedy's approval, the invasion of Cuba began on April 17, 1961. It quickly became a disaster. By the time the ragtag

American Peace Corps volunteers often found themselves in situations in which their skills and resources could barely scratch the surface of the poverty and deprivation in the host country. This volunteer (left) in Colombia worked on nutrition and food programs, as well as teaching macramé and drawing to children.   (ACTION, Photo by Jim Pickerell)

army of counterrevolutionaries hit the shore at the Bay of Pigs, conservative elements with little, if any, support inside Cuba dominated it. Castro's efficient and loyal army had no trouble defeating them. The Bay of Pigs debacle suggested the shallowness of CIA understanding of the Cuban revolution; more ominously, the experience displayed a tendency of moderate alternatives to revolution to evolve into right-wing juntas. Furthermore, Kennedy's hasty approval of covert military actions undercut faith in his Alliance for Progress, announced one month earlier. However, failure in Cuba did not substantially change Kennedy's belief that elite or middle-class groups would willingly create more democratic societies, as the Alliance aid programs hoped to encourage, or that military force was an effective last resort.

Despite the Cuban setback, Kennedy continued to push for a flexible military force, concentrating his efforts on the creation of a special strike force, called the Green Berets. He also tested the waters of censorship, asking a very suspicious and uncooperative group of publishers to institute self-censorship during "our country's peril . . . which knows no precedent in history." When the publishers refused, Kennedy backed off. The new President had learned one lesson at least: to distrust the CIA leadership. Shortly after the Cuban fiasco, he replaced Allen Dulles with John McCone.

Events in the Third World—the beginning of the liberation struggle against Portugal in Angola in early 1961 and trouble in the former Belgian Congo (called Zaire since 1971), Cuba, and Vietnam—buffeted Kennedy's first days in the White House, but the most perilous storms swirled around relations with the Russians. In June 1961, Kennedy agreed to meet Khrushchev in Vienna. By the time the two leaders confronted each other, both had marked off nonnegotiable positions. The President had pushed for an increased defense budget, announced a grandiose space program to bolster American prestige, pressed Congress for a fallout shelter program, and approved the invasion of Cuba. The Russians had proposed a "troika" (three leaders) to head the United Nations, instead of one person, and they began to push again for a final settlement of the German question.

When the two leaders met on June 3, their encounter resembled the preliminaries to a match between two wary boxers. Each leader spent considerable time sizing up his opposite. There were harsh and enigmatic words, but little agreement when the parley ended a day later. Still, the bluster on both sides might have evaporated, had it not been for Germany. Always a special problem in itself, the shared occupation of Berlin symbolized the failure of East and West to agree on a peace treaty with Germany. American policy since Eisenhower promoted the industrialization and rearmament of West Germany, aiming toward reunification and ultimate integration into the Western alliance. The Russians recognized West Germany, but demanded equal treatment for their client state in East Germany. As the West German economy grew rapidly in the late 1950s, West Berlin was resurrected as a glittering showcase of consumer capitalism. Increasingly, the city siphoned off East German intellectuals, scientists, and engineers, whose defection caused an acute crisis in 1960 and 1961 for the East German government of Walter Ulbricht.

On June 21, 1961, Khrushchev acted to help his East German ally by announcing he would sign a peace treaty with East Germany by the end of the year, turning over control of East Berlin to it and access to West Berlin. This would force the Americans, French, and British to recognize the Ulbricht government and its sovereignty over Berlin. Kennedy's advisers were divided in their suggestions. Dean Acheson favored proclamation of a national emergency. Arthur Schlesinger, Jr., Hubert Humphrey, and others suggested negotiations. Kennedy struck out for a middle ground, but leaned toward some tough response. His decision was announced on June 25, during a solemn national television speech requesting increased defense expenditures and higher draft quotas. He also asked for more civil defense funds. Most important, he called up military reserves. It was a slide toward the brink.

Khrushchev's response nineteen days later settled the German problem in a way that angered many Americans. On August 13 and 14, East German workers erected a barbed-wire and concrete wall between East and West Berlin. Thereafter, the flow of refugees slowed to a trickle. In what amounted to a public relations gesture, Kennedy sent 1,500 American troops along the East German autobahn into West Berlin. Short of war, however, he could do nothing to remove the wall. Thereafter, American-Russian relations continued to deteriorate. On August 30, the U.S.S.R. ended its self-imposed nuclear-test ban and exploded the largest weapons ever constructed. On September 12, the United States began underground testing and on March 2, 1962, resumed open-air testing.

Soviet-American hostility peaked during the next summer, this time ninety miles from home. With the approval of the Cubans, the U.S.S.R. began construction of nuclear-missile launching sites in Cuba. Whatever his reasons—whether pressure from hard-liners in his government, desire to probe American defenses, or eagerness to defend the Castro revolution—Khrushchev underestimated the swift and stern character of Kennedy's response. On October 15, 1962, an American U-2 plane positively identified the missile sites, and the President quickly called his advisers to consider American responses. Brushing off Adlai Stevenson's suggestion for broad negotiations with the Russians, aimed at neutralizing Cuba and withdrawing American forces from the naval base at Guantánamo Bay, Kennedy only seriously considered varieties of confrontation. When more hawkish advisers, like Dean Acheson, argued for a surprise air strike against the sites, others, led by Robert Kennedy, counseled caution and a policy more easily justified before international law: a blockade to prevent arming of the missiles. For several days, the advisers debated. Their final consensus reflected sensitivity to international opinion. As Bobby Kennedy put it, referring to the surprise Pearl Harbor attack of 1941: "My brother is not going to be the Tojo of the 1960s."

The President chose a relatively moderate course from among extreme possibilities, but he nonetheless brought the nation to the edge of nuclear war. Preliminary preparations for extensive conflict began: troops massed in Florida, and Press Secretary Pierre Salinger sketched out the functions of an emergency Censorship Advisory Board. On October 22, Kennedy spoke on national television, announcing the discovery of the missile site and the countersteps he had already taken. Ridiculing the Soviet assurances that these were defensive weapons, the President announced a "quarantine" (blockade) of all Cuban ports, insisting that all incoming ships would be searched for weapons.

Kennedy's actions presented the American people with a *fait accompli* and policy steps that could not be debated. At the same time, the President had compelled the Russians to decide for or against war. They could try to steam through the blockade and risk seizure, or they could stop and agree to American hegemony on the high seas. It was a difficult choice, but in this test of wills, the Russians backed off. On October 25, missile-carrying cargo ships of the Russian merchant marine stopped. In the meantime, Khrushchev sent a message to Kennedy promising to withdraw the missiles in exchange for United States guarantees not to invade Cuba. As the President prepared to accept this offer, the Soviet leader suddenly raised his demands, pushing the United States to withdraw its missiles from Turkey. The events of October 27 plunged the administration back into crisis, and Kennedy stepped up plans for military action. At the same time, he wisely decided to ignore Khrushchev's second message, cabling agreement with the first proposal. The Russian leader then accepted Kennedy's guarantees, and the crisis ended. The Russians dismantled their missile sites under the watchful eye of American airplanes. But the world had come dangerously close to nuclear warfare, as two men surrounded by their advisers, sitting in the situation rooms of their capitals, decided on the fate of humanity.

Confrontation seemed to soften the Kennedy-Khrushchev relationship in the months that followed, as both leaders backed down from antagonistic gestures. In December, the Soviet leader suggested a nuclear-test ban treaty. Kennedy's American University speech of June 10, 1963, confirmed a new emphasis upon reaching a peaceful accommodation with the Soviet Union. Although the final agreement, signed on July 25, 1963, excluded underground tests and did nothing to slow the arms race, it did stop the atmospheric discharge of large amounts of radioactive waste. Détente had begun in a small way.

Kennedy's foreign policy helped shape his attitude toward important domestic considerations, such as economic growth and civil rights. He stressed the need to increase America's gross national product in campaign speeches, but he was not clear about why this should be done: to add to defense capabilities or to aid those in the distress of unemployment and poverty. In areas like civil rights he remained cautious, because he did not wish to alienate Southern support for economic and defense programs.

On overall policy, the President gradually accepted the advice of economist Walter Heller and others on the Council of Economic Advisers for his strategy. Heller called these Keynesian tactics the "New Economics," or federal direction of the economy, using fiscal measures. His agenda stressed tax incentives to business for modernization, general tax cuts and reforms, and informal price-and-wage guidelines. Some of these measures might unbalance the federal budget, but Heller persuaded Kennedy that economic growth, stimulated under the program, would more than compensate by bringing in new tax revenues. For success, the program depended upon cooperation from Congress and the business community.

The President's relationship to business, however, was troubled and sometimes acrimonious. Businessmen suspected his liberal rhetoric and promises to use the power of the federal government in the economy. They disliked the activism of his administration, preferring the pleasant drift of Eisenhower's approach. His advisers seemed suspiciously like government planners—indeed, one of them, John Galbraith, was, although Kennedy kept him at arm's length.

Kennedy's initial policy tested the water. In February 1961, he announced plans to begin sailing America out of the economic doldrums. His tack included supplements to unemployment benefits, aid to distressed areas, a higher minimum wage, and more Social Security benefits. All of these measures passed through Congress by September. In other areas, he had less success. Of an investment tax-credit plan, tax reform to provide withholding on stock dividends and interest payments, and revision of expense-account deductions, only the tax credit survived. This plan for a 7 percent increase in deductions on new business equipment found a wide channel of support in Congress.

Nothing in this program should have angered business, yet Kennedy touched a raw nerve of confidence. In late 1961, the new administration had begun to worry about the wage-price spiral. According to this theory, wages that rose above increases in productivity pulled prices upward, in turn inspiring workers to demand higher compensation. By early 1962, Kennedy had accepted his economic council's advice on price-wage guideposts. He advised unions to seek only those wage hikes warranted by productivity increases, and he asked business to hold down prices. He had clearly signaled that economic growth, and not income redistribution, was the administration's aim.

Since the 1930s, the labor movement had been the largest organized component of the Democratic party, from which it demanded special consideration after elections, but the AF of L-CIO had never been close to Kennedy. Nonetheless, it willingly accepted the President's economic leadership. Interested only in selective intervention, Kennedy decided to set an example of wage-and-price restraint in steel. Beset by several long and expensive strikes since World War II, the industry had shut down for 116 days prior to its last settlement in 1959. Kennedy wanted to avoid this trend.

Meeting secretly on January 23, 1962, with Roger Blough, of the giant firm of U.S. Steel, and with President David McDonald, of the Steel Workers Union, Kennedy and Arthur Goldberg thought they had hammered out a noninflationary agreement. Labor's demands would be so low that the industry could maintain its current prices. In his estimation, the President was half-right. On March 31, the union settled for an embarrassingly slight $.10 per hour wage package plus fringe benefits, well within the economic council guidelines.

When he saw an appointment with Roger Blough on his April 10 schedule, Kennedy was surprised. He became furious when he understood the meaning of the meeting, for Blough had come to announce a $6 per ton price increase in steel. Arthur Goldberg, who had been standing by, came into the President's office. Accusing the steel executive of a "double cross," Goldberg attacked Blough for breaking the understanding of the January conference. After a half-hearted effort to justify himself, Blough departed. Kennedy, visibly shaken, called in his staff to announce the price hike, acidly commenting: "My father always told me that steel men were sons-of-bitches, but I never realized til now how right he was." Understandable as it was, this injudicious remark, when it appeared in the press, confirmed business exasperation with the President. Shortly afterward, New York businessmen began sporting buttons proclaiming, "I'm an S.O.B." The deeper message was clear.

Kennedy's off-the-cuff expletives did not embitter business as much as the substantial action he took the following day. At a press conference, the President used his Cold War rhetoric against the steel industry. "In this serious hour in our nation's history," he warned, when servicemen were dying in Vietnam or leaving their homes to join the reserves, a few arrogant men had defied the national interest. "Some time ago," he concluded, "I asked each American to consider what he would do for his country and I asked the steel companies. In the last twenty-four hours we had their answer." Several actions matched these tough words. The Defense Department promised to shift its purchases of steel to any company that maintained low prices. The Justice Department began to investigate whether simultaneous price rises in other companies indicated an illegal conspiracy. The FBI, meanwhile, sent agents in the middle of the night to rouse a reporter who had suggested that Bethlehem Steel wanted to resist the price rise. In the Congress, an investigation began into the monopoly practices of the industry.

Challenged from all sides, the large steel producers broke ranks. On April 13, 1962, Bethlehem Steel rescinded its price rise, followed quickly by U.S. Steel. The crisis ended with Kennedy the apparent victor. But the injury to relations between the administration and business remained an open wound, upon which the President thereafter poured the balm of tax credits and special favors. Partly an aftershock, the stock market began a steep plunge in late May. Restoration of confidence and a new policy were in order.

The President moved on three fronts. He sought to restore business confidence, in a series of speeches, one to the Economic Club of New York, in December 1962, which John Galbraith called "the most Republican speech since William McKinley." In this address, Kennedy called for a tax cut and moderate tax reforms to block the most flagrant deduction loopholes. Inspired by Walter Heller, this program went to Congress in January 1963, featuring $13.6 billion in tax relief, most of it for individuals. Although the tax cut was not enacted until early 1964, several months after his death, Kennedy accurately assessed its effects. During the early years of the Johnson administration, production increased rapidly to around 6 percent a year, increasing tax revenues and decreasing the federal budget deficit. But the program also had a more subtle effect. Instead of pushing investment into useful social production for housing, transportation, or education, it emphasized consumer spending as the route to economic health.

Aside from some minor tax reforms and a Manpower and Development Act, passed in 1963, Kennedy's economic programs remained stalled in the conservative committees of Congress; they emerged for approval only later under the leadership of President Johnson. The reluctance of Congress to act on economic proposals typified relations between the legislature and Kennedy and the suspicions of Kennedy in the business community. He proposed, but Congress refused to dispose, and only a small percentage of his programs survived to return to the Oval Office for his signature. Lacking the skill, political clout, favorable political climate, and persistence of Johnson, he suggested programs for medical care for the elderly, aid to education, an Urban Affairs Department, and most important, a civil rights bill, but could not shepherd them through the legislative corridors of Congress.

In civil rights, Kennedy showed initial promise, as well as quickness to compromise. He attempted to avoid a treacherous and difficult route through Congress, while concentrating on legal desegregation initiatives pushed through the Justice Department. Although he appointed more black ambassadors and middle-level officials than any previous President, Kennedy ceded to compromise with Southern Democrats and named men unsympathetic to black equality to federal judgeships, in such states as Georgia and Mississippi. His caution on civil rights legislation gave way gradually, as the movement for its achievement deepened. Increasingly, the President began to side with these forces, but with a commitment tempered by his need for Southern votes on other issues. For example, only after Congress rejected his proposal for a housing and urban development Cabinet post (to be headed by Robert Weaver, a black city planner) in January 1962, did he finally fulfill a campaign pledge to eliminate by executive order, by "the stroke of a pen," segregation in federally financed public-housing projects.

During this period, Attorney General Robert Kennedy increasingly turned his attention to prosecuting school-integration cases and worked quietly to desegregate such transportation facilities as airline waiting rooms in the South. The administration also integrated the Army reserves and the National Guard, while it pushed desegregation of facilities surrounding United States military camps. But, not until February 28, 1963, did the President propose sweeping civil rights legislation.

By then, Kennedy could not ignore—or chose not to ignore—increasing demands from civil rights advocates all over the country. The force of events and the logic of his own beliefs compelled him to take action. Confrontation over the admission of black student James Meredith to the University of Mississippi required intervention. After the federal courts ordered "Ole Miss" to admit Meredith in the fall of 1962, a hostile mob of white segregationists rebuffed the new student. When state police refused to protect his rights, rioting broke out, eventually leaving two persons dead. Kennedy then federalized the Mississippi National Guard, and under the watchful eye of troops and marshalls, Meredith enrolled.

The drama of Birmingham, Alabama, in the spring of 1963 more than matched this sample of resistance. The Southern Christian Leadership Conference, headed by Martin Luther King, Jr., began a nonviolent protest movement to crack segregation in the city's commercial life. Met by strong opposition from state and local officials—especially "Bull" Connor, of the Birmingham Police Department—the city's black residents began marches and demonstrations. The police countered with arrests, beatings, and police dogs. Behind the scenes, Kennedy worked to arrange a truce. Deploying Cabinet members and advisers to contact their friends in the Southern business community, the President achieved something of a triumph with an agreement, reached on May 10, to integrate rest rooms, lunch counters, fitting rooms, and drinking fountains. Business promised changes in hiring practices, with a biracial committee established to oversee the pact. When state and local officials tried to renege on the agreement, Kennedy dispatched 3,000 troops to the outskirts of the city. Organized resistance crumbled.

Still, the movement continued to push beyond the President. On June 19, 1963, Kennedy proposed new civil rights legislation to strengthen voting rights and school desegregation. Despite a rousing speech on June 11 in favor of civil rights, he declined to endorse or attend the August 28 March on Washington, led by King and other black leaders. This celebration of black rights brought labor leaders, church officials, and thousands of black and white citizens together in the high point of the religiously oriented, nonviolent crusade against segregation. Martin Luther King's speech and sermon, "I Have a Dream," thrilled the enormous crowd by reaching into the very heart of America's moral and religious traditions. In some sense, it was the fulfillment of those traditions. King's biblical cadences intensified his incantation: "I have a dream." "I have a dream that one day every valley shall be exalted, every hill and mountain shall be made low, the rough places will be made plains, and the crooked places will be made straight, and the glory of the Lord shall be revealed, and all flesh shall see it together. . . ." Kennedy held back from joining this vision of Judgment Day, partly because this movement challenged his leadership and partly because he still did not see racial inequality as a moral equivalent of the Cold War.

However, during the last three months of his life, Kennedy increasingly paid attention to questions of social reform. He supported the much amended and strengthened civil rights bill pending before Congress. But, even as tension over the issue built, the administration could not convince Congress to act. Three days before his death, Kennedy instructed Walter Heller to block out legislation for a war on poverty. Pressure to move decisively in this direction had been building in his administration, and Kennedy recognized that poverty had become an important issue. Outside academic consultants and advisers close to the President began informal discussions on a comprehensive attack on persistent joblessness and depressed economic areas in 1962.

A different, more ambiguous legacy of the Kennedy administration was Vietnam. On this decisive issue, Kennedy's reputation seems to stand or fall, yet history cannot judge because of incomplete and contradictory evidence. From the beginning of his term in office, Kennedy personally involved himself in Vietnam, with an increasing commitment to winning the civil war in that nation. But, all the while, his skepticism grew. At the moment of his assassination, he was fast approaching a crossroads; either he increased American participation in the war or gradually disengaged United States forces.

Many of Kennedy's closest advisers, like Robert McNamara and General Maxwell Taylor, agreed with his faith in the special forces and quiet military intervention in the Third World. Rather than Cuba, with which Kennedy showed some signs of desiring an accommodation, Vietnam became the essential test case of this faith. Upon advice from Taylor and National Security Adviser Walt W. Rostow, after their mission to Vietnam in October 1961, Kennedy agreed to increase the number of military and political advisers, but he resisted requests for combat troops. At the same time, he increased pressure on Prime Minister Ngo Dinh Diem to institute social reforms. But Diem realized—if Kennedy did not—an inherent flaw in the policy. He knew that the United States would support him so long as he maintained a semblance of order.

By 1962, Kennedy's policy of material and political support was in full swing; the South Vietnamese Army, supported by American air power, in the form of helicopters and fighters, introduced napalm, defoliants, and a strategic hamlet program designed to isolate the Viet Cong revolutionaries from sympathetic peasants. Optimistic battle reports flowed in, but still the fighting increased, and Kennedy increasingly doubted the figures. By late 1962, Diem's situation grew bleak. When Buddhists rioted against his government in May 1963, Kennedy signaled to his South Vietnam ambassador that he would support the replacement of Diem. When the coup came in early November, the President was shocked at its violence: Diem was assassinated by rival generals.

"Sent to all posts, 11/22/63." This photograph of Vice President Lyndon Johnson (left) and President John Kennedy was one of several similar photographs sent to American information posts throughout the world on the day of Kennedy's assassination in order to stress the continuity of government. *(National Archives)*

How Kennedy would have dealt with the political coup that followed is unknown. The young American President himself was struck down by an assassin's bullet three weeks later, on November 22, in Dallas. Some evidence indicates that Kennedy was reconsidering Vietnam. He had clearly come to distrust the optimistic reports emanating from the battlefield. His speech at American University on June 10, 1963, indicated a new hesitancy and skepticism about the Cold War. Yet the President had been convinced by his own enthusiasm for counterinsurgency to commit almost 25,000 personnel to Vietnam. Furthermore, it is doubtful that the President had even begun to consider how the United States could terminate its intervention: how to do this in an upcoming election year, when right-wing Republicans could be expected to cry sellout to the Communists.

Many of the programs to uproot poverty and end segregation, to reverse the desperate decay of cities, had their initial hearing in this administration, but they were still in an embryonic state in 1963. Unfinished and still unformed, the Kennedy administration was short on legislative accomplishment but far-reaching in its impact on American society. Reality became indistinguishable from the myths that assuaged the collective guilt and shock most Americans felt at the President's assassination. The young President's style and humor, his wife's cultural activities, gave many Americans the impression of great movement and energy. Kennedy was hated by segregationists and revered by many black Americans, but neither reputation was entirely deserved. In economics, the President touched off the same heat lightning. Even his foreign policies were shifting and changing at the moment of his death. Yet, the effect he had was enormous. His energy helped unleash the idealistic forces that created the splendor, but also the failure, of Lyndon Johnson.

9 The Limits of Liberal Politics: Part II

In the terrible moments of November 22, 1963, after the assassination of John Kennedy in Dallas, on the airplane flying back to Washington, and in the days that followed, Lyndon Johnson skillfully managed a transition of leadership while the nation mourned its young President. Johnson quickly took over the duties of office while the nation fixed its attention upon the pageantry of burial. The new President first persuaded the Cabinet, press corps, and White House staff to remain in office. He offered Jacqueline Kennedy any assistance she might need. And, to quiet speculation, he appointed a special commission, headed by Chief Justice of the Supreme Court, Earl Warren, to investigate Kennedy's assassination and the murder of the suspected assassin, Lee Harvey Oswald, by Jack Ruby. Its task was to lay to rest fears of a political conspiracy. Johnson also decided in these early moments to turn the unfinished legislation of John Kennedy into a monument for the slain leader and a justification of his own administration. He promised to complete the program of domestic legislation and civil rights pending before Congress. Five days after the assassination, he called for action on the civil rights bill as a tribute to Kennedy.

This masterful and quiet assumption of command demonstrated Johnson's immense political skill and his position as a Washington insider. The path to this position of power and influence began in the unlikely place of Stonewall, Texas, on August 27, 1908. Johnson's childhood was a happy one, but tension between his parents took its toll. His mother, Rebekah, relished her "superior advantage," as she put it, and saw in her son "the deep purposefulness and true nobility that had shone in her own father's steady brown eyes." Lyndon's father, on the other hand, had few pretensions to culture or superiority; he was a tough, hard-drinking man with a small-time political career. Perhaps biographer Doris

Kearns is right in ascribing Lyndon's lifelong insecurity and desire to be loved to a struggle between his parents for his affection. But Johnson's personality also reflected contradictions of the Southwest frontier—a place where culture stuck like a thin veneer over a vast terrain of frank brutality and struggle. Johnson grew up only partly his mother's boy. Deeply dependent upon her, he nonetheless nourished an abiding suspicion of the intellectual accomplishments she desired for him.

When he assumed the presidency in 1963, Johnson was a large, unhandsome man with a slushy drawl. Another biographer, Robert Caro, contends he also had an overweening ambition. A person with uncommon magnetism and political skill, he had a swollen, but tender ego. Vulgar in private to the point of aggressive crudeness, he became the model of propriety and common-sense morality in public. He could be remarkably generous to those close to him or shockingly brutal. As White House adviser Eric Goldman reported, staff members sometimes left his office white with anger and embarrassment. It amused Johnson to invite the sedate members of his Cabinet or the press corps to swim nude in the White House pool. He often conducted business in the men's room. And White House reporters were always abuzz with his latest homey invective: For example, he declared an opponent so stupid he couldn't "pour piss from a boot with the instructions written on the heel."

Yet, Johnson was a masterful congressional manipulator. Schooled in the politics of the Senate's inner circle, he played the strengths and weaknesses of his fellow senators. More influential than Kennedy or Humphrey or Kefauver, he became the Senate majority leader in January 1955. Not known as a liberal, despite his reverence for F.D.R. and the New Deal, Johnson had been placed on the 1960 presidential ticket to provide geographic weight. The strategy worked well, as Johnson loyally canvassed the South and Southwest for votes. But the results were not satisfactory to him; deprived of his leadership role in the Senate, Johnson agonized over the inactivity and loss of power associated with the vice-presidency. Although Kennedy included him in important decisions, Johnson knew well that some of the President's advisers disliked him, that some mocked his speech behind his back. In return, Johnson disapproved of the late parties, the style and glitter that surrounded the administration.

The chance to be President gave him an opportunity to test himself against the already mythic heroism and accomplishments of Kennedy. In this pursuit, he turned Kennedy's failures into his own triumphs, while Kennedy's hesitations became the new President's passionate goals. On neither score, however, could he disentangle himself from the shadow of his predecessor. Yet, from the beginning, the new President bent his office to his own priorities. It surprised no one when Theodore Sorensen resigned as special counsel to the President in January 1964, less than two months after the assassination. One by one, Kennedy's entourage moved out of office, until only a few of his former closest advisers remained.

Johnson's first address to Congress as President came on November 27, five days after he assumed office. Stressing the theme, "Let us continue," he pledged enactment of the "ideals" of the Kennedy administration: action on civil rights, taxes, medical care, education, and jobs. He also underscored the need for firmness in Vietnam, warning "those who seek to impose upon us or our allies the yoke of tyranny." Johnson's thrust, however, was to promise success where his predecessor had failed.

If faintly critical, this tone went unnoticed, and Johnson earned praise for eloquently picking up the mantle of power. And, he made good his promises. Reform legislation flowed steadily in 1964, as the President skillfully rolled over legislative roadblocks. By the summer, Congress enacted three large and important programs: a major tax cut bill that reduced the withholding rate from 18 percent to 14 percent and lowered corporate and individual taxes by $11.5 billion; the Civil Rights Act, signed on July 2; and the Equal Opportunity Act, of August, establishing the Office of Economic Opportunity to coordinate the President's "war on poverty." Johnson had guided the passage of reform legislation on a scale matched only by Franklin Roosevelt's first administration during the 1930s.

Johnson's most spectacular victory came in civil rights. Portraying Kennedy's death as a martyrdom and subtly playing upon the desire of Americans to exonerate their society through some formal act of generosity, he called in political favors and applied strong pressure. Johnson succeeded because he worked both aisles of Congress, acquiring crucial Republican support from Republican Charles Halleck, of Indiana, in the House and Everett Dirksen, of Illinois, the minority leader in the Senate. Bypassing Southern opponents, his forces closed off a filibuster and then enacted the most powerful civil rights legislation since the 1860s. The act, essentially the same as introduced in 1963, although sharpened by amendment, created an Equal Employment Opportunity Commission, increased the power of the Civil Rights Commission, strengthened federal capacity to push the desegregation of schools, outlawed segregation in public facilities, and strengthened voting rights through strict regulation of literacy tests. If the act did not achieve integration at one stroke, it did nonetheless knock down most of the visible barriers to equal opportunity.

On taxes, Johnson again proved his mastery of the sideline run. By promising budgetary restraint and lowering projected federal expenses below the plus $100 billion mark for 1964, Johnson effectively neutralized potential opposition to a tax cut from Virginia's Senator Harry Byrd, chairman of the Senate Finance Committee. The effect of the bill matched the anticipations of Johnson and his advisers. It helped increase economic growth and consequently increased federal tax revenues, so that until 1967, the budget deficit was slight: $5.9 billion in 1964, $1.6 billion in 1965, and $3.8 billion in 1966. Unemployment shrank from 5.7 percent to 3.8 percent in 1966, and the inflation rate remained low.

The war on poverty, first suggested by Kennedy, but developed by Johnson, became his most ambitious and original program. Suggested in his State of the Union speech on January 3, 1964, the program began before it had firm legal standing. The President appointed Sargent Shriver, of the Peace Corps, to direct the effort when it became law. In a special message to Congress on March 16, accompanying the proposal for an Economic Opportunity Act, Johnson defined his plans. The major purpose of the legislation would be to centralize scattered and uncoordinated federal antipoverty activities into one new executive branch office, the Office of Economic Opportunity (OEO). Various titles of the act offered a wide assortment of training programs and support services. The act would set up a job training corps for young people between the ages of sixteen and twenty-one. It encouraged formation of community action groups to assist local agencies in the distribution of comprehensive social services to the poor. It provided grants to farmers to purchase agricultural materials and offered incentive loans to businesses willing to hire the hardcore unemployed. As well as a variety of educational benefits, it offered job training for heads of households currently on public assistance. Finally, the Equal Opportunities Act created VISTA, a domestic peace-corps volunteer service for work in poverty areas. Associated programs, such as Head Start (1965) and Upward Bound (1966), were later

In the late 1960s and early 1970s, many universities became increasingly involved in the affairs of their surrounding communities. Students like this one at the University of Nebraska at Omaha often received academic credit for working as volunteers in the community.   (ACTION)

attached to the general program. As *Time* magazine put it in 1964, the OEO reflected the uniquely American belief that "evangelism, money and organization can lick just about anything."

Using a ceiling of $3,000 per year income for a family of four in 1964 as a definition of destitution, this ambitious program proposed to eliminate poverty in America in time for the bicentennial celebration of 1976. Its stress on education, self-help, and equal opportunity represented a culmination of the optimistic, social engineering hopes of modern reformers. Viewed dispassionately, however, it set unrealistic goals. As the authors of the various programs understood, ending poverty was a complex and long-term proposition. While parts of the OEO touched these complexities, for example, by promoting community action and the organization of the poor, other aspects were too limited to have much effect. As conceived and legislated, the OEO never attempted to alter the income shares of rich and poor through taxation, although such a drastic route was probably the only way to eliminate poverty quickly. Nonetheless, presidential rhetoric and media attention to programs implied that the OEO meant to soak the rich and the middle classes. Thus, much of the controversy surrounding the programs came from public misunderstanding of their scope and purposes.

Despite the genuine successes of some OEO programs, difficulties in job corps centers and controversial activities of community action groups brought on increasing opposition. In 1966, leading Republicans effectively attacked the program. By 1968, it was clearly in trouble; President Johnson's attention by then focused almost entirely upon the war in Vietnam. The deterioration of the total approach to poverty began when pieces of the OEO were lopped off and programs, such as Head Start, were transferred to the Department of Health, Education, and Welfare in early 1969.

As the war in Vietnam began to suck funds out of the federal budget, programs like the OEO became domestic casualties. Johnson could not keep his promise of guns and butter. But, beyond funding and administrative problems, thinking about poverty was seriously limited. Being poor in America was not just bad luck or the accident of birth; it had fundamental structural and cultural causes, compounded by race and class divisions, that the war on poverty could not eliminate. Yet the President's grandiose rhetoric seemed to indicate his commitment to radical change. This created bewilderment among those supposed to be the recipients of change and angry opposition from thousands of taxpayers convinced that their hard-earned dollars were budgeted for a social revolution.

Early in 1965, however, President Johnson remained exhilarated with his legislative victories and his enormous electoral triumph over Republican Barry Goldwater in the fall presidential election. Now a President in his own right, Johnson pushed another wave of legislative programs through Congress, including Medicare, establishing compulsory hospital insurance for the elderly and voluntary medical insurance. Along with this program, Congress passed Medicaid for those below the age of sixty-five unable to pay for medical services. Other legislative victories included a new Civil Rights Voting Act (August 1965), which eliminated literacy tests, as well as other restrictive practices designed to keep blacks away from the polls. In August, Johnson fulfilled another Kennedy promise by securing a law to create the Department of Housing and Urban Development, authorized to subsidize the rents of low-income families. More legislation followed: federal aid to higher education, the Urban Mass Transportation Act of 1966, a Demonstration Cities Bill, the Clean Water Restoration Act, the Highway Beautification Act, and others. This remarkable burst of lawmaking, touching everything from the arts to education, from air pollution to poverty, testified to Johnson's power and versatility. Johnson's programs epitomized the notion that social reform could be achieved by technical adjustments to the economy. Based upon his own experience during the 1930s, his genuine commitment to ending poverty and racism, and his own immense self-confidence and belief in the effectiveness of federal government programs, he orchestrated a national attack on a myriad of serious social problems. But, like Johnson's thinking about his office, his programs lacked coherence and sustained support. Once created, an innovative program required careful funding, caretaking, and coordination. The "Great Society," as Johnson named his collective efforts, required executive talents and attention beyond his capacity. In this way, the social reform of the mid-1960s increased social tensions by promising more than it could deliver.

Poor and black Americans gave Johnson an early and sharp indication that his programs raised frustrations as well as hopes. The programs that gushed through the federal pipeline probably intensified black demands. As much as Johnson sympathized with the poor or adopted the rhetorical goals of the early civil rights movement, he could not contain the revolution of rising expectations, whose fires he stoked. Beginning in the summer of 1964, American cities began to explode one after another, as if tied to the same short fuse. These riots intensified each year, through the summer of 1968, making the Johnson years among the most violent and unsettled of this century.

Urban riots, destruction of property, and intractable demands of black civil rights organizations in the North distressed and confused many Americans. Gallup polls from 1963 onward reflected this anguish. Americans consistently included civil rights agitation with the most serious and worrisome problems—crime and lawlessness, the war in Vietnam, high prices and unemployment. Public opinion also indicated that Kennedy and Johnson moved further and quicker on civil rights than most Americans wanted. Indeed, white resentment over integration crested in 1964 and 1968 in the presidential candidacy of Governor George Wallace, of Alabama. Wallace not only articulated anti-integrationist sentiment, but he also attacked federal interference in state and local affairs.

The polarity in American society that President Johnson tried to reduce with legislation and encouraging words revealed itself in the report of the National Advisory Commission on Civil Disorders, headed by Governor Otto Kerner, of Illinois. Appointed in late July 1967, after severe urban rioting across the nation left sixty-three dead, hundreds injured, and thousands arrested, Kerner and his board of labor and business leaders, law-enforcement officers, and prominent blacks considered evidence and reported in 1968. Warning against the possible degeneration of American society into two distinct and warring civilizations, one white and the other black, the Kerner report confirmed what many sociologists and political leaders already felt about official investigations. They repeated shopworn advice and warned about possibilities that already existed. Although the Kerner Commission argued that "white racism" lay behind the riots, opinion polls taken in 1968 discovered that only about one-third of Americans agreed with this conclusion.

Confusion about integration degenerated into bitter resentment and backlash by the end of Johnson's administration, but the President continued to propose more civil rights legislation. After the summer riots of 1967, the President angrily warned lawbreakers that they would be punished: "Violence must be stopped, quickly, finally, and permanently." Yet, his solution remained political: a legislative "attack—mounted at every level—upon the conditions that breed despair and violence."

Liberal legislation and more programs constituted Johnson's panacea for racial turmoil, but they represented an end to—not a further evolution of—broad attacks upon inequality. In the last year of his administration, he successfully sought a new civil rights act, signed on April 11, 1968, barring discrimination in most American housing. Yet this last act was consummated in tragedy. On April 4, Martin Luther King, Jr., was assassinated by a sniper in Memphis, Tennessee. King's death touched off riots in over 120 American cities. In this angry reflex, urban disorder resulted in more deaths and arrests. This time, however, the riots seemed to have a lasting, splintering effect. After 1968, civil rights legislation stalled, and the black movement sputtered.

Urban riots, assassinations, rising crime statistics, and mounting antiwar protests on college campuses etched a picture of America in violent colors. After the murder of Senator Robert Kennedy on June 5, 1968, by a Jordanian immigrant, Sirhan Bishara Sirhan, President Johnson appointed another national commission, instructed to explore the causes of violence in America. Headed by Milton Eisenhower and including clergy and legislators, the commission was charged to discover what caused Americans to "inflict such suffering on ourselves." Reporting a year-and-a-half later, the commission summarized the conclusions of its various task forces. Many of its proposals sensibly aimed at solving underlying social problems—even questioning large defense expenditures and calling for reordered social priorities. Anything of the sort, however, fell on deaf ears. In 1969 and 1970, concern for violence had evolved into a national obsession with law and order. Congress increasingly became hostile to anything resembling a change in priorities. As early as 1967, for example, the House refused to consider a $40 million rat extermination program for urban ghettos, even after (much to its embarrassment) Washington newspapers revealed the substantial sums spent on rat control in the Capitol building itself.

☆   ☆   ☆

If anyone, President Johnson inadvertently reordered priorities in his own administration by focusing attention on the war in Vietnam. Over and above his enviable legislative victories, the war loomed larger and larger, until it almost entirely blocked his vision. Johnson's initial decisions about Vietnam established the character of American escalation: increased force applied to a deteriorating situation. Not privy to his predecessor's growing frustration with the war, the new President had to make the decisions that would have eventually revealed the scope of Kennedy's reservations. In late 1963 and early 1964, Johnson tried to maintain quiet on the Vietnam front, in order to consolidate his administration and gather dependable advisers around him. This came to mean shifting men who had enthusiasm for a tough line on Vietnam into prominent positions on the White House staff. A serious complication emerged outside the administration. Preparing for the Republican party convention in 1964, enthusiasts for Barry Goldwater built a powerful, conservative movement. Should Johnson demonstrate weakness on Vietnam, he might be ambushed in the presidential election. By downplaying the war, however, he could present himself as a moderate.

The President's own views, as he revealed them, defined Vietnam through a scrim of 1930s analogies. He repeatedly invoked the "Munich" analogy, based upon belief that British and French appeasement of Hitler had brought on World War II. This he combined with Eisenhower's "domino theory," a simplistic view of containment that pictured Communism as a single force emanating from the Kremlin, and able, with increasing momentum, to topple one strategic nation after another. Behind both analogies lay a deep suspicion that Western capitalism lacked force and resolve to prevent the spread of Communism.

The other half of Johnson's view derived from a positive vision of the 1930s. He hoped to offer the Vietnamese—if they accepted American intervention—a Southeast Asian version of the New Deal. "I want to leave the footprints of America in Vietnam," he said in 1966. "I want them to say when the Americans come, this is what they leave—schools, not long cigars. We're going to turn the Mekong [River] into a Tennessee Valley." A Mekong River Redevelopment Commission would prepare a massive system of dams, power plants, and water projects to rebuild the country once the war ended.

Inside the administration, Johnson listened carefully to the leading hawks among his advisers. As he told reporters early in his tenure, "I have found the myth of McNamara to be true." The myth he referred to was the belief in McNamara's absolute administrative competence.

Early in 1964, Johnson made several moves up the ladder of escalation. In January, he approved plans to step up covert harassment of North Vietnam. He began more and more to depend upon men in the defense and foreign relations bureaucracy who had convinced themselves that increased bombing would cut off the Viet Cong from supplies and strengthen the generals now controlling Saigon. This interpretation rested upon two questionable assumptions: that the Viet Cong rebels actually depended upon the North and that bombing would not touch off increased infiltration of arms and armies from the North. The President also shifted leadership inside the American command in South Vietnam, replacing General Paul D. Harkins with General William C. Westmoreland. In this new position, Westmoreland pushed his strategy of open and increased American combat.

These decisions were either hidden or downplayed, but they set the stage for a public event during the summer that provided Johnson with authorization to wage war. On July 30, 1964, South Vietnam P T boats attacked bases in the Bay of Tonkin area of North Vietnam. Almost simultaneously, an American destroyer, the *Maddox*, steamed into the area on a mission to disrupt North Vietnamese communications. On August 2, North Vietnamese P T boats attacked the *Maddox*, probably interpreting its presence as cover for the South Vietnam attack. The *Maddox* returned fire and sank one of the attack ships. Receiving news of the attack, Johnson ordered the *Maddox* to remain in the area, while he sent another ship, the *C. Turner Joy*, into the bay. On August 3, both destroyers reported that they had been attacked. Johnson and his advisers then decided to use this skirmish as a pretext to retaliate, sending bombers into North Vietnam to destroy naval targets. That evening, the President summoned Congressional leaders to inform them of the incident—minus any background details about the activities of the American or South Vietnamese navies. He requested their support of his bombing raids, and he suggested that Congress specifically confirm his power to protect American interests in South Vietnam. Despite spirited opposition by Senators Wayne Morse, of Oregon, and Ernest Gruening, of Alaska, the resulting Bay of Tonkin Resolution, sponsored by Foreign Relations Committee chairman William Fulbright, of Arkansas, sailed through the Senate on August 7. Johnson had a mandate to pursue full-fledged war in North and South Vietnam.

In addition to providing legal justification for policy, the Bay of Tonkin incident perfectly fit the pattern of American escalation: an incident provoked by North Vietnam, the Viet Cong, or the United States itself became justification for increasing firepower or troop levels. And, as American forces became stronger and more active, the Viet Cong also mobilized, while North Vietnam began to infiltrate troops and material into the South in large quantities. In turn, this buildup on both sides weakened the South Vietnamese government, requiring further American intervention. Thus, pretext became cause in a never-ending upward spiral of men, arms, and destruction.

For most of 1964, after the Tonkin Resolution, Johnson played down America's Vietnam role. As anticipated, the Republicans nominated Arizona conservative Barry Goldwater for president. Also, true to predictions, Goldwater proved unwilling and unable to distance himself from the right-wing John Birch Society, which had canvassed for his nomination. Goldwater rewarded these followers with a widely quoted line in his acceptance speech: "Let me remind you," he said, "that moderation in the pursuit of justice is no virtue, and I would remind you that extremism in the defense of liberty is no vice." The Democrats didn't need to sling charges in his direction; Goldwater had declared himself an "extremist." Even the Republican National Committee seemed fated to smear its own candidate. When it adopted the slogan, "In your heart you know he's right," it inspired a rhapsody of parodies on other parts of the body: "In your guts you know he's nuts," for example. In case the American public missed the point, the Democrats exhibited a television commercial showing a small girl plucking the petals from a daisy, followed by a picture of an atomic blast, followed by words urging voters to support Johnson. The implications of this political montage couldn't be clearer: A vote for Goldwater meant a vote for war.

Nothing the Republicans could do would have changed the election, for Johnson's legislative successes, his sensitive, self-assured role as executor of John Kennedy's political legacy made him an unbeatable candidate. The mood of the country was polarized, but still largely liberal. By choosing Hubert Humphrey as his running mate, he confirmed active aid of the Democratic party's liberal and labor wing. The results disclosed one of the great landslide victories of American electoral history: Johnson gathered 61 percent of the vote and Goldwater only 38.5 percent. Whatever the American public thought were the issues of the campaign, however, a vote for Johnson was not a repudiation of war.

With a landslide victory behind him and a vigorous Democratic majority in both houses of Congress, the President moved ahead quickly on his legislative program. At the same time, he walked straight into a bog of war. For the next four years, escalation continued, and the effects of war returned home in a rising tide of inflation, protest, and uncertainty. At first reluctant to commit American troops to a ground war in continental Asia, Johnson also refused to consider withdrawal without face-saving concessions from the North Vietnamese. Daily, he became more preoccupied with selecting bombing sites or reading reports on "body counts"— enemy casualties that were puffed up by American commanders in Saigon. Increasingly too, Johnson cut himself off from his great strength in the political wisdom of Congress. He defined hesitation and dissent as weakness and honest press coverage as hostile bias. The President had changed his own personal priorities, sacrificing good political sense to the prosecution of a victoryless war.

Never friendly to intellectuals, Johnson became the butt of their scorn and satire. His reaction was angry, yet cautious. Early in his administration, he invited historian Eric Goldman to act as liaison with the academy. Goldman convinced him to sponsor a White House Festival of the Arts in June 1965. Johnson liked the idea. It had a Kennedy ring to it, and it would establish the President as a patron of the arts. But Johnson was shocked and infuriated when poet Robert Lowell, one of the invited guests, published a letter stating his refusal to attend. Other intellectuals followed suit, explaining that their principled opposition to the war in Vietnam made it impossible for them to come.

Those who opposed the President were reacting to a series of escalations undertaken over the winter. Convinced by his advisers, among whom only Hubert Humphrey—temporarily—and George Ball—openly—dissented, Johnson agreed to more troops and more bombing. In February 1965, after a Viet Cong attack at the American base in Pleiku, the President ordered retaliation raids against Northern targets and authorized regular bombing sorties one week later. In the spring, he agreed to Westmoreland's call for offensive American action, dubbed "search and destroy" tactics, in the oblique parlance of the war. By the summer, the United States had

General William C. Westmoreland (center right) thanks entertainer Bob Hope for his many years of service to American troops in the field. Vietnam, December 24, 1965. (U.S. Army Photograph, Photo by Sp4 Ralph Boatwright)

over 30,000 troops in South Vietnam and over 185,000 by the end of the year. When Johnson claimed that nothing had changed and that conditions were improving, the reverse was true.

Johnson's embattled foreign policy in Vietnam pushed him into hasty action elsewhere. In the Dominican Republic, during the years following the 1961 overthrow of dictator Rafael Trujillo, that country experienced instability and political turmoil. In April 1965, open conflict erupted between forces supporting reformer Juan Bosch and those backing more conservative army officers. As the conflict grew, the American ambassador hastily wired Washington that American lives were in danger: "The time has come to land the Marines." The President agreed and ordered in American forces, not just to prevent attacks on American nationals, but to prevent Bosch from steering the small republic on a leftward course. Eventually 22,000 Americans landed, and their presence enabled a government acceptable to Washington to assume power. Foreign aid, private investment, and stability eventually returned.

In his State of the Union message in January 1966, Johnson began a long review of foreign affairs with a strange sentence: "Tonight," he solemnized, "the cup of peril is full in Vietnam." It was indeed, but the President himself had already drunk deeply from its bitter brew. Promising not to rob resources from social programs to pay for the Asian war, he was, in fact, preparing to do so. He grossly underestimated the costs of Vietnam at around $5.8 billion a year, and he advocated no new taxes. Putting the most favorable appraisal on the face of conflict, he declared: "The enemy is no longer close to victory."

Nothing in the remainder of the year warranted this optimism. Convinced by Westmoreland and Defense Department experts, the President committed 385,000 American troops to the conflict by the end of the year. Expenditures for stepped-up air strikes and naval maneuvers added to the cost of this expeditionary force. At home, military expenditures distorted the federal budget; with no new revenues, the government escalated deficits and borrowing. Inside the administration, Johnson faced increasing uneasiness. National Security Adviser McGeorge Bundy quit to take a position heading the Ford Foundation. Johnson replaced him with Walt Whitman Rostow, an enthusiast for the war. In the fall, critic George Ball quietly left his position in the State Department. Feeling it useless to issue a blast at Vietnam policy, Ball reluctantly admitted his ineffectiveness in the administration. The most

Vietnam, 1966

CHINA

Nanning

Loakay

Thanuyen

Pingsiang

Yen Bay

Dienbienphu

Hanoi

GULF OF
TONKIN

NORTH
VIETNAM

Paksong

Ban
Ban

Thanhoa

HAINAN

Luang
Prabang

Nan

LAOS
Vang Vieng

Sama

Vinh

Vientiane

Donghoi

Udon

Vinhlinh

THAILAND

Hué

Haiphong

Danang
Tamky
Chulai
Quangngai

Ta Khli

Ratchasima

Pakse

Kontum

Pleiku

Ankhe

Quinhon

Stungtreng

Bangkok

Battambang

CAMBODIA

SOUTH
VIETNAM

Tonle Sap

Nhatrang

Kompong Cham

Camranh Bay

Pnompenh

Bo Duc

Preyveng

Bencat

GULF OF
SIAM

Beinhoa
Saigon
Tan Son Nhut

Vinhlong

SOUTH
CHINA
SEA

Rachgia

Cantho

- - - Demarcation Line of 1954
→ Ho Chi Minh Trail

Camau

0   50   100   150   200 mi.

General Lewis Hershey, head of the Selective Service System, indicates his own birthday and position on the draft eligibility chart. The lottery system of determining draft eligibility by birthdate, while continuing the policy of student deferments, made conscription controversial during the war in Vietnam. (Courtesy, Ted Green)

important doubter was Robert McNamara. After a trip to Saigon in October, where he repeatedly questioned bogus body-count figures and unwarranted optimism, the Secretary of Defense returned, shaken, although not yet a convinced opponent of the war. He did, however, order a careful historical study of American policy in Vietnam and assigned Daniel Ellsberg to the task. Taking his own doubts to his research, Ellsberg uncovered a secret history of intervention and deceit revealed in classified documents. So disturbed was he, that he later defied all rules of security and passed his report to *The New York Times* for publication in 1971. The result was the *Pentagon Papers*. McNamara himself gave way to serious questioning in 1967; on learning this, the President abruptly moved him out of Defense and into a job as head of the World Bank. But even his replacement, long-time Democratic party stalwart Clark Clifford, appointed in early 1968, worked on the inside to prevent further escalation of the war.

Defections from his administration, mounting criticism in Congress, the loss of forty-seven House and three Senate seats in the 1966 elections, at first did nothing to deflect Johnson from his course; they only isolated him further. The master politician succumbed to the ideologue, and Johnson turned his large talents to the single purpose of winning the war. During 1967, escalation continued, with about 100,000 more American troops pouring into the beleaguered country. From the North, Communist units continued to infiltrate south, despite the fury of American air strikes. As draft calls mounted at home, critics took stronger and stronger stands, compelled, they felt, by the crumbling social and political consensus. An important sign of the times appeared when Martin Luther King, Jr., joined opponents of the war, stating that the United States had become "the greatest purveyor of violence in the world today." In King's mind, the administration had sacrificed the struggles of black Americans to a war in Asia.

Nonetheless, Johnson persisted. Orchestrating bombing pauses, often followed by more devastating raids, the President offered negotiations to the North Vietnamese in December 1966, February 1967, December 1967, and finally, again in March 1968. The North Vietnamese, led by Ho Chi Minh, however, rebuffed his offers. They refused to accept a permanent, separate, anti-Communist enclave in South Vietnam, allied to the United States. On this point, they were adamant.

In early 1968, the United States had stationed over 500,000

Two Viet Cong suspects captured in Hobo Woods during Operation "Crimp." (U.S. *Army Photograph, Photo by Sgt. Bernie Mangiboyat)*

Soldier-artists and Army photographers sometimes recorded their shock and dismay at the war in Vietnam in their work.

Left—"*Death in the Delta,*" *by Col. Robert Riggs, Vietnam, 1963.*   *(U.S. Army Photograph, Army Art Collection)*

Right—"*The Parentless Ones,*" *by Col. Robert Riggs, Vietnam, 1963.*   *(U.S. Army Photograph, Army Art Collection)*

troops in Vietnam. Inflation and budget deficits mounted so rapidly that Johnson acceded to demands of his economic advisers and pushed for a tax surcharge. In effect a 10 percent war tax, the bill remained stuck in Congress for a year, but the message was clear enough: Johnson finally admitted the real cost of war. Early spring brought worse news from the battlefield. During the Tet lunar New Year holiday, a massive Viet Cong offensive destroyed the credibility of Johnson's assurances about the war. Beginning in January and lasting for almost a month, the struggle challenged American forces everywhere. Viet Cong forces besieged the American Embassy in Saigon and took over several urban centers, including the ancient ceremonial city of Hue. Although American and South Vietnamese armies eventually won back the cities, the Viet Cong had delivered a serious blow to American willingness to fight, a lesson replayed nightly in television news broadcasts, which cut deeply into the confidence and sense of purpose many Americans had felt about the war. When General Westmoreland requested more troops in the thousands, the futility of United States strategy was apparent.

For Johnson, the battle presented a shock that demanded attention. Deception, half-truths, and secrecy no longer protected him from critics. On March 12, in the New Hampshire presidential primary, liberal Minnesota Senator Eugene McCarthy shepherded antiwar sentiment into a large vote that almost upset the incumbent. With opposition rising in his own party and Congress rumbling, Johnson exercised the political acumen that had escaped him for several years. In late March, he summoned his Senior Advisory Group on Vietnam to Washington. In a moment reminiscent of Truman's first conference on the Cold War, military men and political figures joined Dean Acheson, Arthur Dean, McGeorge Bundy, Douglas Dillon, and John McCloy in informing the President that his policy had lost the support of a great many Americans, including the business establishment. Johnson realized that he could not continue. As a candidate for reelection, he would tear open the Democratic party. On March 31, he announced his withdrawal from the race. It was perhaps the saddest moment, but still a brave one, in his political life.

The withdrawal was even more bitter, because he abandoned the field to Robert Kennedy. While Kennedy waited until the shock of New Hampshire to announce his own candidacy, he immediately captured support in primaries and from powers in the

Democratic party. Once a zealot in pursuit of labor union racketeers, Kennedy had gradually adopted a position of strong support for integration and opposition to the war. He was, by 1968, the liberal and humanitarian alter ego of his brother, and he was a favorite of many party leaders.

Johnson's step, however, settled nothing. Bitter months followed with violent urban riots and the final confrontation at Chicago between the police of Mayor Daley and protesters supporting the candidacy of Eugene McCarthy. As convention delegates moved inexorably to nominate Hubert Humphrey, the nation watched a pitched battle between police and protesters.

The political exit of Lyndon Johnson in a hail of controversy obscured significant foreign policy events of his last years: the containment of the June 1967 conflict in the Middle East, when Israel defeated Egypt, Jordan, and Syria; the Nuclear Nonproliferation Treaty with the Soviet Union in 1967; and the successful return of the crew of the spy ship *Pueblo*, seized in early 1968 while on mission near North Korea. All of these events were buried in an avalanche of bad news from Vietnam.

After eight years, the words spoken by John Kennedy at his inauguration became eerily true. In 1968, the world had entered a dangerous and terrible period, when civilization seemed threatened. But the rhetoric of idealism evoked on that cold morning in 1961 and reaffirmed every year since, had soured into clots of opposition and bitterness. By 1968, the political system was impoverished and exhausted, and Americans prepared to select a new President by default.

10 *The Awakening: Beyond Liberalism*

One of the most successful science fiction movies of the 1950s, *The Invasion of the Body Snatchers* (1956), pitted moral bravery against conformity. In this disturbing tale of mind-controlling invaders from outer space, the whole population of a town is gradually replaced by blank-staring replicas of human beings. This destruction of the soul entirely deprives each citizen of privacy. With no resistance and no conscience, each individual acts out the prearranged plans of conquest. Mindlessly happy, the transformed person becomes a willing participant in the film's horrifying version of mass society. Only one man escapes, fleeing up onto a freeway buzzing with fast-moving cars. Vainly trying to stop someone, to wake the nation to a threat it should have anticipated he cries, "They're here already!" Perhaps the "they" is Communism, or the manipulators of mass culture, but whatever the inspiration, the fear takes the shape of conformity: unfeeling, unemotional inaction. In this film, inability to act or focus moral attention on duty is a typical community failing. Only the solitary individual perceives the threat.

The conformity depicted in this film expressed itself during the 1950s as an ideology of compromise. Yet, the 1950s were also a time of enormous social ferment. Much of this ferment began as a reaction to the low-key politics of the Eisenhower administration and the limited appeal of contemporary liberalism. Around a variety of issues, a number of new movements organized to challenge the status quo in religion, politics, and culture. Some of these favored right-wing causes; some favored more radical causes; some focused primarily on cultural or religious issues. But all of them shared a sense of the inadequacy of American politics—the prevailing liberal theories of the day—to solve the larger problems of society. All of them shared a yearning for a moral, ethical, even religious awakening. By the late 1960s, these movements had become the most important phenomena in American culture.

The wave of idealism that swept American society in the 1960s had its origins in the feeling that conformity masked moral and political inertia. Despite appearances, America in the early 1950s was still reacting to the profound disturbances and aftershocks of World War II. The unfinished business of war, the ideological challenge from Third World revolutions and Communism, and the unresolved domestic inequities required resolution. Beset by these demands, many Americans began a reevaluation of their institutions in a fashion that invoked some of the oldest political and religious traditions of the nation. This movement, beginning in the 1950s, had all the confusion and contradictory facets of earlier awakenings, as in the 1830s and 1840s, when a similar extraordinary mix of women's rights, radical democratic ideas, communitarian experiments, concern for black Americans, and conservative evangelical religion burst into the mainstream of American politics. During the 1950s and 1960s, these same causes reappeared in a new guise. Once again, millions of Americans reaffirmed an old and traditional faith that society could not be guided by politics alone. Whatever the bias of their politics—left or right—they occupied the edges of the same culture that envisioned America as the beacon of hope and rectitude for the world—the single grand exception.

One of the leading students of such reform periods, Arthur M. Schlesinger, Jr., wrote *The Vital Center* in 1950. This justly renowned tract examined the nature and resilience of American society. To Schlesinger, the political philosophy of liberalism (embodied in the New Deal interventionist state) constituted the "vital center" of American society. Providing a lighted path between the darkness of left and right philosophies, liberalism, he wrote, could solve most domestic social problems and face the ideological challenges of the Cold War. Schlesinger recognized that liberalism occupied the center of American politics in the 1950s—even the Republicans accepted its basic premises. He also realized that liberalism seriously needed an infusion of vitality and energy.

Understanding this, Schlesinger hoped to found a new, lean, and combative liberal philosophy in religious insights. Borrowing some of the theological premises of Reinhold Niebuhr, he adopted a tough-minded, even pessimistic stance toward achieving a just society. He also affirmed Niebuhr's suggestion that the balance attained in welfare capitalism by the competing claims of labor unions and capital would ultimately benefit all of society. Aware of individual sin and social evil, modern society should proceed cautiously toward the goals of justice. To Schlesinger, Niebuhr's neo-orthodox Protestantism affirmed vital liberalism; it sustained a belief in American ideals at "a high pitch of vibration."

Many Americans in the 1950s and 1960s agreed with Schlesinger that liberalism occupied the center of domestic political philosophy, but they disagreed that it had either the political vitality or moral breadth to solve the immense social problems of the day. In its ascendancy in 1950, by 1968 liberalism was being besieged from all sides. Schlesinger's firmest assumption became the era's most persistent doubt: was liberalism vital?

A search for the vital center of American civilization preoccupied a multitude of authors in the late 1940s and early 1950s. Reevaluations of democratic society streamed from the pens of American historians, sociologists, philosophers, and political scientists. This purpose even inspired a new academic discipline, American studies, dedicated to defining the distinct features of American civilization. Begun in earnest during World War II, at institutions such as Princeton and Vassar, the study spread rapidly after the war to several large state institutions. By 1949, it had a journal, *The American Quarterly*, and by 1951, a professional association. Probably the most famous work in this field was Henry Nash Smith's *Virgin Land*, published in 1950. This book explored the nature and uses of agrarian myths in the United States and, by implication, suggested some of the reasons for the distinctiveness of American culture.

Not only political liberals and academics sought to define an essential Americanism during these years. The same goal energized Senator Joseph McCarthy and his anti-Communist movement. McCarthyism and liberalism shared the premise that essential American traditions should be revered and foreign ideas rejected. Yet, in the hands of the Wisconsin senator, the notion of orthodoxy became the inspiration for inquisition. He turned his tactics of bluster, intimidation, and innuendo against a Democratic party establishment that surely did not merit the accusation of being soft on Communism. He transformed "un-Americanism" into a partisan issue. Gathering support on the state and local level, in the press, and in the Catholic hierarchy, McCarthy linked anti-

Communism to suspicion of Easterners, ethnic and racial minorities, and political radicals, in a mixture that threatened to create a "know-nothing" coalition of broad proportions.

McCarthyism also precipitated a crisis in liberal philosophy by challenging its claim as the vital defender of tradition. The question of rights of free speech for American Communist party members and sympathizers seriously split the liberal community. Firings of left-wing professors and the intellectual justification for intolerance of opinion divided liberal organizations like the American Civil Liberties Union. Verbal warfare between intellectuals reached a fevered pitch as such journals as the *Nation* rushed to defend the rights of Communists, and others, such as the *New Leader*, denied them. The most sophisticated justification for denying rights to Communists probably came from philosopher Sidney Hook's book, *Heresy Yes, Conspiracy No*, published in 1953. Despite his intelligence and care, the book lent intellectual stature to the elusive and impossible attempt to define true Americanism.

What some defended as vital orthodoxy, critics of American culture and society denounced as conformity. In February 1951, *Fortune* magazine published a scathing attack on the new impulse to conform. Contemporary Americans, wrote the editors, had lost touch with society. No one, they complained, could explain the meaning of American principles. Other social critics shared *Fortune*'s puzzlement about conformity. Beginning in 1951 and 1952, marked at mid-point by Alan Valentine's *Age of Conformity* (1954), and rising to a peak in 1956 and 1957, scores of books and popular magazine articles deplored the blandness of American society, the insipid quality of opinion, and the decline of intellectual curiosity. When the *Reader's Digest* discovered the problem in December 1958 and published "The Danger of Being Too Well Adjusted," the discussion of conformity reached barbershops, doctors' waiting rooms, and millions of homes.

Yet few observers could agree about the causes of conformity. Opinion ranged from David Riesman's picture of the *Lonely Crowd* and philosopher Hannah Arendt's perceptive remarks about mass society to religious assaults on conformist Christianity, corporate second thoughts about large enterprise and government regulation, and popular fears about the impact of television. There was no real accord on defining the conformity syndrome, just a vague set of symptoms without a prescription for cure. To critics, conformity symbolized a lack of motion in society, the effects of McCarthyism, and the soporific effects of Eisenhower's low-keyed presidency.

To theologian Will Herberg, conformity had transformed even competing religions into a vague "civic religion." As he understood it, civic religion was a shared Jewish, Protestant, and Catholic theology that "validates culture and society, without in any sense bringing them under judgment." Looking at the 1950s, Herberg noted that major American religious sects had gradually grown together; all of them accepted tolerance and pluralism; all of them claimed religious belief as a fundamental part of citizenship; all of them believed that religion validated the American way of life. As Dwight Eisenhower put it: "Our government makes no sense unless it is founded in a deeply felt religious faith—and I don't care what it is." Or, in the words of the popular song "I Believe," released in 1952: for the flowers that grow and candles that glow, for prayers that are heard, for leaves, for sky, for babies' cries. In other words, faith was nondoctrinal—simply belief in belief. Perhaps most typical of nondenominational uplift was Norman Vincent Peale's *The Power of Positive Thinking*, published in 1952. Culminating almost two decades of work in religious broadcasting and publishing, Peale's book combined elements of modern psychology, self-help religion, and traditional Protestantism into a prescription for happiness and success.

Statistics measuring religiosity moved upward during the 1950s. Church membership rose from 57 percent to 64 percent of the population. Bible sales increased suddenly and dramatically from 1949 to 1953. Church attendance remained high throughout the decade. In 1954, 96 percent of persons interviewed in a Gallup poll declared their belief in God. In 1964, 63 percent claimed they prayed frequently; only 6 percent admitted they never prayed. As late as 1968, America topped Greece, the European nation with the highest recorded extent of belief: in God, the existence of afterlife, and the reality of hell. New church construction approached $1 billion in 1958, over twice the funds devoted to construction of public hospitals and a little less than one-third devoted to public school construction. In 1953, a religious fiction book, *The Robe*, made the best-seller list for the first time since 1943, while, in that same year, five of six nonfiction best-sellers had a religious theme.

Despite this placid surface of tolerance, conformity, and civic religion, conservative and evangelical sects grew rapidly, indicating dissatisfaction with the religious status quo. Lutherans, Baptists, Catholics, Latter-Day Saints, and the Church of Christ gained members much more rapidly than liberal, suburbanized congregations. Thus, while the liberal National Council of Churches worked out a revised standard and updated version of the Bible, moved toward eliminating differences between faiths, and took liberal stands on social issues, many conservative congregations rejected this aspect of civic religion, searching for faith in more traditional experiences of revivalism.

Revivalism during the 1950s drew upon the particular strength and talent of two great evangelistic preachers: Baptist Billy Graham and Catholic Monsignor Fulton J. Sheen. Both men combined a conservative political orientation, fundamentalism, and media appeal that made them as much cultural celebrities as religious leaders. Both skillfully used television to bring vitalized religion into millions of American living rooms.

Fulton Sheen's weekly television series, *Life Is Worth Living,* began in 1951 and extended through 1957. A leading television personality of the day, Sheen often outdrew Milton Berle's comedy show at the same hour. Sheen was an experienced radio showman, as well as a television star, and he credited both media with spiritual attributes, calling them "beautiful examples of the inspired wisdom of the ages." Projecting a relaxed and friendly image, he examined moral and political problems, spicing his serious remarks with poetry, jokes about Milton Berle, and amusing asides about his role as a TV priest.

Born in the small town of El Paso, Illinois, and educated in St. Paul, Minnesota, Catholic University in Washington, D.C., and in Europe, Sheen was known for his firm anti-Communism. No doubt this reputation helped account for the most famous conversions he precipitated: Clare Booth Luce, the playwright, and Louis Budenz and Elizabeth Bentley, two renowned anti-Communist witnesses for the House Committee on Un-American Activities. Dismayed by the progress of Communism worldwide, Sheen doubly felt America's need for spiritual revival. He explained the drift of American culture as a movement into "spiritual vacuum." In his first television show, he asked a question that troubled many other observers in the 1950s: "Is life worth living, or is it dull and monotonous?" To Sheen, the answer was emphatically: Yes! Life has a purpose. He repeated this message through his nondoctrinal religiosity, his comforting moralisms, and his patriotism.

Another brilliant master of religious drama, and even more widely known than Bishop Sheen, was revivalist Billy Graham. Born in 1918 into a strict Scotch Presbyterian family, Graham experienced a deep religious conversion at the age of sixteen. Relinquishing thoughts of becoming a professional baseball player, he dedicated himself to spreading the news of his awakening. After Wheaton College in Illinois, he worked on a weekly radio religious broadcast, *Songs in the Night*. His growing reputation then led to an invitation to join Youth for Christ. By 1944, he achieved his first success as a revivalist preacher in Chicago. By 1948, Graham had put together a large organization for the production of revivalist meetings. In 1949, he completed a three-week crusade in Los Angeles, with song leader Cliff Barrows and soloist George Beverly Shea, converting thousands of men and women and attracting the attention of William Randolph Hearst. Spotlighted by Hearst's national newspaper chain, Graham became a celebrity by 1950, planning international crusades and meeting with important world leaders. Measured in numbers, Graham's success was remarkable. By 1955, his national headquarters in Minnesota had 125 employees and a budget of $2 million annually. His radio show, *The Hour of Decision*, beamed into 1,000 stations with 20 million regular listeners.

At the beginning of his career, regular Protestant churches often refused to welcome Graham, but as his success increased, so did his acceptance. Relying primarily upon public conversion, he preached a message of anti-Communism, antimaterialism, and faith in the capacity of conversion to overcome moral perils, like divorce and juvenile delinquency. He rejected reliance upon progress, political institutions, and social reform.

Graham's sermons reflected a keen awareness of contemporary social issues, and the format of his radio and television shows incorporated the cultural tastes of his audiences. His homey language suggested companionship and intimacy. For example, in his *Talks to Teenagers*, he depicted Christ as a sort of baseball star: "Christ is the Hero and Idol of my heart."

Attuned to some issues, Graham often remained silent on social questions, such as integration. Touting "rugged individualism," he criticized powerful labor leaders, strikes, and "socialistic" legislation. Consequently, he was a welcome guest at the Republican White House during the 1950s and a frequent golf partner of Vice-President Nixon. By the late 1960s, he had become something of a Protestant confessor to Nixon, who recounted that Graham, during long walks on the beach in 1968, had helped him decide to make a race for the presidency. Graham's social and cultural conservatism did not, however, become completely partisan. His first priority was souls, not votes. Deeply disturbed by the smug, complacent attitude of the 1950s, he sought to restoke the fires of revivalism.

☆   ☆   ☆

To the avowed right wing, the problem of complacency and conformity resulted from twenty years of Democratic liberalism, as well as religious lassitude. The ascendancy of William F. Buckley—witty, sarcastic pundit on the right—quickened right-wing thought in the 1950s. Buckley's new magazine, *The National Review*, begun in 1955, lent coherence and direction to conservative criticism of liberals. His first book, *God and Man at Yale*, appeared in 1951, a youthful but interesting attack on his alma mater. Offended by the liberal economics and social reformism espoused by his professors, Buckley lectured his readers on the merits of academic reorganization. He proposed to reconstruct Yale as the mirror of business corporation. In his model, the alumni who financed the school occupied the position of owners of the corporation; students were its consumers. This left the professor in the anomolous position of employee, hired to create a product—that is, to teach the ideals defined by the alumni. In Buckley's estimation, these ideals ought to be private enterprise, individualism, and religion. Existing academic freedom, which allowed professors to teach their own ideals, subverted this purpose. Therefore, teachers should be required to subscribe to established notions or should be invited to leave to find another university that espoused their principles.

This sacrifice of free speech to the free marketplace reappeared as the basis of a second book, published in 1954. In this tract, *McCarthy and His Enemies*, Buckley once again proclaimed his intolerance of ideas that he felt were generally despised. Defending McCarthy, Buckley could not agree that American Communists had the right to civil liberties.

Like many conservative intellectuals of the day, Buckley devoted his efforts primarily to right-wing journalism, not serious political organizing. Nonetheless, important right-wing political action groups flourished in the 1950s and 1960s, and toward the middle of the 1960s, they made serious inroads into the Republican party. Several of these organizations relied heavily upon radio broadcasting, such as the Twentieth-Century Reformation Hour of Reverend Carl McIntire and the Christian Crusade of Reverend Billy James Hargis. Some, such as the White Citizens councils, stood strongest in the South, appearing principally to oppose integration. Others, such as the Minute Men, a clandestine paramilitary group much discussed in the press in 1966, were organized to prevent a leftist takeover believed brewing in Washington. Although these groups issued similar political jeremiads, denouncing moral degeneration and conjuring images of a Communist-liberal conspiracy in government, they rarely cooperated with each other. Well financed by conservative benefactors, most remained obscure, regionally contained, or peripheral to American politics.

The John Birch Society proved an exception to this general rule of political impotence. The Birch Society successfully defined a national program and established outposts in every section of the country. At its height in the mid-1960s, it comprised perhaps 4,000 semisecret chapters and almost 100,000 members. Beyond this, its influence extended into police forces, school boards, state and national legislatures, and into the Republican party. More than any other group, it represented a broadly based, right-wing rejection of liberalism. To Robert Welch, its founder, the liberal vital center had betrayed American principles, and he organized a political movement to destroy it.

For men like Robert Welch, the early 1950s seemed an age of the Apocalypse. Eisenhower's defeat of Taft in 1952 and the demise of McCarthy in 1954 shattered their confidence in the Republican party. The party, they felt, had succumbed to the enticements of government planning and high taxes. Rejuvenation could only come from the outside. Thus, Eisenhower's modern Republicanism played the role of catalyst in the creation of the John Birch Society. Its attacks on the President came from Welch's belief that Eisenhower had sold out individualism and militant Christianity for a hollow crown of political office.

Welch's career up to the official founding of the Birch Society in 1958 prefigured his later controversial activities. Raised as a fundamentalist Baptist, Welch was something of a child prodigy, enrolling at the University of North Carolina at the age of twelve.

After graduation, he went to Harvard Law School. After a confrontation with Harvard Professor Felix Frankfurter (later a Supreme Court justice), he quit law school in 1921 for a career in candy-making. Success in this field eluded him until the mid-1930s, but by the early 1940s, Welch was a wealthy and widely known business executive. Named "Candy Man of the Year" in 1947, he served two terms as chairman of the National Association of Manufacturers' Advisory Committee. In 1950, he ran unsuccessfully for the Republican nomination as Massachusetts' lieutenant governor.

During World War II, Welch began his public crusade against collectivism and political democracy. His electoral defeat in 1950 derailed his strategy, but Eisenhower's 1952 landslide confirmed a new direction in his thinking. When he discovered the controversial career and death of the missionary John Birch (after whom he named his political organization), he knew what he wanted to do; he now had a cause.

John Birch had been a Baptist missionary in Asia during World War II and worked closely with American forces operating in China. When the war ended and the Chinese civil war flared up, Birch was caught in a skirmish and killed by Communist troops on August 25, 1945. The U.S. War Department reported the death. After closely examining the facts, Welch concluded that Washington had hushed up the incident for its own dark purposes. To explain why this was so, Welch plunged into a sea of conspiracies, emerging with a theory that Communists and their handpicked stooge, Harry Truman, dominated Washington. To Welch, the "mysterious" death of John Birch revealed the tragic infiltration of America by Communist agents. They had entered, camouflaged by a bankrupt liberal tradition that stretched back into nineteenth-century English philosophy. Only militant Christianity, joined to anticollectivism, he wrote, could save America and generate a "spiritual resistance."

To spread the word, Welch began his periodical, *One Man's Opinion*, in 1956, changing the title to *American Opinion* in February 1958. That shift marked the formal beginning of the John Birch Society, organized during a marathon meeting at the home of an Indianapolis friend. By 1960, the secret organization had spread nationwide, undertaking an "Impeach Earl Warren" campaign because of the Chief Justice's role in civil rights and First Amendment decisions. In 1960, the society also initiated a campaign to control local PTAs and, in 1963, enjoined its members to organize support for local police forces. Strongest in California, Arizona, and suburban areas of the industrial East, the society received bad press and publicity and was often subjected to hostile investigation.

Nevertheless, in 1964, the Birch Society's influence in the Republican party was so strong that presidential candidate Barry Goldwater would not repudiate its support. In 1965, after the disastrous results of the November election, leading conservatives in the party denounced Welch. In October of the same year, William Buckley attacked Welch in the pages of the *National Review*. Public disapproval of Welch and his organization rose to a crescendo in 1966, after leading society members made remarks interpreted to be anti-Semitic. Thereafter, Welch's conspiratorial interpretation of politics, once convincing to thousands of Americans, became confused and hesitant, and the movement began to crumble. But it left a legacy that resurfaced in American politics a decade later.

Attacks on liberalism by conservatives generated considerable energy and attention in the 1950s, but their wrath struck especially at the Supreme Court. Under Chief Justice Earl Warren, appointed in 1953, the Court transformed the procedures of democracy and redefined citizenship in ways that neither Congress nor the President dared to undertake. Of all the institutions of government, the Court was the most vital in transforming American society—and the most controversial. Accused of legislating where it should only have adjudicated, the Chief Justice and the majority that voted with him stepped actively into the major social issues of the day. It is no accident that by the early 1960s, Earl Warren had become the leading enemy of conservatives.

Nothing in Earl Warren's early career suggested this aggressive judicial liberalism. Born in 1891, the son of an upwardly mobile railroad worker, he attended the University of California. Attorney General and then Governor of California, he was a large, fair-haired, stolid, but kindly-appearing man. Not known for liberal ideas, on the Court he became the leader of one of the most activist phases in the institution's history.

The Warren Court's notoriety rested on decisions in four areas: civil rights and school integration, legislative reapportionment, criminal justice procedures, and protection and extension of the rights of free speech. In *Brown* v. *Board of Education* (1954), the

Justice Earl Warren.   *(Historical Pictures Service, Chicago, Illinois)*

Court rejected the legal and moral justification of segregation. According to Warren, the 1962 decision *Baker* v. *Carr* was the most important in his tenure. Affirming the doctrine "one person, one vote," the Court redefined the nature of legislative representation. In *Miranda* v. *Arizona* (1966), the Court closely defined the rights of arrested persons and circumscribed the power of police. In the category of free speech, the Warren Court generally struck down obscenity laws, banned Bible reading in public schools, and extended legal rights of political dissidents.

☆   ☆   ☆

The most important challenge to the vitality of the American political center came from the civil rights movement. Although the movement allied itself to liberalism frequently during the 1950s and 1960s and black voters most often cast their ballots for Democratic candidates, the relationship remained a coalition rather than an agreement on principles. The demands of black Americans for social justice constantly pushed against the confines of liberal politics. Liberals supported many of these demands, but not all of them, and with differing degrees of fervor and urgency. The result was an uneasy truce between principle and party.

The roots of the civil rights movement lay deep in twentieth-century struggles for equality: in the legal activism of the NAACP, in the skillful pressure on F.D.R. exerted by A. Philip Randolph for job equality during World War II, in the growing numbers of black voters in northern cities, in the political commitments of the Democratic party, and in the emerging sophistication of black leaders. Influenced by anticolonial revolutions in the Third World, touched by the same forces awakening many white Americans, black leaders also drew from a deep well of Christian consciousness. The moral and political vitality of this movement came also from the strange position of American blacks: once the objects of scorn, in the 1950s and 1960s, they became the subjects of conscience.

If the civil rights movement of the 1950s had a pivotal point, it was the desegregation decision of the Supreme Court in 1954. The civil rights movement, however, had to assume the initiative in enforcing the rights of black citizens, because Congress and the executive branch procrastinated. The Court ordered desegregation, but black Americans had to seize their rights through confrontation with local, state, and even national officials.

At the same time as it demanded enforcement of existing laws, the civil rights movement pushed ahead of the political center with demonstrations, passive resistance, and even violence to achieve more than simple integration. Living at the edge of politics, the civil rights movement courted liberals and often won their support. At the same time, its own priorities sometimes alienated this support. Ultimately, this precarious existence split the black movement into competing groups, reflecting the deeper divisions, aims, and generations that constituted the black community itself.

Undoubtedly, the central figure of the civil rights movement was Martin Luther King, Jr. Born in January 1929, King grew up in a family deeply anchored in the traditions of Southern fundamentalism. A handsome, bright youngster, who fancied himself something of a ladies' man, King attended Atlanta's Morehouse College. Switching from medicine to sociology and finally to the ministry in his senior year, he graduated in June 1948. Next, he went to Crozer Theological Seminary, in Pennsylvania. There, he discovered the religious and philosophical writings that influenced the remainder of his life: theologians Reinhold Niebuhr and Walter Rauschenbusch and the Indian pacifist Mahatma Gandhi. In fundamental ways, these thinkers contradicted each other, but King, choosing portions of each, created a tough-minded passive resistance strategy that became the mark of the early civil rights struggle. Finishing his studies with a Ph.D. in philosophy at Boston University, he married a young civil rights activist, Coretta Scott, in 1953 and took up the pastorate at Dexter Avenue Baptist Church in Montgomery, Alabama, the following year.

Commanding complex philosophic concepts, but drawing out a rich skein of imagery from slave songs and Biblical stories, King became a widely known preacher in a city where such a position connoted power in the black community. Events quickly proved this point. On December 1, 1955, Rosa Parks entered a Montgomery city bus but refused to move to the rear seats set aside for blacks. Following her arrest, Montgomery black citizens began a protest boycott of the bus system. Community leaders brought King into the leadership of the movement, and he quickly assumed an important role. Emerging as the prime mover of this protracted struggle, King gained international attention and praise for his nonviolent tactics. Already strong in his belief that pacifist means could topple the empire of Jim Crow, he was doubly receptive to the influence of pacifists Bayard Rustin and A. J. Muste, of

Martin Luther King, Jr.   *(UPI)*

the Fellowship of Reconciliation, who visited him in Montgomery during the struggle.

After a hard-fought agreement with Montgomery's white business leaders desegregating the city, King received invitations to visit Ghana in 1956 and India in 1959. With other black ministers in 1958, he organized the Southern Christian Leadership Conference (SCLC), the organization that served as an umbrella for his civil rights activities until his death in 1968.

In the first years of the Kennedy administration, the civil rights movement greatly enlarged its demands. Southern segregation flourished, despite the desegregation decision and the Civil Rights Act of 1957. Waiting rooms, transportation facilities, rest rooms, fitting rooms, drinking fountains, hotels, schools, restaurants, clubs, universities, political organizations, voting regulations, and jobs were divided by the accident of birth and skin color. King's group, now joined by the Student Nonviolent Coordinating Committee (SNCC) and the Congress for Racial Equality, demanded a redress of the segregationist imbalance.

Very quickly, King and other leaders discovered that Kennedy's campaign promises of 1960 had to be extracted, painfully, from the new administration. Certainly friendlier to the cause of civil rights than Eisenhower had been, Kennedy avoided new legislation. During 1961 and 1962, civil rights leaders sought the President's moral support. After the integration marches and freedom rides in Albany, Georgia, and Birmingham, Alabama, dragged out into violent and brutal police attacks on pacifist demonstrators, the President intervened. Even in August 1963, however, Kennedy could not be persuaded to address the March on Washington organized by King and other black leaders. With broad support from white religious figures, liberals, and labor leaders (George Meany of the AF of L-CIO, however, was conspicuously absent), the march was the high point of King's career. His great address, coming at the end of the day, was an unforgettable and moving sermon on the political rights and duties of the nation. For his efforts, he received the Nobel Peace Prize in 1964.

Growing criticism of King inside the black movement tarnished the glory and accomplishment of such moments. Faulted for conservatism and an overbearing attitude, he was sometimes referred to as "De Lawd" by some of the younger SNCC members. Yet, in 1964, King had begun to push harder for economic demands. As the black movement spread northwest and began to soak up the bitter and violent frustrations of big-city ghettos, King found himself the chief spokesman for a movement that divided deeply over demands, needs, and traditions. Regardless of public appearances, President Johnson distrusted King, and in 1964, FBI chief J. Edgar Hoover, who had long counted King a subversive, blurted out that the black leader was the "most notorious liar in the country."

These troubles mounted in the last years of King's life. The black movement split along generational and tactical lines. King's criticism of the war in Vietnam cut him off from influence over the administration after 1966. More important, the urban riots, beginning in 1964, demonstrated that civil rights agitation could not satisfy many black Americans. An end to second-class citizenship demanded a deep revision of priorities that even the most liberal politicians scarcely considered, and never discussed, in public. Himself a victim of the bitter backlash against civil rights in 1968, King had long since ceased to preside over a movement that knew what it wanted or where it was headed. It had accomplished much under his leadership, but the next steps were for others to take.

King's tragic assassination in 1968 left the civil rights movement in disarray and America's large cities smoldering with fires of revenge. It removed the most vital political figure of the era. But splits in the movement had long been apparent. Some of these represented old divisions, extending back to the controversy over the Marcus Garvey movement during World War I. Extolling the virtues of blackness—in culture and physical appearance—Garvey devoted considerable organizing skills to the project of a reverse migration to Africa. When his venture failed in the early 1920s, he left millions of black Americans, touched by his promises of a new future, without leadership. But the idea of a separate black nation did not disappear.

Revived again briefly during the 1930s, black separatism grew rapidly in the late 1950s and early 1960s. Inspired by Malcolm X, one of the leaders of Elijah Muhammad's Nation of Islam, thousands of followers joined the movement. In the guise of Islam, this philosophy of self-regeneration and self-help appealed particularly to lower-class, urban blacks who rejected integration because it offered no solution to their problems of grinding poverty, violence, crime, drug addiction, and alcoholism. An entirely black, separatist nation—inside America—seemed to offer hope for the future, and Malcolm X, who had been a drug addict and a convict himself, painted these dreams in a moving fashion.

Partly because of political differences and partly because he threatened the hold of other leaders in the movement, Malcolm X was expelled from the Nation of Islam in 1963. During the next year, he traveled widely in Africa and on speaking tours to college campuses. Early in 1965, he established the Organization of Afro-American Unity, designed to promote a united front of black organizations. Although still committed to black separatism, in the last months of his life, Malcolm X had begun to speak more generously about working with white radical groups or other black civil rights organizations. Before anything could come of this, however, he was struck down by assassins in February 1965.

The Student Nonviolent Coordinating Committee, begun as a pacifist organization, absorbed some of the black nationalist ideas articulated by Malcolm X. Under the leadership of Stokely Carmichael, who popularized the slogan "Black Power" as a rallying cry in 1966, SNCC expelled its white membership. Moving from an integrationist organization with religious orientation, SNCC evolved into a group devoted to community organization and independent political action. Members linked American struggles to Third World revolutions against European colonial powers. As the Vietnam War intensified, groups such as SNCC tried to establish ties with Third World revolutionaries.

From this position, it was a small step toward the founding of the Black Panther Party, in 1966, by Huey P. Newton and Bobby Seale. Proposing self-defense against attacks by white police or vigilante groups, the Panthers rejected Islam and the African heritage in favor of revolutionary nationalism. Opposed to cultural exclusiveness and favoring revolutionary socialism, the Panthers, by 1969, expressed willingness to ally themselves (if hesitantly and temporarily) to white radical groups. Never a large movement, the Panthers suffered serious decline after hostile press coverage, police infiltration and confrontation, and meager results from their political alliances.

The variegation of the black movement—Southern, Northern, Christian, Islamic, integrationist, separatist, cultural nationalist, and cultural integrationist—reflected the diverse aspirations of the very complex black experience in modern America. But all of these movements, in one way or another, challenged the integrity of American culture. They provided energy and example to other protest movements. More important, however, they burst through the liberal political center to challenge its very premises.

One federal official, J. Edgar Hoover, chief of the FBI, believed it his special calling to oppose the activities of these groups. As head of a national police force, Hoover only minimally acted to enforce civil rights and instead devoted a good measure of his bureau's energies toward collecting dossiers on Martin Luther King, Jr., and other black leaders and political radicals. Hoover, the self-appointed guardian of American liberties and morals (his high school yearbook referred to him as a "gentleman of dauntless courage and stainless honor") lived and died for the federal bureaucracy.

Living alone with his mother until her death, he never married, devoting himself entirely to what Chief Justice of the Supreme Court Warren Burger called "the American dream of patriotism." For Hoover, this dream depended upon a mastery of public relations and the survival skills of a longtime bureaucrat. Whether they wished to or not, American presidents, from Roosevelt on, dared not replace him. Issuing periodic denunciations of Communism, crime, and moral decay, Hoover represented a strong force at the heart of government, opposing civil rights and anti-Vietnam War activists until his death in 1972.

    ☆   ☆   ☆

To many Americans, forces clamoring for change represented a chance to revitalize culture, to move beyond the limitations of political compromise. What Hoover denounced as lurid conspiracy, they saw as fulfilling old promises. For them, black self-consciousness and civil rights activism promised a regeneration that would carry the nation beyond liberalism.

The Beat writers of the 1950s were one such group that drew upon the energy of the turbulent black urban community. They nourished their poetry and prose with sympathy for America's underclasses: the poor, exploited, and down-and-out. There was precedent for this identification. In the poetry and prose of the twentieth-century American writers, the immigrant, the working man or woman, the tenant farmer, have appeared as symbols for humanity, as sparks of energy and authentic experience in a muddle of middle-class culture. The Beat poets and writers saw black culture as the same symbolic force. Cohering around several New York writers, especially William Burroughs, Jack Kerouac, and

Allen Ginsberg, this literary movement celebrated jazz, drugs, and the street life of urban ghettos. Its uniform of a T-shirt and Levi's proclaimed its authenticity. Its characteristic style, typified in the novels of Kerouac, sought spontaneity that resembled jazz improvisation in prose. Poet Allen Ginsberg used the black experience as a symbol for his own generation. As he wrote in his famous poem, "Howl," published in 1956:

> I saw the best minds of my generation
>   starving hysterical naked
> dragging themselves through the negro streets
>   at dawn looking for an angry fix,
> angel headed hipsters burning for the ancient
>   heavenly connection[1]

The public first noticed the Beat writers, in 1952, in an article written for *The New York Times Magazine*. By 1957, when *Life* magazine and other journals featured photo essays on Kerouac and his friends, the movement became something of a fad. Literary critics greeted the publication of "Howl" and Kerouac's novel *On the Road* (1957) with derisive reviews, but the books sold widely. In fact, the movement suffered transformation into popular culture in the guise of the "beatnik" movement, a term coined from "Sputnik" and expressing what one journalist described as its unearthly, far-out qualities. By the late 1950s and 1960s, scores of low-budget films and TV dramas featured beatnik characters—usually violent, unkempt petty criminals or dope addicts.

More authentic versions colored the acting of Marlon Brando and, especially, James Dean and Sal Mineo, whose search for authenticity projected beyond the particular roles they played. Unlike other Hollywood stars, with lives punctuated by publicity stunts and marriages arranged in studio casting, these new stars seemed to be outsiders, much like the roles in their films.

Unlike public caricatures of them, the Beats attempted serious literary innovation. Built upon such traditional American poets as Walt Whitman and heavily influenced by a variety of Eastern religions and modern psychologists (Wilhelm Reich, etc.), they celebrated the immediate impulse, the instanteous life experience. Like so many other groups in the early 1950s, their celebrations had strong religious overtones. When called to define his movement, Kerouac proclaimed: "The Beat Generation is basically a

religious generation. Beat means beatitude, not beat up. You *feel*
this. You feel it in a beat, in jazz—real cool jazz or a good gutty
rock number." Mixing drugs, music, and Eastern religion; cele-
brating outsiders and the affinity for the black experience; aiming at
self-liberation, the Beats laid the foundation for the counterculture
of the late 1960s. They directly influenced Bob Dylan and the
Rolling Stones and lent their name to the most famous group of
that later era, the Beatles. Kerouac's reference to a generation
of writers contained an important clue to the appeal of the Beat
movement for the 1960s. What society interpreted as vulgarity in
music, delinquency in young people, or mindless spontaneity during the 1950s was transformed by a very complex process into
counterculture, radicalism, and liberation in the 1960s.

☆　　　　　　　　☆　　　　　　　　☆

The search for authenticity and vitality that infected literature in
the late 1950s and early 1960s also disturbed American theology.
Two transformations in American Protestantism, and to a lesser
extent in Catholicism, coalesced to translate generational politics
into religious experience. The first of these was the "God is Dead"
movement of the early 1960s; the second was the situation ethics
developed to justify the new, looser morality of the decade.

Taking the slogan, "God is dead," from the proclamation of German philosopher Friedrich Nietzsche, several Protestant theologians argued that the God worshipped by early Christians had
disappeared from modern worship; in their words, Christianity
had become a social religion, with churches acting as businesses to
accumulate wealth, buildings, and prestige. For William Hamilton, one of the leading figures of the movement, revived Christianity should affect "life-styles" and change behavior. The center of
Christianity, he wrote, was Christology, or the consent of God to
suffer as humans suffered. God was dead because modern society
denied the essence of human experience, its sin and suffering.

A second important idea to challenge theology in the early 1960s
was the new morality. In part inspired by Pope John XXIII's example—his efforts to update church doctrine and strike a middle position in the Cold War—and by the writings of Protestant theologians,
the new morality rejected tradition and authority in favor of individual conscience. As John Fletcher wrote in his book *Situation
Ethics*, in 1966, the commandments of conscience far outweighed
legalistic biblical injunctions: "Always do the most loving thing in
every situation," he advised.

This advice fit the changing behavior of the day. Franker public discussion of sex, relaxation of media and film censorship, the widespread adoption of contraceptives indicated different attitudes toward human relationships. In 1961, the National Council of Churches affirmed the right of women to employ a wide variety of birth-control measures, including oral contraceptive pills and intrauterine devices. Despite the injunction of the Catholic Church, even a majority of Catholic women used contraceptives by 1965. By 1970, 65 percent of white women and 60 percent of black women regularly employed contraceptives (primarily the pill or the IUD).

By emphasizing personal and authentic religion outside institutions and traditions, the new religious morality joined hands with forces in the churches that focused on the war in Vietnam. The intense commitment of many nuns, priests, and ministers to ending the war drew some of them out of organized churches and into radical groups. The conservatism of the Catholic hierarchy in some cities, plus Pope Paul's encyclical *Humanae Vitae* in 1968, reaffirming the Church's absolute opposition to birth-control devices, raised a storm of protests. When the National Association for Pastoral Renewal lobbied to change the celibacy rules of the Church, the papacy refused to bend. To many Catholics and Protestants alike, the path to authentic religion led out of the churches and into a more political, private, and self-satisfying experience. Daniel and Philip Berrigan made the most famous odyssey away from the traditions of the Church and toward a self-authenticating experience. They moved from the traditional priesthood to join the New Left in protesting the war in Vietnam, ending finally in Danbury Federal Prison—for destroying Selective Service records on May 17, 1968, at Catonsville, Maryland. Deeply influenced by the worker-priest tradition in European Catholicism and by experience in organizing the American poor, the Berrigans confronted ecclesiastical authority and state power as they demonstrated for civil rights and protested against the war in Vietnam. In 1964, they organized the Catholic Peace Fellowship, opposing escalation of the conflict. Working inside the Church, the Berrigans helped focus opposition to the war for the next three years. Their step into direct action in 1968 flowed naturally from their beliefs, or as Daniel said, it was something "I believe Christian and Gandhian ethics demand." To exist apart from the struggle would betray its meaning.

The Berrigans expressed in religious terms something very close to the intense idealism and political fastidiousness that distinguished the New Left. This complicated political movement also originated as a protest against the politics of compromise and the ideology of the liberal center. It drew sustenance from the black movement, from the quickening of cultural and religious dissent, and from the vast changes inherent in the demographic shift of the early 1960s. This demographic change separated the 1950s and 1960s and their dominant attitudes like a fault line. During the 1950s, the population gravity of the country edged toward the thirty-five- to forty-year-old age group, reflecting the high birth rate immediately after World War I. By the early 1960s, however, the center shifted down abruptly to the seventeen-year-old age group, because of the post–World War II baby boom. As the population became younger, attitudes of large numbers of Americans, then reaching maturity, began to prevail. Born into a wholly different world of relative peace and prosperity, largely suburban or urban in origin, and attending universities in large numbers, this group felt little in common with its elders. Authenticity was in some sense, then, a function of generational conflict.

Writer Paul Goodman argued this very point in his widely read *Growing Up Absurd* (1960). Hostile to organized society, he warned that young Americans were not permitted to grow up. Society had "missed" necessary revolutions. As a result, young people donned the garb of antagonistic, absurd roles; they became Beats or delinquents.

As so many other movements of the day, the New Left proclaimed the insufficiency of politics alone to transform critical domestic and international problems. During the 1960s, the New Left became a student movement housed primarily in the largest and most prestigious American universities. Here, middle-class students, predominantly studying liberal arts subjects, joined organizations like Students for a Democratic Society (SDS) and demonstrated for civil rights and against the war in Vietnam. By the late 1960s, these demonstrations intensified into an assault on the university structure itself, and the ideology of the movement deepened into a call for revolutionary socialism.

Students first roused themselves to political protest in the late 1950s. They joined the Student Peace Union, founded in 1959, at the University of Chicago, and participated in scattered campus demonstrations against compulsory ROTC training, the activities of the House Committee on Un-American Activities, and the loyalty-

Street theater, such as this performance in front of the Selective Service headquarters in Washington, became a part of every major protest march against the war in Vietnam. Television and the media in general tended to focus on these dramatizations. (Courtesy, Ted Green)

oath provisions of the National Defense Education Act. Other roots of dissatisfaction were nourished by the growing counterculture of the late 1950s, whose heroes—like James Dean and Jack Kerouac—conveyed the alienation, anger, and desire for authenticity that many young people felt, growing up in the suburbs, conscious of the conformity of their environment.

Another trail to the New Left passed through older radical movements. During the 1930s and early 1940s, many Americans had joined or sympathized with the Communist or Socialist parties or one of the smaller left splinter groups, and many more were enthusiastic partisans of the experimental liberalism of the New Deal. Their children were now of college age, and this younger generation had an ambiguous attitude toward their parents; intrigued by the left-wing politics of the previous era, they also judged their parents as backsliders and compromisers.

Intellectually, many sources fertilized the new radical movement, but none so copiously in the late 1950s as the works of sociologist C. Wright Mills and historian William Appleman Williams. Mills, a professor at Columbia University, in a series of widely noted writings, blasted the social science professions for their lack of theory and their reliance upon the cold tools of mathematics and precise measurement to analyze large, complex problems of the social order. He persistently asked: Who ruled America and how? The answer he gave rejected the pluralist hypothesis of 1950s liberalism. The supposed competing forces of government, labor, and business, he wrote in 1956, in *The Power Elite*, actually constituted a small group of powerful and wealthy leaders, sharing the same ideology and determination to rule. Their vision of the world amounted to "crack-pot" realism—the logical policies that flowed from false and misleading assumptions. As someone who sought to explain "the moral uneasiness of our time," Mills had begun a serious reevaluation of Marxist writings toward the end of his life. Although premature death, in 1962, cut short any further movement in this direction, his intellectual life marked off an exemplary path to many of the young radicals who read his works.

William A. Williams, of the University of Wisconsin, even more deeply sounded the moral and idealist frustration of the new radicals. In his *Tragedy of American Diplomacy* (1959), the historian explored a paradox that he and later radicals of the 1960s found between the noble aspirations of American principles and the sordid reality of interventions and compromises dictated by the Cold

War. His theory of American foreign policy contrasted moral possibilities with the tragedy of reality in a way that helped shape later criticism of the war in Vietnam. Two grand ideals, humanitarian impulses and the desire to spread self-determination, were everywhere undercut by the demands of an economy that overproduced and underconsumed. Thus, the inequalities of American society projected outward onto the world the guise of imperialism. Foreign adventurism, to Williams, signaled weakness, not strength.

In the context of these intellectual stirrings, students reacted to the Cuban Revolution of 1959, the election of John Kennedy, and the increased vigor of the civil rights movement. Aroused and yet distressed by Kennedy's idealism, the New Left, when it formed, did so by rejecting its liberal parentage. In 1962, when Tom Hayden, editor of the student newspaper at the University of Michigan, formulated a position paper for a new organization to be called the Students for a Democratic Society, he evoked a mood of betrayed puzzlement. The "Port Huron Statement" he helped to write reflected the moral dilemma that Williams had depicted. American young people were "uncomfortable" in their inherited world. Shocked out of complacency by black activism and the possibilities of nuclear terror, they had begun to ask why society was unjust and overarmed. Dismissing liberals as apologists for the status quo, Hayden, echoing Mills' words, denounced the ruling elites who had created such a system. He exhorted students to restore a democratic society in America.

The initial phase of student activism in the early 1960s disrupted and then paralyzed the University of California at Berkeley. Within a few miles of San Francisco, the campus occupied a cardinal point on the compass of political radicalism and counterculture developing in the Bay area during the period. In part, the Free Speech Movement sprang from the highest standards and liberality of the campus. University President Clark Kerr, a noted sociologist with expertise in labor relations, had helped establish the national preeminence of the university. In 1959, he broadened his liberal reputation by securing an end to preemployment loyalty oaths, previously required of all professors. But Kerr's ambitions for the university raised serious questions about the uses of knowledge. Speaking shortly before the crisis of 1964, he defined his efforts to transform Berkeley into a knowledge factory. The aim of the university, he claimed, should be to enhance national purpose. Knowledge created by professors should contribute to national economic growth, and professors should lend their services to industry and government. As elite institutions with democratic trappings, "cities of the intellect," universities had become "the port of entry" into the professions. Stepchildren of "middle-class pluralism," these institutions established permanent links to the burgeoning knowledge industry.

Kerr's optimism was well founded. In the flush, post-Sputnik era, federal grants to university departments in the sciences, social sciences, and medicine flowed lavishly. Total expenditures for higher education during the 1960s in the United States rose from $6.7 billion to $24.7 billion, multiplying over 3.5 times. Scientists and engineers employed by universities increased from 30,000 to about 80,000. And, enrollments in public universities jumped from about 2 million to over 5 million in 1970.

Much of the funding granted to universities in the 1960s was earmarked for defense industry or defense policy research. Smaller amounts went for much more controversial purposes. Secret funds given to Michigan State helped provide South Vietnam with technical and political assistance. Other government money, laundered

Federal Funding for Universities from Federal Government for Research and Development

Date	Directly to Universities ($ millions)	To Federally Funded Centers Run by Universities ($ millions)
1954	160	141
1956	213	194
1958	254	293
1960	405	360
1962	613	470
1964	916	629
1966	1,262	630
1968	1,572	719
1970	1,648	737

Source: Historical Statistics of the United States, *Bicentennial Edition,* Vol. II, p. 965.

through bogus foundations, financed the National Student Association, founded in the late 1940s. Policymakers aided student organizations because they wanted an anti-Communist group to speak for American students.

Trouble at Berkeley began in the fall of 1964. During the summer, a number of students had participated in the Mississippi Freedom Project to register black voters. It had been a brutal experience—3 persons killed, 35 shootings, 1,000 arrests, 30 houses burned, and only 1,200 black voters registered. Participants returned to campus frustrated and angry. When students picketed in an area of the university traditionally designated for soapbox speeches and political recruitment, administrators changed the rules. No one could solicit funds or members on Bancroft Way. As students returned to fall classes, they openly defied the ruling; the university then called in the police. Tempers flared, administrators stiffened regulations, and students organized. Led by philosophy student Mario Savio, their Free Speech Movement attracted thousands of members and eventually forced the university to rescind its limitations on advocacy.

Once formed, part of this movement edged off into the counterculture, beginning a campaign to use salacious words in public. This "Dirty Speech Movement" reflected the apolitical interests of the cultural revolution springing up in San Francisco. The remainder of the movement, however, turned its attention to the stepped-up war in Vietnam. It was joined by a chorus of protests from major colleges and universities throughout the country.

Although students warred against university administrators at Berkeley, the new radical left generally felt comfortable in its academic environment at first. During the spring of 1965, this affirmation increased with the "teach-ins" held at Michigan, the University of Wisconsin, and scores of other colleges, culminating in a national teach-in held in Washington in June. Under this format, university professors addressed students and each other, declaring their opposition to the war and their serious quarrels with American society. Publicity given to this organized doubt did much to activate student radicals, although it had no immediate effect on Johnson's policy of escalation. Furthermore, it convinced many students that American universities were enclaves of liberalism and intelligence in a world of strife and misinformation.

Civil rights activism conscripted many of the new radical students, but the real war became Vietnam. After 1965, many of

them began to join SDS chapters, to read Marxist literature—
particularly the neo-Marxist writings of philosopher Herbert Mar-
cuse—to subscribe to and edit underground newspapers—like
New Left Notes and *Radical America*—and to join demonstrations
against the war—such as the large campus protests in the fall of
1965. As the news of American actions in Vietnam filtered back
into the United States, the nightly TV news in dormitory lounges
all over the country became the pretext for intense and personal
debate. Borrowing language from the black movement and the
cultural underground and ideas from radical theoretical writings—
haunted by conspiracy theories that hovered over the indecisive
and contradictory Warren Committee Report of the Kennedy
assassination—the New Left created a culture of student radicalism that dominated many American campuses through the early
1970s.

This new tone of intellectual dissent on campus was matched by
a curious dependence upon the war for the generation of styles
and behavior. As has sometimes been the case with popular movements, protesters adopted the styles and even the dress of their
opponents. In the middle 1960s, students increasingly began to
wear cast-off military clothing in mockery of the real army. Many
were attracted to the guerrilla warfare doctrines outlined by Mao
Tse-tung and Cuban revolutionary Che Guevara. Most important,
some students accepted violence as a legitimate form of political protest. Thus, the protest movement at home came to be a
caricature of the war abroad.

By 1967, SDS had become a large organization whose greatest
problems reflected its successes. Attractiveness to students and loose
membership requirements brought it over 100,000 members by
1968. But this made it a haven for political recruiters from established leftist sects. The most important of these, Progressive
Labor, following an Americanized version of Maoism, made key
inroads into the organization in 1968. Success also frustrated SDS.
Able to organize large numbers for demonstrations in the spring
mobilization of 1967, when three or four hundred thousand people
demonstrated against the war, the movement could not stop the
war. Moreover, the university appeared less a haven than before,
as radical journalists uncovered secret defense projects on campuses and watched administrators protect recruiters for defense
contractors, like Dow Chemical (principal manufacturer of
napalm), visiting campuses in search of future employees. Kerr's
multiversity, it appeared, existed everywhere.

Pent-up anger and frustration engulfed Columbia University in 1968. Two issues were at stake: the university's plan to construct a gymnasium in an adjacent park, thus taking land away from one of Harlem's few green spaces, and the deep involvement of the school in defense-related research. Borrowing civil rights tactics, the demonstrators occupied several buildings, to be removed finally forcibly by New York City police. Similar takeovers of university buildings occurred at other major universities.

Even this tactic was only a temporary stage in the evolving movement. By the late 1960s, students had resorted to firebombings and "trashing" of university buildings or businesses in university towns. Thus, the conflagration that burned the black ghettos in the late 1960s spread into middle-class university sanctuaries. In some ways, the flash point was the same: deep moral outrage, which politics could not contain. In the process, students had sullied their own sanctuaries. Whatever legitimate grievances they had and however much they speeded up much needed academic reforms, students failed ultimately to enlist the universities in their cause, and they became isolated from this potential constituency. In doing so, they lost the moral leadership of the antiwar movement. They raised the cost of pursuing the war, but made its termination into a political issue of ending civil turmoil at home.

At this turning point, the movement halted as if to reexamine the many roots that had entwined in its creation. In the moment of its greatest success, the New Left split into a variety of groups. Some members merely dropped out. Others wandered into religious sects. A few became confirmed revolutionaries, such as the Weathermen of 1969. Women, particularly those who had consciously submerged their own agenda of demands for transforming America, split off into the separate and growing women's movement. Some simply outgrew the movement or accepted America's scaled-down physical presence in Vietnam after 1969. But, perhaps the strongest lure was the counterculture, a vast and variegated life-style revolution that affected millions of Americans in the late 1960s and early 1970s.

☆   ☆   ☆

The counterculture, avowed its leading advocates, represented a revolutionary force for change, encompassing but moving beyond the New Left. Hailing Beat culture, the drug life of Haight-Ashbury in San Francisco, and the musical genius of late 1960s

This engraving and photograph illustrate the common use of images of pollution and waste to symbolize the destructive aspects of American civilization during the 1960s and early 1970s.

"Aftermath," by Donald Sexauer. Vietnam, 1971.   (U.S. Army Photograph, Army Art Collection)

Smoke rises from Redding, California, city dump, December 13, 1965.
(Environmental Protection Agency)

rock and roll, counterculturists also borrowed extensively from old and respectable American protest traditions. They advocated health foods, rural living, communal family styles, spiritual perfectionism, and the interchangeability of sexual roles that typified some of the most famous experimental and religious communities of the 1830s and 1840s revival. Joined to a vaguely leftist orientation, the counterculture promised a powerful amalgam in reversing the contemporary evolution of American culture. Hostile to technological culture, bureaucracy, careers, and middle-class lifestyles, the counterculture was, ironically, as much the child of television and the electronic media as it was the child of rural innocence, Eastern mysticism, drugs, or the generation gap.

The admixture of these themes formed the foundation for Charles Reich's enormously successful *The Greening of America*, published in 1970. Going back to the roots of dissatisfaction with vital center politics, the Yale law professor portrayed established American culture as the enemy of the human spirit. Responsible for the war in Vietnam, it had pressed logic, reason, and science to the point of madness. In opposition, a growing revolutionary culture had emerged, devised by a young generation raised in the permissive environment of the postwar years. The young militants of the new consciousness, he claimed, would inherit the earth; America would change dramatically when it accepted their nonviolent, loving culture. The trumpet blast of the new consciousness would crumble the walls of the corporate state.

Aggressively apolitical, Reich reflected a flame that burned brightly, but extinguished itself in the 1970s. The counterculture burned for a moment with the incandescence of a religious awakening. Reich heightened its intensity by articulating its moral premises. His work reveals the degree to which the new consciousness was an old moralism smoldering deeply in American tradition. The "greening" of the nation that he predicted did not occur. The structure of society and the economy did not shift. Instead, American culture absorbed the counterculture like an estranged but familiar child. Rather than the announcement of something new, Reich's book delivered a postscript to the rhetoric of idealism that had pervaded the 1960s. American culture in the next decade changed enormously, making pursuit of new lifestyles, individual freedom, and social experimentation far more acceptable than ever before. But the sum of these changes did not constitute the political revolution that Reich had predicted. Indeed, they contributed to a mood of national malaise about the direction of social evolution.

In 1979, Hollywood provided another postscript to the period by remaking *The Invasion of the Body Snatchers*. The new version made several significant changes in the original plot. The location was readily identifiable: San Francisco, formerly the center of the counterculture. Unlike the original, the end was hopeless; no one could hope to escape transformation into an automaton. Struggle became useless in this confrontation with the invaders of the self. Thus, the film appeared to emphasize the end of a period. Protest and the counterculture had come full circle, ending where they began in the trancelike state of conformity. Light from the great western city on the hill once more passed behind an obscuring cloud.

11 *Modern Times*

In *Modern Times*, a film released in 1936, Charlie Chaplin created an unforgettable caricature of American industrialism. In the film's most hilarious scene, Chaplin plays a worker desperately trying to keep up with the pace of a speeding assembly line. Literally bound to his workstation, Chaplin struggles heroically to turn bolts and screws on passing machines until his whole body dances into motion. The point is obvious: Modern industrialism had transformed the worker into an extension of the machine. Only Chaplin's bungling prevents the complete subjugation of the worker to automation. Only comedy preserves the human spirit.

This vision of the automated factory with workers transformed into living machines remained a haunting vision of the future during the tentative moves to automation during the 1950s and 1960s. But in the 1980s, a remarkable transposition of images occurred. When IBM launched its television and magazine campaign to sell home computers, it adopted the Chaplin figure as its advertising mascot. The ad campaign began purposely where the film left off with the comic figure deluged by cakes and hats on a speeding assembly line. This chaos and humor recalled the dehumanization of the assembly line and the crisis of old-fashioned industrial work. But when the ads demonstrated the use of computers, the assembly line disappeared. The message was simple: Now more technology could eliminate the problems of modern industrialism. Charlie Chaplin of the 1930s had become a computer programmer of the 1980s.

But the problems that IBM cleverly dismissed in its comic juxtaposition of two historical periods were not trivial. In fact, the worlds of the 1930s and the 1980s contrasted immensely. One form of industrial society had been superseded by another. The paradigm of heavy industry, with huge applications of energy applied to large-scale enterprises, had been replaced by miniaturization, robotics, and information. Although this transition certainly began earlier, during the first phase of automation in the 1950s, its implications became unmistakable in the 1970s.

Simultaneous revolution deeply influenced responses to these changes. Many of the institutions such as family, ethnic group, and community, which had provided a haven for the individual, now appeared to be weaker. In part this was a result of affluence, social mobility, and rapid change. The result was the appearance of a new sort of personal autonomy in which individuals were, more than ever, defined by possessions, social mobility, education, and wealth, and less by traditional categories.

Consequently, every step taken in the direction of personal liberty—of elevating individual rights over the claims of custom and tradition—marched in tune with an expansion of the marketplace into individual lives. Among other things, for example, integration of black Americans also meant integration into the mainstream of commercial culture. Sexual liberation brought more, not less commercial exploitation of sexuality. When more women entered employment, they established a new relationship with the commercial market. The more each individual group emerged from the obscurity of tradition or the control of others, the more each exchanged these older ties for new links with a commercial nexus.

This process of change has been a familiar one in American history. Throughout the nineteenth and twentieth centuries, society experienced a similar spread of the marketplace and disruption of private institutions. But during the 1970s, this process accumulated to the point where it caused a visible and serious reaction. Perhaps no other theme is more striking during this era than the attempt to redefine the personality to fit this new social reality—from the "counterculture" attempts to restore a balanced relationship between individual and nature of the 1970s, to new definitions of sexual roles, to the rebirth of the ninteenth century evangelical personality. Thus, the simple change pictured by IBM in fact disguised a revolution in the economy, as well as culture and personality. In fact two societies existed simultaneously: the older industrial world with its established social institutions and a new society with emerging institutions and new problems.

From the 1960s through the 1980s, a new industrial revolution swept through the factories and plants of the United States. It generated major transformations of work and management that differed from the first industrial revolution. Almost every major industry applied computers to planning, production, distribution. At the same time, American production shifted away from heavy basic industries and durable consumer items commonly produced now in the plants of Japan or developing Third World countries. Such basic industries as steel and autos declined. Newer items, such as television sets and radios, were manufactured abroad as a glut of world production affected one product after another. Even computer components were sometimes constructed abroad in factories owned or licensed by American corporations. Inside the United States, technological change cut jobs for blue-collar workers but did nothing to slow a dramatic expansion in government, managerial, and lower-paying service jobs. Certainly this situation did not fulfill Walter Reuther's predictions about the dangers of automation. But neither did the new automation generate a smoothly operating and balanced economy. It continued to deliver low-priced opulence to millions of Americans. But behind it also brought unemployment, recession, and insecurity. As in other eras in American history, technological progress tested social and spiritual resources, and called forth new responses.

The transition to the new economic order can be seen clearly in the automobile industry where opportunities and problems were exaggerated. Moreover, the automobile has played a profound psychic role in the American spirit. The most seductive and attainable vision of the "American dream" has been the mobility and luxury offered by the automobile. Since the 1920s, images of mobility—a consumer's democracy—provided a tantalizing impression of American life. Not that it is inaccurate. Automobile transportation as recently as the 1970s had absorbed as much as 10 percent of the average family budget, and as many as one in six American jobs depends upon the automobile and related industries. From the steel and chrome boxes of the 1950s to the sports cars and interstate cruisers of the 1970s the automobile expressed the aspirations and accomplishments of many Americans.

Then in the 1970s, the American automobile industry—and the American dream that depended upon it—received shocks from which neither may ever recover. During the 1960s, the U.S. car market suddenly became saturated. Those families wishing to buy automobiles generally possessed one or two already. New sales therefore had to concentrate primarily on replacements or marginal expansion into such untouched markets as utility vehicles—campers, trucks, sports cars. The frontier in auto markets had closed.

Competition from foreign imports assembled and designed in Europe or Japan constituted another serious problem. At first American purchasers and producers treated these imports with contempt. And well they might have, for when Renault of France and English Ford tried to penetrate the American market in the 1950s, they failed miserably. By the 1970s, however, importers offered a different product. Low-priced Japanese and German vehicles boasted more than competitive prices; their workmanship and fuel efficiency surpassed many American makes. At the top of the line, European luxury autos set standards for comfort, prestige, and design.

Despite ample warning, automakers acted as if this foreign competition would fade away. In 1971, the domestic market for autos leaped to 8.6 million units. But just the next year, sales by Ford, General Motors, Chrysler, and American Motors slumped disastrously. The public clamored for safer, more efficient products, and this reaction was understandable. From 1966 to 1973 about 30 million cars and trucks had to be recalled by manufacturers for serious repairs. To some consumers, the industry seemed more interested in sabotaging efforts to curb air pollution or limit profitable gas guzzlers than in improving their products. It is not surprising that the number of German Volkswagon and Japanese Toyota and Datsun imports increased rapidly between 1968 and 1970. Of 6.7 million cars sold in America in 1960, only 500,000 were imported. In 1982, of 8 million sold, 2.2 million were imported.

General Motors, in response, decided to build a competitive American version of a small, high-quality car. It was announced that the new Vega would be produced at an ultramodern Lordstown plant in Ohio in 1970.

The fate of this new model underscored the seriousness of the problem. Quality controls, robotics, and computers made this plant GM's most up-to-date production unit. Unfortunately, difficult snags developed in the switchover to high technology, and the Vega did not entice American consumers away from imports. In 1972 a bitter strike was fought out in the nation's press as workers complained of high-handed management and intolerable working conditions, and General Motors denounced lackadaisical workers—an "industrial Woodstock" they claimed, where employees refused to work.

Worker alienation, absenteeism, and sloppiness (whatever their source) at Lordstown suggested a general, industrywide crisis in management and labor. The Chrysler Corporation's near bankruptcy in 1979 underscores this impression. Only massive loan guarantees of $1.5 billion from the U.S. government, private financing, and union givebacks of wages and benefits prevented the liquidation of the corporation. Something had to be done to revive the industry. In the late 1970s, the industry looked abroad for solutions. It borrowed new management techniques, such as quality circles and group production units, from the Japanese and Swedes. These changes in the workplace allowed workers to suggest changes in design and production control. However, such fine tuning did not reverse a general decline of the industry. Imports by the 1980s maintained a steady quarter of the market. American companies increasingly farmed out production to branch factories in Mexico or other Third World nations with labor costs at only a fraction of U.S. standards (one fifth to one third in Mexico). The number of permanent jobs in the American auto industry fell from about 940,000 in 1978 to about 500,000 in 1982, with little hope for a future increase in employment. Certainly the automobile remained the American dream machine—a symbol of affluence and mobility—but the industry that produced it had diminished in power and importance.

Other economic forces shook the position of the American automobile industry during the 1970s and 1980s. During two serious shortages of gasoline supplies in 1973 and 1979, engineered by price-rigging and embargoes by the Organization of Petroleum Exporting Countries (OPEC), oil-rich suppliers demonstrated the dependence of the American economy on foreign supplies (about 36 percent of gasoline and fuel oils were imported in 1974). Dependence upon imported raw materials that had once seemed boundless and cheap made it suddenly much more expensive to operate Detroit's inefficient vehicles. Crude oil went from $3 a barrel in 1973 to $28 a barrel in 1979. This disastrous inflation echoed through the rest of the economy.

Indeed, inflation became an American way of life during the 1970s, responsible for much of the uneasiness that greeted the new economy. Government borrowing to pay for domestic social programs and indexing of welfare and social security payments, defense spending (including the Vietnam War up to the mid-1970s), high wage settlements in industry, corporate fixing of high prices, shortages and bottlenecks in supply and production, and low productivity and wage increases pushed prices higher—up to 13 percent annually by the early 1980s. This led to a psychology of inflation. Americans came to expect higher prices partly because the periodic recessions of the 1970s did not (as they had after World War II) depress wages and prices. Only the severe recession of 1981–1982 finally accomplished this. But generally, the economy failed to respond to fine tuning when the government raised and lowered interest rates, imposed price and wage controls, and raised or lowered taxes. Inflation and rising interest rates imprinted the public mind with the impression that American standards of living were actually declining. In fact, the question is debatable. During the 1970s, the American per capita income rose by about 26 percent, compared with 32 percent in the 1960s and 19 percent in the 1950s. Certainly some of this increase resulted when large numbers of women entered the labor force. But whatever the figures, rising prices and public uneasiness over high interest rates during the unstable years of 1979 and 1980 gave the impression of economic decline. And in economics, impressions are all that matter.

By 1975 the new term *stagflation* had entered the economic lexicon. This clumsy verbal concoction combining "stagnation" and "inflation" demonstrates something of the bewilderment of economists who discovered a situation that defied their textbook predictions. Slow growth or stagnation usually induced recession and lower prices, but the 1970s combined the worst of both worlds: diminished growth and continued inflation.

Some economists blamed government policies—such as abandonment of a fixed dollar-gold exchange rate in 1971; the 1972 Russian export wheat deal that sent American bread prices skyrocketing; the roller-coaster policies of the Nixon administration, which fixed and then rescinded price controls; and the incoherent initiatives of the Carter Administration. A growing legion of conservative economists attacked high taxes and rapid growth in the money supply. Not unexpectedly, they called for a return to old verities of a balanced federal budget and an end to controls and regulations, as if this could rescind new realities and restore the less regulated economy of the early twentieth century.

The new economy of the 1970s and 1980s existed in a precarious and competitive international climate. From a global point of view, the United States economy continued to perform relatively well despite serious shortcomings. However, the United States had lost part of its huge postwar share of the world economy. Production and consumption remained the largest in the world, but the economy increasingly showed strains of maturity and diminished buoyancy. As the economy relied more and more upon foreign trade, its leading productive sectors (such as calculators, computers, autos, and

"Made in U.S.A." Manufacturers appeal to patriotism to sell their products in American markets, which are increasingly dominated by Asian and European exports. (AP/Wide World)

steel) experienced stiff competition. Many American companies were ill-equipped for the contest because of high labor costs, antiquated plants, and shortsighted management decisions. One result was slower growth in productivity—output per worker—when compared with Japanese and European rates.

In part, slower productivity suggested the need to increase fundamental investments in human and productive resources. Training and education of workers, upkeep of transportation facilities, and modernization of plants lagged. Serious labor difficulties, high crime rates, drug problems, and the subtle injuries of racism diminished the human capital for high growth rates. Finally, shortages of such natural resources as petroleum and high grades of metal ores raised the prices of manufacturing and forced the economy into an incurable dependence upon foreign suppliers.

In summary, the industrial sector of the American economy had matured, exhibiting entrepreneurial conservatism and slow growth. From 1970 to 1980, about one tenth of the American Gross National Product flowed into investment into new plants and research. But defense work siphoned off one fourth of this sum. By comparison, Germany and Japan earmarked from 15 to 20 percent of their national incomes to modernize. During this period, Switzerland, Denmark, West Germany, and Sweden surpassed the American standard of living and life expectancy.

If the American economy, in traditional heavy industries, experienced only slow expansion or actual decline, other areas had rapid growth. Much of this activity had a specific geographic orientation. Throughout the 1970s, industries continued to flee to the Sunbelt—the South, Southwest, and California. They sought nonunion, lower-wage labor scales, low state and municipal taxes, and less stringent pollution and safety regulations. However, the federal government also pushed investment in this direction by awarding much of its immense defense budget to Sunbelt industries. Attracted by government policy, labor costs, and plentiful energy in the oil-rich South and West, industries created new jobs at twice or three times the rate of increase in the North, Midwest, and New England. The bright spots remaining in the Snowbelt reflected rapid expansion of the information and computer industries in Massachusetts and New York.

By no means was this a new phenomenon. After World War II, northern cities began to lose population and tax revenues as booming new southern cities were conjured up out of dusty small towns and crossroads. Facing diminished resources and jobs, those least able to migrate—the unskilled industrial workers—remained behind to occupy low-paying service jobs. Northern cities, more than ever, served as administrative and banking centers, with a daytime population of commuters, and a nighttime population divided between the poor and the city gentry crowded into separate enclaves. The problems and opportunities of the new economy posed important questions. Could—or should—the United States compete with newly industrializing nations in the production of such basic commodities as steel and textiles? Should it maintain these remnants of historic industries behind steep tariff walls? In this time of somewhat slower economic expansion, could the nation maintain adequate living standards and employment opportunities for its population?

This last question intensified the problem of distributing income in the United States. In the early 1980s, the United States had the least equitable income distribution of major Western industrial nations. Wealthier Americans earned a larger share, and the poorer groups had a lesser share than their counterparts elsewhere. Of course such figures are relative. The real standard of living depends upon employment, social security, and income transfers, such as food stamps. Yet, the problem of distribution remained crucial, particularly for an economy that experienced the skewed growth of maturity. Job openings in this new economy clustered in middle and upper management and at the lower end of the employment scale in fast food and health care. As Socialist leader Michael Harrington warned, the "working people of the middle class" risked losing status and importance. What he meant was that the old industrial order had passed. The behavior of the economy in the first four years of the 1980s underscores this contention, as the relative share of income of the bottom 60 percent of the population diminished slightly.

Despite its problems and readjustment, the economy in the 1970s performed remarkably in one area providing almost 20 million new jobs. Women filled a great many of these. In 1960 about 35 percent of jobs were held by women, but in 1981, this figure rose to about 44 percent. In other words, women now performed close to half the paid employment in the American economy. Although many of these positions were extensions of traditional occupations, such as health care, food processing and service, and secretarial work, women made striking gains in previously male-dominated fields—

including computer technology, insurance, real estate, advertising, banking, and law.

Nonetheless, these broad advances did not yet compensate for the inequitable pay that women received—only a little more than half the income of men. This differential came partly from traditional low pay in women's occupations and from the concentration of females in parttime positions, but a measure resulted because employers did not reward comparable work with comparable pay.

When women went to work, they left the traditional American family behind. Quite often their salaries were necessary to maintain or increase the family's standard of living, but their absence unmistakably changed the nature of the American family. There were other indications of the diminished importance of the traditional family. For example, unrelated persons living together increased rapidly as a category during the 1970s. On the other hand, family for a great many Americans came to mean a single-income, single parent household that bore much of the burden of poverty. Almost 70 percent of these households were headed by women, many of whom had never married. (This is underscored by the alarming fact that almost half of all births to teenagers were to unwed mothers.) By 1980, about a quarter of all American children resided with only one parent; for black children, the figure was more than 57 percent.

Obviously, the American family structure had been revolutionized, partly by necessity and partly by opportunity. The traditional version of the married couple, with an employed father and a mother at home tending the children, shrank to a small proportion of American households. Even the percentage of families among all households declined to about 75 percent, as nonfamily living arrangements became more popular during the decade.

Inevitably, one of the most discussed political and social issues of the 1970s was the family and the changes in social, sexual, and generational roles it experienced. Some women fought for and welcomed these changes. Their growing independence and significance to society was signaled in September 1981 by the appointment of Judge Sandra Day O'Connor to the Supreme Court and the nomination of Representative Geraldine Ferraro as Vice-President on the Democratic ticket of 1984. These were hard won and controversial victories.

The woman's movement, which must be credited with many advances, appeared in the early 1960s and claimed national attention in 1966 with the foundation of the National Organization for

Women. Like most other important social movements, the woman's movement existed on two levels with visible organizations that pressed demands and a large sympathetic population that supported more equality for women but viewed some of the organizations with suspicion. As always, change bred outright opposition.

Early agitation for equal rights emerged in part from a revolution in middle-class consciousness, inspired by Betty Friedan's *Feminine Mystique*, published in 1963. Part repudiation of the shallow suburban life of the 1950s and part rejection of traditional portrayal of women as weak and incompetent and mere sex objects, Friedan's critique generated an awakening among American women—a recognition of the possibilities of equality. In fact, at first the revolution seemed to come too easily and too fast. In 1963, Congress passed the Equal Pay Act; and in 1964, Title VII of the new Civil Rights Act outlawed sex discrimination in jobs. A new Equal Employment Opportunity Commission (EEOC) was appointed to enforce this principle. Then, on March 22, 1972, Congress passed the Equal Rights Amendment to the Constitution and submitted it to the states for approval. In 1973, the Supreme Court ruled in *Roe* v. *Wade* that neither states nor the federal government could deny women the right to seek an abortion. The first result of this decision was to eliminate back-alley abortions, but the public sanction of abortion also generated a huge and continuing controversy.

Initial victories did not necessarily spell social and economic equality for women, however, nor did they unite all elements of the women's movement behind a single program. The modern movement had historical and ideological roots in the suffrage campaign of the Progressive Era. But the restatement of the cause came as a result of World War II, with its opening of employment and then the aftermath of firings and displacements that induced women back into the home. By the 1950s, women were once again returning to the workplace in increasing numbers, for their incomes had become crucial for the support of their families. Although economic motivations lay behind some of the demand for political and social change, the press (and the movement) did not always focus on the issue of equal pay for equal work. More spectacular news stories, such as that of women who protested against the Miss America Pageant, often crowded out the more mundane and serious aims of the movement.

By the early 1970s, the feminist agenda had become overcrowded with cultural issues. Women had to confront such questions as

Legal Abortions in the United States, 1972–1980*

1972	1973	1974	1975	1976	1977	1978	1979	1980
586.8	744.6	898.6	1,034.2	1,179.3	1,316.7	1,409.6	1,497.7	1,553.9

*Numbers in thousands.

Source: Statistical Abstract of the United States (1984), p. 71.

Legal Abortions: White and Black and Other Women, 1972–1980

	1972	1976	1980
Rate per 1,000 women (white)	11.8	18.8	24.3
Rate per 1,000 women (black and other)	21.7	56.3	56.8

Source: Statistical Abstract of the United States (1984), p. 71.

sexual orientation when small groups of lesbians or gay women's caucuses formed inside leading women's organizations. For many, relationships seemed to subordinate issues of the workplace. Consciousness-raising and discussion-support groups formed to help women fight the psychological barriers to self-assertion.

By the mid-1970s, the initial struggle over peripheral issues subsided. Most women and men recognized that the agitation involved more serious questions than who should exit from an elevator first or whether a husband should open a car door for his wife. These more serious problems defied ready solutions, for they were deeply anchored in culture and tradition. Even as women pushed into nontraditional areas of skilled work, including construction jobs and managerial positions, male dominance remained etched into differential pay. Even as women increasingly won election as mayors and state governors and Congressional Representatives, the U.S. Senate and other places remained almost entirely "gentlemen's" clubs. In culture, progress looked dramatic, but the results were also mixed. For example, in the mid-1970s, an enormously popular television series, "Charlie's Angels" portrayed women as detectives—certainly a nontraditional role. Yet these programs represented some of the most sexually exploitive shows ever to appear on television.

If American institutions could not yet completely accept the revolution of women's rights and behavior, it was partially because women disagreed about the ultimate consequences of their progress. Most women favored equality and recognition in the workplace. However, there was neither consensus on what should replace the traditional female role, nor consensus that it should be replaced. Many women suspected the women's movement was too radical. A large contingent of women as well as men worried about changes in social and sexual roles. They feared that new life-styles or living arrangements would permanently undercut the already fragile family. Many focused on male and female homosexuality as the greatest threat to traditional religious and social values, and they blamed the women's movement for its increased visibility. Almost inevitably, the Equal Rights Amendment gradually accumulated serious opposition as it moved through passage in state after state. Indeed, the ERA became a great symbolic issue in the clash of two cultures and two economies.

The woman most responsible for lighting the backfire that defeated the Equal Rights Amendment was Phyllis Schlafly. A right-wing publicist during the 1950s and 1960s, Schlafly exemplified the postwar revolution in women's lives. A competent organizer and speaker, she was by no stretch of the imagination the traditional woman she defended. Through her writings, such as *Power of the Positive Woman* (1977), and her Stop-ERA movement, Schlafly gradually gained attention by leveling serious charges against the proposed amendment. She contended that it would legalize homosexual marriage, it would require mixed public toilets, and would dictate a female military draft. It would also, she warned, condemn housewives, forcing them to abandon their families for the workplace.

Although her claims distorted the intent of the ERA, she articulated the deepest fears of men and women who distrusted and disliked the social change of the 1970s and early 1980s. Unwilling to attack the complex causes for the evolution of family structure and sexual roles, Schlafly and her followers settled for victory over the ERA. Unable to impede the changes that had given birth to the women's movement, they successfully prevented passage of the ERA in the few remaining states and thereby defeated the amendment by 1982.

Legal access to abortion was an even more deeply controversial element included among women's rights. Once again, new individual rights clashed with deeply held traditional values. The privacy principle enunciated by the Supreme Court elevated the claims of each woman above those of the prospective father, the church, the society, and the fetus, which many believed to be a living, but unborn, child. Conservatives and traditionalists denounced this reversal of values. Catholics and evangelical protestants asserted the rights of the "unborn" and the family over those of the mother.

By the 1970s "right to life" groups mounted a strong and emotional political campaign. Sometimes they took extreme actions, including picketing and bombing abortion clinics. The bulk of the movement, however, sought redress in a constitutional amendment. However, even in the conservative years of the first Reagan administration, Congress refused to enact their demands. In fact, few plans to legislate traditional values won acceptance. Movements to end abortion and institute prayer in the public schools set the tone of political debate, but gained few victories.

During the 1970s, American men also changed. Clothing styles for men evolved rapidly after the muted and dour 1950s. Men increasingly wore bright colors and jewelry, purchased perfumes (sold as "masculine scents"), and spent hours on their hair with shampoos, rinses, and blow dryers. These superficial changes existed atop more serious alterations in what had become stereotyped male roles. Many men took up cooking and baking, and some shared housework and child care with their wives. A popular film, *Kramer v. Kramer* (1979), put this revolution in social behavior in the form of a question: Could a divorced advertising executive who won custody of his seven-year-old son develop the sensitivity to become a real parent?

During the 1970s, psychologists and social observers frequently commented on the more open expression of emotion by contemporary men. This psychic revolution certainly touched Americans unequally, but middle class males certainly experienced serious role changes. Even popular culture began to reflect such shifts. One of the most popular evening television programs of the 1980s, "Hill Street Blues," transformed the stereotypical, tough-guy, police show into a soap opera that explored the depths of male emotional expression. Each week, the male society of police officers showed feelings that would have been unthinkable twenty years earlier. In that earlier age, Jack Webb's "Dragnet" character, Joe Friday, set the stereotype of the modern cop: a character whose trademark was a voice and manner completely devoid of emotion. Yet this change was far from universal. Many men continued to celebrate traditional male roles of bravery, toughness, and camaraderie. Thus popular culture also had its football heros, its icy detectives like Clint Eastwood, and its unquestioning patriots like Sylvester Stallone.

Some of the new social and sexual roles defined in the 1970s and 1980s represented the absorption of the counterculture. The counterculture turned the traditional self inside-out. It celebrated repressed emotions. Personal liberation had been its signpost, and liberation justified anything from drug taking to new social and sexual relationships.

Yet two symbolic events in the final days of 1969 demonstrated that the counterculture comprised more than a simple celebration of personal liberation. In mid-August, 400,000 young people invaded the tiny community of Bethel, near Woodstock, New York. Gathering at a 600-acre farm, the "tribe" of the new Woodstock Nation heard a three-day concert featuring rock stars Janis Joplin, Jimi Hendrix, and the Jefferson Airplane. Braving mud and rain, short supplies of food and inadequate toilet facilities, the young people created a community devoted to sharing and pleasure—an intentional contrast to the war-weary society obsessed with Vietnam and the getting and spending of suburbia. As *Time* enthused, the "phenomenon of innocence" triumphed over the work ethic.

Yet, a gathering for individual pleasure and self-expression is hardly a community. To experiment with new forms of consciousness or the deep, momentary friendships made by necessity scarcely constituted a permanent response to the anguish or the ambitions of this young generation. In fact, lack of community feeling characterized the next major rock concert held four months later. A free concert by the Rolling Stones at Altamont, California, inverted the benign survivalism of Woodstock. The Stones hired the Hells Angels motorcycle gang for protection, and this group intensified bad drug trips and confrontations of the spectators into serious physical violence and one death.

Certainly, Altamont did not destroy the counterculture. But it demonstrated that the celebration of natural foods, country life, the liberation of the psyche through drugs, and rural communitarian experiments could scarcely counteract the changes in American society challenging traditional social order. The counterculture, in addition to preaching individual freedom and an end to repression, intensified some of the forces of separation and segmentation that aroused feelings of alienation during the late 1960s and 1970s.

It could be argued that at its most extreme America had generated a society of autonomous individuals and that each person claimed priority over the whole. Traces of this new culture may even be discovered in the new attitude toward celebrity. The genius of contemporary painter, designer, and media personality Andy Warhol was to declare every American a potential celebrity. Every invididual could aspire to ten or fifteen minutes of media attention. One example of what he meant is illustrated by the annual *Guinness Book of World Records*, which listed records of genuine athletic and artistic accomplishment alongside scores of endurance records for pointless activities. Celebrity could also be purchased. A widely printed ad announced in the mid-1970s (in *Rolling Stone Magazine*, for example), explained how to order celebrity as if it were a swank drink: "Liza [Minnelli] introduced us to White Rum and soda at an Andy Warhol party. She was wonderful and sincere and became one of our best friends," the ad copy bubbled. She—and the drink— conferred immediate importance to the potential consumer.

During the 1970s, the mass media redefined public heroes in terms of the new celebrity. Such sports stars as football quarterback Joe Namath, tennis champion Billy Jean King, and baseball player

Jim Palmer, as well as politicians, entered a world once reserved for movie and television stars. This mingling established a celebrity elite. Noteworthy men and women, whatever their accomplishments in theater, films, sports, television, and politics, became interchangeable personalities appearing on television talk shows or celebrity sports or charity events.

Renewed interest in physical culture and jogging introduced another form of celebrity. Of course both activities demonstrated a growing awareness of the physical problems of a sedentary, urban life. But they also promoted the self; they were sports without spectators or standards in which every participant could be a champion.

Of course, as many Americans recognized, self-promotion cast a negative shadow too. Advice books for invigorating the psychological, social, sexual, or religious self regularly topped the best-seller lists. Millions of Americans bought popular journals with intimate titles like *People* and *Self*, but just as many—perhaps including some of the same consumers—also wondered where it all might end. Historian Christopher Lasch, in his book the *Culture of Narcissism* (1979), provided one answer. Preoccupation with the self mirrored a prevalent psychological disorder in which the personality depended upon others for definition. The popular culture of self-liberation, he claimed, only worsened the situation.

For Lasch, social toleration of special groups of individuals who celebrated marginal life-styles, brought no special virtue to society. In fact, society desperately needed cohesive values and vital institutions to express them, not more diversity. But the difficulty remained: What were these values and where were these institutions?

A search for answers to this question preoccupied much of the culture of the 1970s, as the uneasy transition to a new society perplexed many Americans. Very different solutions were suggested, which swung between the extreme of absolute toleration and the dogmatic claim that only traditional social institutions had value. Both extremes contended, but neither prevailed. Thus, the decade rang with the same arguments that filled Edith and Archie Bunker's living room with comic tension. These two characters, from the immensely popular TV series, "All in the Family," symbolize the two sides of America's search for understanding of social change. Edith Bunker stood for tolerance and sympathy. Archie upheld conservative values, yearning to return to a past of shared verities. Although the show satirized both views (its producers shared Edith's values), the strength and popularity of Archie's character spoke for many

"Pumping iron" was probably not the goal of most American feminists. But the relaxation of strict gender roles brought attention to a variety of possibilities for women athletes. *(Jean-Pierre Laffont/Sygma)*

Americans who, through the fog of nostalgia, saw no evil in the old-fashioned treatment of women, blacks, and other exploited or repressed social groups.

Although the demands of new groups (gays, for example) underscored social division and sometimes incited angry responses, traditional racial and ethnic divisions of society remained the most serious divisions. The advances of black Americans in the 1960s had been remarkable, even revolutionary. But these advances did not affect every person equally. Of course, each American benefited from the suppression of legal racism with its daily reminders of caste apparent in the simplest actions of voting, shopping, riding a bus, or drinking from a public water fountain. Accommodation of middle-class, well-educated blacks proved not to be terribly controversial. Hundreds of blacks took positions of political leadership. They won important victories in mayoral elections in Philadelphia, Chicago, Birmingham, Washington, D.C., Atlanta, and Los Angeles. Black athletes, rock stars, and television personalities became the heroes and role models for young Americans, black and white. Universities and colleges opened their doors to talented black scholars. But discrimination was hewn in the bedrock of American society. In 1980, blacks still clustered around the lowest rungs of the employment ladder, serving as 53 percent of household servants, 40 percent of laundry workers, 35 percent of garbage collectors, and 29 percent of nurses' aides and hospital orderlies.

Those left behind suffered from the decline in the black family. The forces that destabilized the American family in general bore heaviest upon the black and Hispanic populations. For example, 17 percent of all births in 1980 were out of wedlock, but this figure reached 55 percent for black births. More than half of all black children lived with only one parent, and female-headed households made up more than 41 percent of all black households. High crime rates, dependence upon degrading welfare programs, disease and death rates, infant mortality, all ravaged this vulnerable population. Given the impoverishment of so many, it is not surprising that the income share of black families stalled at about 58 percent of that of white families during the 1970s.

Beyond economics lay the psychological and cultural struggle for equality. Beginning in the 1960s, some black intellectuals had begun to celebrate blackness, the African heritage, and consciousness of distinct dress and hair fashions. Even "black English" was promoted as a discrete and valuable dialect for a short time. This cultural renaissance aimed to erase class lines in the black community by invoking help from those who had benefited from integration for those still mired in poverty and exploitation. However, consciousness-raising and demands for a redistribution of income also helped to initiate a backlash among those whom political commentator Michael Novak has called "the unmeltable ethnics." Novak pictured a political texture that had frayed because of extraordinary attention paid to black Americans. Other ethnic groups, feeling left out, became more self-conscious, more visible, and more politically active.

Nothing fused their anger more than court-mandated busing for school integration in northern cities. In Los Angeles, Boston, and Chicago, public schools remained segregated by neighborhood. Ghettoized populations meant ghettoized schools, black and white. The court-approved solution mixed the school populations and tried to distribute them evenly, but this could only be accomplished by elminating neighborhood schools. In 1975, during antibusing riots in Boston, the anger and hatred etched on the faces of mothers and factory workers watching their children being bused out of neighborhoods expressed far more than racial animosity. They were bitterly protesting the destruction of a cherished ethnic institution.

Busing and other challenges to traditional institutions sharpened consciousness of community identity, but Alex Haley's *Roots* provided an awakening of this spirit. This immensely successful novel, transformed into an even more popular television serial shown over consecutive evenings in 1977, demonstrated through black history how to recapture ethnic pride. Haley's saga of his ancestors, dragged from their idyllic pastoral society in Africa into cruel centuries of slavery, was a fascinating tale of survival, and, finally, success. It also bore the telltale compromises of Hollywood fantasy. Although it was sentimental, stereotypical, and exaggerated and sometimes sacrificed historical accuracy, these flaws made the story all the more appealing and familiar to the mass television audience.

Haley's family success story illustrates how the tale of one black man's search for his roots could inspire other segments of American culture to explore their roots. During the 1970s, millions of school children constructed family trees to establish their roots. Genealogy became a popular pastime, and a national museum on Ellis Island (where millions of European immigrants first disembarked) in New York Harbor promised to be one of the most popular new tourist attractions in that city.

Preoccupation with roots had other causes than the appeal of a popular television program. Perhaps Americans sought historic identity because they recognized the fragility of that identity in their own lives. The rapid decline of the traditional family, high divorce rates, rapid social mobility for some blacks, changed social and sexual roles for women and men, economic instability and inflation, geographic mobility, political confusion, and a costly war pushed questions about identity and social order into consciousness. In a different reflex, American popular culture began a major exploration of fantasy and escapism. Although it is difficult to quantify such things, some periods of history, are more likely than others to express social and psychological preoccupations with the language of magic, science fiction, and cult religions. This occurred in the 1970s despite the enormous emphasis upon technology and science elsewhere in the culture.

An extreme example of escapism freezes the imagination. The Reverend Jim Jones fled with his followers to Guyana in South America in the mid-1970s to escape from American society and culture. Like some other religious-political cults, Jonestown empowered its charismatic leader, but in this case with deadly authority. In 1978, Jones feared a threat to the community from American authorities. In a frenzy, he ordered the mass suicide and murder of the whole community of 400 men, women, and children.

Other expressions of fantasy certainly had less horrible results. A benign example was the film *The Exorcist* (1973). The first in a series of popular films about supernatural and natural super forces like earthquakes and fires, *The Exorcist* turned upon the implausible possession of a young girl by the Devil. The movie was only slightly sillier than a more cerebral earlier film of 1968, *Rosemary's Baby*, which was a grotesque and sophisticated adventure in Satanism. However, *The Exorcist* generated a new popular genre that filled the screen and television airwaves with haunted houses, monsters, and irrational fears.

Science fiction also returned, but refreshed and quite distinct from the atom bomb films of the 1950s. Each summer of the late 1970s and early 1980s featured the release of another successful science fiction or fantasy film—from updated versions of the popular "Star Trek" television series, to the Empire costume pageants of George Lucas, to the swashbuckling fantasies of Steven Spielberg's *Raiders of the Lost Ark* (1981). None of these films possessed the murky seriousness of earlier science fiction; none were morality plays on Hiroshima; but most surprising, none was inspired by the very real, but pedestrian looking, space adventures of American astronauts and Russian cosmonauts.

The new fantasy and science fiction was aimed at juveniles. Hollywood, in its eternal quest for audiences, courted the family through its children. The industry recognized that its most loyal audiences (and taste setters) were below the age of 20. Nonetheless, there is more than successful merchandising involved in the huge expenditures and success of these films. Adventure, set completely outside institutions, politics, and the serious adult world, but intended for the whole family, suggested a desire for playfulness and imagination that was lacking, or threatened, by the real world.

The best example of this escapist quality can be seen in the charming film *E.T.: The Extra-Terrestrial* (1982). A thinly disguised adaptation of *Peter Pan*, it pictured a thriving child's world beneath a sometimes menacing adult reality. Into this joyful environment floated E.T.; a dark-skinned space voyager, accepted and befriended by the children. When they discover him, adults treat him with cold and cruel rationality, practically murdering him. His greatest desire, however, is to return home, and he finally abandons his sad playmates. While the film brims over with suggestive meanings, none are quite drawn out. The theme of home and belonging is raised and then dropped. The film obviously suggests the problems of accepting beings with different physical characteristics, but such implications dissolve in the morality play between the disapproved world of the adults and the rapturous child's world of imagination.

This same ambiguous approach to modern society defined the modern romance novel sold primarily to women. These paperback books marketed by the millions each month in grocery and drugstores earned publishers almost $300 million in 1983. As many as 140 new titles appeared monthly. As one publisher put it about his series: "Silhouette and Campbell Soup are exactly the same," by which he meant that both products belonged with the family's weekly purchases. Of course, romance had long sustained midday dramas, such as "General Hospital." Television soap operas held their audiences in thrall with romance, conflict, tragedy, weakness, and pictures of evil. The modern romance aimed at the same audience but stressed a different emotion. It pictured only handsome heroes and beautiful, vulnerable, but contemporary women. As one successful editor described his typical literary heroine: "She must not be naive and virginal but rather a mature young woman, and even though she may have lost her first love, she must never be portrayed as depressed or depressing." A taste of reality added relish to romance. At the same time, these books may have indicated mixed feelings of readers about the contemporary advances in social and sexual equality.

If popular culture equally expressed a fractious individualism, traditional values, and escapism, one group in American society allowed for no ambiguity. Evangelical protestant groups gained members and power during the 1970s by stressing conversion (to be "born again") and a simple but rigorous, fundamentalist theology. In social matters, these churches warred against the symbols of a new morality sexual promiscuity, homosexuality, equality for women, rock and roll, and drugs. Imbedded in rural Southern and Southwestern culture, they sometimes opposed racial equality, government social security systems, and in general, much of modern life.

This did not prevent them, however, from skillfully exploiting modern mass communication, including television and mass mailings. Unlike Billy Graham, who had defined his position at the political margin as an adviser, these groups defiantly called themselves the "moral majority." By this, they meant a political majority. The alliance between evangelical ministers and publicists cemented this powerful new force. As the Reverend Jerry Falwell wrote in 1981, "The godless minority of treacherous individuals who have been permitted to formulate national policy must now realize they do not represent the majority." Publicist Richard Viguerie noted, "Because conservatives have mastered the new technology, we've been able to bypass the Left's near-monopoly of the national new media."

These activities and accusations in the late 1970s and early 1980s helped to redefine the American political agenda. Facing a conflicted family and unchanging ethics, they proposed a program of "traditional" family values. Their effort to overcome what they saw as the drift and divisiveness in American society focused on dismantling those public institutions created after World War II that had aimed at social equality. They took a harsh, fatalistic view of international relations, blaming the Soviet Union for the problems of American foreign policy and pressing for massive defense expenditures. However, their clearest call rang out for a new religious community based upon the revived family structure and underwritten by the power of government, a "Christian America."

Of all the movements of the 1970s to call for a new personal orientation toward social change, this one illustrates most sharply the cultural dilemmas of the era. Social and economic evolution constantly undercut established values and principles, leading to a society of contending individual claims. But how could this process be halted without foreclosing on progress? On this pivotal point, the evangelical right shared a problem with political liberals who had also rediscovered the virtue of the family during the early 1980s. In the face of enormous diversity in American households, what was the family? What were the proper roles for men and women? The traditional structure of patriarchy had practically disappeared. To call for its restoration meant simply to flail against a swarm of demographic trends. Ironically, the energetic capitalism that both conservatives and liberals supported, the consumer economy they cherished, increased the radical new personal and social relationships that challenged traditional institutions. Variety in human relations mirrored diversity in consumption and production. To turn time back might involve extraordinary government intervention into the clockworks of society and the economy.

There was no certainty, either, that a revived family structure would rejuvenate community feelings. Retreat behind the four walls of kinship represented no real answer to problems that demanded national solutions. Society was not, in the 1980s, simply the family writ large. Yet faced with the complexity and alienation of modern life, the temptation to seek familiar terrain remained strong. Thus, American culture began to look away from public and political solutions to problems—an emphasis that had prevailed since the end of World War II. Or at least, the old answers, provided by liberalism appeared to demand revision. Now the future seemed to depend upon restoring private institutions. The ramifications of this response had profound political effects.

12 Treading Water

In the early morning hours of June 6, 1968, weary tabulators finished counting the California primary returns. Robert Kennedy had taken the election, and with it the possibility of a presidential nomination on the Democratic ticket. So the victory celebration was joyous and exuberant, especially as the candidate prepared to make his way through the crowd of well-wishers. Suddenly, shots exploded and Kennedy fell, mortally wounded. A young Jordanian immigrant, waving a revolver, was subdued by Kennedy's entourage. Grief and despair swept the nation when it heard. Americans repeated the bewildering question of the 1960s: Why this terrible season of violence?

After a ceremony at St. Patrick's cathedral in New York City, another ritual: A slow funeral train wound its way, bearing Kennedy's body to Washington, D.C. From Union Station on Capitol Hill, the body was escorted through the city and then to Arlington Cemetery for burial next to John Kennedy. Several thousand miles away, in London, on the same day, Scotland Yard apprehended James Earl Ray, the murderer of Martin Luther King, Jr.

Still the circle of political violence had not closed. At the end of August in Chicago, the Democratic party nominating convention met to select a candidate for president. Vice-President Hubert Humphrey gripped the winning cards. Chicago's Mayor Richard J. Daley tightly controlled the proceedings, while President Johnson insisted that the convention ratify his Vietnam policies—if not himself. Humphrey, a knowledgeable, experienced, and skillful leader—the very soul of the party's liberal wing—compromised himself by his visible impotence. If independence was ever a state of his mind, he did not show it. Outside the convention hall, 10,000 protesters invaded the city parks for rallies and a rock concert to denounce Humphrey's politics as usual.

Daley and the party bosses packed the floor and the aisles of the convention hall, but they could not control the protest outside; nor could they direct national attention to their proceedings. Rather than a perfunctory nomination of Humphrey—the dull piling on of inevitable words and ballots—the American public watched protest in the streets turn into riot, with police violence, tear gas, and bloody casualities. Thus on Wednesday, August 28, 1968, Humphrey gained his cherished nomination while a huge national television audience watched protesters assault his party.

The Kennedy assassination and Humphrey's fragile victory seriously weakened the Democratic ticket. In the last moments of the election, the Democrat pulled close to his competitor Richard Nixon, but too late. Yet chance was not to blame. The Democratic party could neither compromise between opponents and supporters of the war nor between its competing constituencies. So a season of missed chances and rigidity ended an era—an age that began in 1932, when the Democratic Party defined the policies that governed the nation for 35 years. This disintegration of the political center guaranteed a decade of political instability and demanded a new politics.

Yet, to emphasize 1968 would be to mistake the surface for the dramatic undercurrent of destabilizing forces. The Democratic debacle of 1968 did not begin the disintegration of party and political community. The Democratic coalition of the 1930s declined because political consensus fractured, creating a multitude of contending, self-interested groups. Evidence of this process can be found in the 1964 election, when the decline of party affiliation and lower voter turnout became recognizable trends in American politics. By 1967, for example, 37 percent of eligible voters sat on the political fence as independents, neither Republicans nor Democrats. They tended to jump into the camp of a single issue or follow a candidate rather than support the fortunes of a party. Thus, creating and maintaining coalitions became much more difficult. Even more striking, the percent of voters who actually marked ballots in presidential elections declined gradually. Participation sank from 62.8 percent of eligible voters in 1960 to about 53 percent in 1984. In other words, almost half of all potential voters stayed home. This was hardly the behavior of a vigilant, democratic electorate.

Several explanations for this behavior can be advanced. Some observers suggest that most nonvoters are disaffected Democrats. Still others argue that nonvoters are alienated from the political process or believe that there is little meaning to the solitary act of voting.

Vice President Hubert Humphrey won the nomination but probably lost the 1968 election because of violence in Chicago pictured on national television. (AP/Wide World)

Another explanation suggests that traditional, coalition politics could no longer encompass the interests of very different constituencies. Hence the rise of protest movements within parties and third-party candidates. Advocates of this theory point to the popularity of Governor George Wallace of Alabama, who won about 11 percent of the presidential vote in 1968 and 2 percent in 1962, and independent candidate John Anderson, who gained 7 percent in 1980. George Wallace struck at the heart of the Democratic coalition by gathering the votes of northern industrial workers as well as white Southerners. His success provides some evidence that the goals of white ethnic groups and black Americans were very difficult to compromise.

Lacking consensus and compromise, parties paid more attention to new sorts of interest groups. Political lobbyists for corporations and labor unions and veterans groups have been an indigenous species in Washington, D.C. However, newer interest groups now arrived on the political scene. When they included black Americans, the elderly, consumer groups (such as Ralph Nader's organizations), environmental groups, women, homosexuals, right-wing political action groups, and evangelical Protestants, they inspired controversy. Rising in importance, they displaced or at least competed with traditional groups, and many Americans interpreted this new power as their own loss.

The shift in party alignment also had a demographic basis in the continued drift of population West and South and the ongoing trek of the white and black middle classes to the suburbs. Behind such tangible reasons lay something else though—a troubling assumption that government had become the enemy, not the servant of the American citizen. This was more than a reassertion of traditional individualism or even a new regionalism. It expressed a paradox for the times: As government tried to resolve the tensions of race, class, sex, and region, it appeared to become remote and bureaucratic.

It is no surprise, therefore, that candidates in each election from 1968 to 1984 tilted against a vague foe named Washington. Presidents Nixon, Carter, and Reagan all mounted successful campaigns by suggesting that they were political outsiders aiming to reconquer government for the American people. Even Senator George McGovern, the losing Democratic candidate for 1972, when he attacked the continuing war in Vietnam, implied that faceless government bureaucrats had imposed that distant struggle on the nation. Moreover, he gained the nomination only because rules changes in the Democratic Party allowed amateurs of seize its machinery.

Such politics had serious risks, as the case of Richard Nixon proves. Nixon was a politician of immense talent and versatility, but he was a man who harbored slights and resentments. Despite his successes, he could not overcome the frustrations and checks of public life. During most of the 1960s, he had stood in the wings—if not exactly sulking, then nursing his loss to Kennedy in 1960 and his failure to capture the California governorship in 1962. This was no time of exile, however, for Nixon continued to cultivate Republican candidates and officials. The understudy remained ever ready to play a role when the major players stumbled. He waited loyally through the terrible Republican debacle of 1964 and won the Presidential nomination of 1968.

Nixon sensed the implications of Goldwater's 1964 loss. He also recognized the source of George Wallace's popularity surge in early 1968. Consequently, he and his advisers designed a strategy to cement conservatives and disaffected voters in the South into a coalition containing traditional Republicans from the Northeast and Midwest but avoiding the extremism associated with Goldwater. He selected Spiro Agnew, governor of Maryland, as his running mate, and articulated two fundamental promises. The first—law and order—represented an issue for all sentiments. It implied control of student demonstrations against the Vietnam War, vigilance against urban riots and crime, even the suppression of civil rights demonstrations. Nixon also proposed to resolve the conflict in Vietnam, but he evaded any clear policy statement. Both positions, however, confounded the Democratic candidate Humphrey, who could neither distance himself from the war, which he supported, nor Lyndon Johnson's "Great Society" programs, which he fervently approved.

In his first term in office, Nixon encountered serious problems. Some were of his own making, but overall the term should be judged a success. He faced a hostile Congress that remained solidly Democratic. The fate of his agenda, therefore, fell into the hands of the Southern/Republican coalition born at the end of the 1930s. A workable coalition, it nonetheless lacked stability. The press presented a much greater obstacle. By any measure—especially the President's—reporters treated Nixon without enthusiasm. As his adviser Secretary of State Henry Kissinger later commented acidly: "There is no question that generosity of spirit was not one of Nixon's virtues; he could never transcend his resentments and complexes." Kissinger undoubtedly had Nixon's strong resentment against the press in mind.

Finally, the new President had an insight that unfortunately turned to bitterness. No President better understood the problems of governing the huge administration that he inherited. He realized that the chief executive could not simply step into office and thereby command changes. He had to win control of large, powerful, and competitive executive bureaucracies, such as the State Department, which had powerful constituencies in Congress and elsewhere. He understood the need for continuing political struggle in his own party. However, the slow progress and marginal victories of bureaucratic in-fighting led first to frustration and then to clandestine and illegal activities, and then to the colossal blunders of the Watergate burglary and cover-up.

Nixon owed his election in part to the confused but strong national backlash against the war in Vietnam. Despite his vague promises to end the war, however, his initial plan called for stepping up American participation. Nixon's strategy was shared by Kissinger, his most important adviser in foreign policy and head of the National Security Council. William Rogers, an old friend, acted as Secretary of State, but Kissinger systematically excluded him from important decisions. Kissinger and Nixon formulated foreign policy at the White House. They negotiated through special "backchannels" or informal top-level communications that bypassed the State Department for direct talks with foreign governments. These personal, high-level contacts followed from Kissinger's strategic and geopolitical theories: "I attempted to relate events to each other, to create incentives or pressures in one part of the world to influence events in another."

This grand plan had virtues and faults. Kissinger recognized the complexity of world events; he brought into policy planning a sophisticated estimate of America's diminished ability to cope with each international crisis. His greatest successes flowed from his astute recognition of important divisions in the Communist world. On the other hand, the same global perspective led him to overestimate the ability of the Russians, for example, to control the North Vietnamese. Regrettably, therefore, the most difficult problem facing the Nixon administration—the war in Vietnam—did not respond to the rules of Kissinger's grand game.

Nixon's first impulse was to redirect, not end, the American policy of seeking victory in Vietnam. He hoped to convince the North Vietnamese, the Chinese, and the Russians that he would react swiftly and unexpectedly to any National Liberation Front (Viet

Cong) or North Vietnamese victories in the field. At the same time, he and Kissinger knew the price of continuing the war meant removing American troops from combat. This paradox of escalation and withdrawal became the policy of "Vietnamization." In the summer of 1969, the President began removing American troops from South Vietnam: 25,000 of about 540,000, and then in rapidly increasing numbers until the last combat troops embarked in 1973. Undeniably, this policy undercut the South Vietnamese war effort. So in compensation, the administration increased the ferocity of the air war. On March 18, 1969, Nixon ordered Air Force B-52s to bomb the border areas of neighboring, neutral Cambodia. These areas had been used by the North Vietnamese to shift supplies and men to the South. The President had both widened the war and increased its stakes, while lessening its immediate impact upon Americans.

When South Vietnam, aided by the United States, invaded Cambodia in April 1970, the implications of this policy became apparent. The invasion began the fatal degeneration of Cambodia into coup, revolution, anarchy, and its practical destruction by frenzied internal strife. The sought-for cache of arms and National Liberation Front headquarters proved elusive. In the United States, massive protests struck American campuses, as the antiwar movement rekindled and burned brightly.

Disaster occurred in the heat of this anger. During a demonstration at Kent State University on May 4, students faced the troops of the Ohio National Guard, who opened fire on the crowd, killing four students. Within a few days, strikes swept across campuses, shutting down many of America's most important colleges and universities. More than 100,000 protesters assembled in Washington for a national protest. Late on the night of May 7, before the march, Nixon ordered his driver to conduct him to the grounds of the Washington Monument, where marchers were gathering. He climbed out of the automobile and wandered among them, aimlessly chatting about the environment and travel—about everything except the war at home he had intensified.

The protests surprised and deeply bruised the President. He reached deep into his inner resources for strength and courage, but he also found anger and incoherence. The President recovered from this desperate moment, but with little sympathy for his opponents. In fact, during the next months he taunted opponents of the war, questioning their patriotism and striking at the American press, which reported the protests. Then (in early 1971) his rancor against the press took on a more pointed purpose, partly in revenge for the publishing of the devastating "Pentagon Papers". This history, culled from secret documents, indicted a generation of national leaders and advisers for their clandestine involvement in the Vietnam struggle. From the early 1950s, policy decisions appeared confused and even sinister. Leaked to the press by Kissinger protégé and former defense official Daniel Ellsberg, the papers did not compromise figures in the Nixon administration, but they seriously undercut its rationale for the war.

As a result, Nixon tightened White House security. He endorsed secret wiretaps of executive branch members and their contacts in the press. He drew his close advisers even closer: Kissinger, Attorney General John Mitchell, and White House aides (known to insiders as the "German Shepherds") John Ehrlichman and H. R. "Bob" Haldeman. Eventually, the White House organized a secret investigative unit dubbed The Plumbers, assigned such tasks as breaking into the office of Daniel Ellsberg's psychiatrist to search for damaging records.

Nixon also encouraged Vice-President Spiro Agnew to counterattack student protesters and the press. Using carefully chosen invectives, Agnew elicited guffaws of delight from the converted, but he chilled the climate of political civility. He delighted audiences of war supporters with his description of students as "an effete corps of impudent snobs" and later, as the "curled-lip boys in Eastern ivory towers." However, this confident public posture masked very serious private worries. These words, half believed by the beleaguered administration, pushed it to misunderstand the origins of public outcry against the war.

So the President held true to his course. By the end of 1971, only 175,000 American soldiers remained in South Vietnam, but the U.S. forces escalated bombing missions when the North Vietnamese stepped up infiltration of men and matériel into the South. In March 1972, the North Vietnamese launched a major attack on the South. The President responded with bombing of the North, mining its major port Haiphong, and blockading the nation from the sea. At the same time, using backchannel contacts, he and Henry Kissinger continued negotiations with the North Vietnamese and the National Liberation Front. In fact, both sides reached a tentative agreement shortly before the U.S. elections in the fall of 1972, but negotiations broke off in October. President Thieu of the South, realizing that the draft agreement left him in jeopardy, refused to accept it. So the war dragged on for several more months with saturation bombing of the Northern cities during Christmas ("Operation Linebacker"). Finally, both sides signed a treaty in January 1973, basically the same one negotiated in October.

This remarkable document granted most of what the North Vietnamese and National Liberation Front sought. Four agonizing years of bombing (4.6 million tons were dropped from 1969 to 1973), the invasion of Laos and Cambodia, millions of dollars spent, the fabric of American society slashed open, and the Nixon administration exhausted and suspicious—all for the sake of an undisclosed policy that in the end brought withdrawal of American troops and allowed the North Vietnamese to maintain troops in the South.

Most of the other Nixon and Kissinger foreign policies were conceived and executed in secret. One of these gained a dubious victory in Chile when the socialist government of Slavador Allende was overthrown. Although the CIA did not direct his overthrow and assassination, it tried to engineer his defeat at the polls. Failing this, the administration embarked on a campaign of boycott and economic disruption. Finally, a military coup toppled the government in 1973. After three years of pressure, Nixon could be pleased with his policy.

This was a curious lapse into the old, narrow anti-Communism of the 1950s for a man who achieved major successes in policy with the Soviet Union and Communist China. To Nixon's credit, he recognized and acted upon the principle that the two largest Communist nations were part of the world community. Using backchannel contacts, Kissinger negotiated first with the Chinese. His discussions brought a surprise trip by the President to China in February 1972. He undertook a similar dramatic tour of the Soviet Union in May 1972. Results followed immediately: Tentative steps toward recognition of Communist China and a huge grain sale to the Soviets. In May, Nixon and Soviet Premier Leonid Brezhnev signed the first Strategic Arms Limitation Talks accord (SALT I), limiting the number of antiballistic missile sites. An Interim Agreement ended competition between the two sides to build land-based intercontinental ballistic missiles (ICBM's). Although neither agreement achieved actual disarmament, the documents recognized military parity and dependence on "mutual assured destruction" (MAD), in which rough equality would assure no surprise attack by either side.

Foreign policy in a different arena had profound domestic repercussions. America had two contradictory aims in the Middle East. It wished to defend Israel and protect oil-rich Arab kingdoms. But the mortal enmity between Israel and its neighbors made this a risky course. At a minimum, therefore, American policy opposed the influence of the Soviet Union in the area. Kissinger and Nixon succeeded in diminishing Soviet power, but they could not achieve peace. In fact, war between Egypt and Israel broke out in October 1973. At first the Egyptians gained several striking successes, but Israel counterattacked and crushed the Egyptian army. President Anwar Sadat of Egypt had to sue for peace. Defeated, he turned on his Soviet suppliers and advisors.

America's growing dependence upon Mideastern oil raised the price of support for Israel. Arab nations that had just recently completed nationalizing foreign oil companies now united in a boycott, stopping exports of oil to nations that supported Israel. President Nixon made a "patriotic appeal" for "united action by all," asking for immediate conservation measures. Eventually, states passed 55-mile-per-hour speed limits and banned Sunday gas sales, but lines of cars circled gas stations to buy scarce fuel. Truckers demonstrated against speed limits. The American public became angry, frustrated, and suspicious that oil companies were using the occasion to raise prices.

If President Nixon should receive cautious good marks for steering around some foreign policy difficulties, he found domestic problems more intractable. One of his campaign slogans promised to control violence and crime and combat rising costs of welfare and family assistance. At first, the President made significant gestures in both directions. He proposed a family assistance plan (which neither liberals nor conservatives in Congress favored) to simplify and even expand federal aid to impoverished families. He did convince Congress to stiffen the criminal code of the District of Columbia; but when he attempted to appoint conservatives to the Supreme Court, Congress rejected his first two nominees, Harrold G. Carswell and Clement F. Haynsworth, on the grounds of incompetence and hostility to racial integration. Two other appointees, Harold Blackmun and Warren Burger did, however, temper the liberalism of the old Warren Court.

On economic matters, the President never developed a consistent, long-range plan, but the economy constantly preoccupied him. Contemporary problems defied textbook answers. Historically, prices fell in times of recession. Beginning in the late 1960s, however, stagflation (slow growth and inflation) gripped the economy. During the President's six years in office, he first sought to spur growth with a nudge of increased federal expenditures. Then by mid-1971, inflation, a serious balance of payments problem, and a weak dollar undercut his efforts. In Phase I of his economic program, he ordered a freeze on wages and prices for 90 days, a 10 percent surcharge on imports to the United States, and devaluation of the American dollar. The second phase, begun over the summer of 1973, instituted wage and price-hike ceilings. However, little could be done to combat the enormous surge in prices pushed by swollen oil prices during 1973 and 1974. Over the whole period, economic growth remained slow, and inflation floated near 5 percent.

Despite Nixon's self-proclaimed conservatism, his intense dislike of the liberal eastern establishment, and his desultory attempts to undo Lyndon Johnson's Great Society programs, he did advocate reform. Two important acts, in 1972 and 1973, extended reform. The Equal Employment Opportunity Act of 1972 gave the Equal Economic Opportunity Commission power to enforce antidiscrimination laws through the courts. When Title 9 of the Education Amendments of 1972 prohibited discrimination in education programs, women's collegiate sports began to receive a fair share of funding. The Comprehensive Employment and Training Act of 1973 granted revenues to the states for training unskilled and underskilled workers. The creation of the Environmental Protection Agency in 1971 further extended government regulation of the environment and the workplace. These and other programs did not quite constitute mainline liberalism, but neither were they ultraconservative.

By 1972, Nixon's reelection was secure. Perhaps the Democrats had the chance to rally around Senator Edmund Muskie of Maine or the eventual standard bearer, Senator George McGovern of South Dakota. However, such crucial constituencies as big labor, city bosses, and the traditional South rejected McGovern, fearing a takeover of the party of liberal elements pushing the rights of women and an end to the war to the detriment of traditional ethnic, labor, and regional interests. The success of Governor George Wallace in the Florida primary, running opposed to school busing, was an omen of this debacle. He came close to winning the liberal state of Wisconsin, and he did gain majorities in Maryland and Michigan. Only a would-be assassin's bullet in May halted a campaign that might have split the party down the middle. Although Wallace ran as a Democrat, the passions he aroused in 1972 were inherited by Richard Nixon.

Then why Watergate? Why use underhanded and illegal tactics, in an election that was all but decided? These questions go to the heart the enigma of Nixon. Much after the fact, Nixon reflected on the events of 1972: "I brought myself down. I gave them a sword and they stuck it in. . . . I let down my friends; I let down my country. . . ." This curious confession betrays a puzzling man. The undefined "them"—the enemy—is perhaps the press or the liberal establishment that he despised. Yet, the confession is astonishingly superficial: Nixon could only see an error of judgment where many others discovered the subversion of justice and principle. His tragic failure was to misunderstand the moral dimensions of American politics.

In fact, there were two Nixon administrations—public and private—and two governments—known and clandestine. There were also two Nixons: There was the public puritanical, moralistic persona, the upholder of law and order; and there was the private connoisseur of fine wines who indulged in vulgar language. Watergate simply merged the two administrations and the two selves in full public view. In the end, the President succumbed to rumor, innuendo, and public trial by press, all tactics he had thrived on. Certainly, Nixon aroused great anger in opponents to the war in Vietnam, but his real crime was to compromise the traditions of government he was elected to uphold.

On the night of June 16, a District of Columbia police officer caught five men burglarizing the offices of the Democratic National Committee located in the plush Watergate office complex. After a court hearing for the burglars, *Washington Post* reporters traced the culprits to the White House. They were either former members of the Committee to Re-elect the President (CREEP) or former low-level staff members. Although the paper published this information, the break-in remained an obscure issue. Nixon won the fall election with a huge majority, 60.8 percent to 37.5 percent for McGovern. Such issues as law and order, family values, and foreign policy accomplishments provided the huge margin, but Watergate eventually stopped Nixon from translating this victory into a mandate for a more conservative administration.

In fact, the administration began to unravel in early 1973. One by one, higher and higher officials were implicated in the scandal. A tough federal judge, John J. Sirica, convinced one of the Watergate burglars, James W. McCord, to cooperate with a District of Columbia grand jury and a special investigating committee of the Senate headed by Democrat Sam Ervin of North Carolina. One confession begat another accusation. Witnesses implicated U.S. Attorney General John Mitchell, chief White House aides Haldeman and Ehrlichman, and the President's chief legal counsel, John Dean. All were charged with arranging the break-in or seeking to cover it up. Finally, only the President himself remained.

Washington buzzed with rumors after White House aide Alexander Butterfield disclosed on July 13, 1973, that the President had secretly tape-recorded White House conversations. Suspicions grew about what was on these tapes, however, as Nixon found one legal excuse after another to prevent Congress or his own special prosecutor, Archibald Cox, from hearing them. To protect himself, he was forced to fire Cox. The new prosecutor, Leon Jaworski, merely resumed the quest. Even the disclosure of many of the tapes did not satisfy the Congress or the prosecutor. Eventually, the Supreme Court forced Nixon's hand. In July 1974, the Court ordered the President to release the remaining tapes. The House Judiciary Committee began voting articles of impeachment.

The recordings revealed what many Americans already suspected. Nixon had participated in the coverup of White House staff involvement in Watergate as early as June 23, 1972. The tapes also disclosed an unpleasant, bitter, ill-willed man, anything but presidential in temper. Clearly, the President could not be saved. Members of his own party signaled that they would support impeachment. He could either resist or resign.

The last weeks in office visibly affected the President, whose face showed deepening signs of distress. As late as August 6, he remained indecisive, although his power was crumbling. Just to be safe, the Joint Chiefs of Staff and Defense Secretary James Schlesinger agreed to scrutinize any executive orders from the White House, but the end was inevitable. On the evening of August 7, the President called Henry Kissinger into the Lincoln Room of the White House. Asking the Secretary of State to join him in prayer, they knelt down. Thus, two of the world's most sophisticated men ended their period of joint power in a mumbled prayer. After this bizarre, final moment, which Kissinger called "heart-rending," the President announced that he would resign. He left the White House at 9:36 the following evening.

Nixon had lost the long struggle for credibility, and a few of the nation's principal newspapers could justly boast that their persistent investigations had turned the tide. The political establishment, led by the *Washington Post* and *The New York Times* had, in effect, impeached a president. But this process also released a long wave of public anger, some of it directed at the press. As an aide to Nixon said, "The *Washington Post* would have loved a guilty statement. But even a guilty statement wouldn't have satisfied them. What they wanted was a ceremony on the South Lawn, with the President incinerating himself and Ben Bradlee (the *Post* editor) toasting marshmallows in the flames."

Although Nixon clearly understood the ramifications of what he had done, he never admitted to anything more than errors of judgment. In his defense, it can be said that other presidents, at other times, had engaged in underhanded dealings with political opponents. Yet few had been so systematic, and none had been caught.

The man who stepped into the presidency was Michigan Representative Gerald Ford. Ford replaced Vice-President Spiro Agnew when he left office in October 1973, indicted on charges of fraud, bribery, and payoffs committed while he was governor of Maryland. The new President inherited an administration in shambles and a nation exhausted by Watergate and deeply suspicious of government and politicians. Ford had been a popular choice to stand in for Agnew, but to assume control of the national temper, Ford needed more skill and experience than he possessed. Ford had neither time nor ability to calm political tempers and deal with the problems of stagflation, the calamitous termination of the war in Vietnam, and broadening revelations of malfeasance in the American government.

There is something reminiscent in Ford of an amiable, minor league baseball manager. An instinctive mid-Western conservative, he belonged to the moderate wing of the Republican party. The Congress he faced after the fall of 1974 was aggressive, Democratic, and unwilling to allow the stand-in President to pick up Nixon's programs. Ultimately, Ford compromised his leadership by pardoning Richard Nixon. "My conscience tells me it is my duty," he announced, "not merely to proclaim domestic tranquility, but to use every means that I have to ensure it. . . ." The pardon deprived Americans who demanded the truth about Nixon. For Gerald Ford, the issue hung over the election of 1976 in the form of misgivings about his judgment and honesty.

Nor could Ford escape his reputation as a bumbler, which was reinforced by a lack of success in the face of serious economic problems. With inflation continuing, he tried to institute voluntary conservation of oil, a 5 percent tax surcharge, and a tight money policy. Congressional Democrats successfully opposed most of these programs. During 1975, the nation plunged into recession, with unemployment rising to 9.2 percent of May.

While the President struggled on the domestic front, foreign policy problems flared. During the spring of 1975, North Vietnamese troops and tanks crushed the South Vietnamese army and pressed toward Saigon. Ford could do nothing except, in a futile gesture, request financial aid for Thieu's failing government. Congress refused. In late April, the United States evacuated the last Americans and Vietnamese officials and supporters from Saigon. Television caught the final, desperate moments as hundreds of terrified Vietnamese leaped to catch the runners of departing American helicopters. Then on April 30, 1975, Saigon fell, an event the United States had struggled to prevent since 1954.

These were hours of bitter self-doubt and national reassessment. Then in May, when the Communist government of Cambodia seized the American ship *Mayaguez* and its 39 crew members, Ford acted almost by reflex, sending in U.S. sea and ground forces. On May 14, American forces rescued the 39 crew members, but at the cost of more than 40 casualties. This act of bravado restored a part of American confidence, but most Americans by 1975 probably wanted to forget, not revive, the spirit of Asian intervention.

At home, Watergate continued to radiate political fallout. Investigations disclosed that the CIA had harassed and infiltrated domestic political groups and directed plots to kill Fidel Castro and to throw the election of Salvador Allende. It was further revealed that J. Edgar Hoover and the FBI maintained political dossiers on American political figures, such as Martin Luther King, Jr.

Fighting the inertia of these events in the fall of 1975, Ford sought to establish direction to his administration. He reorganized the cabinet, firing some of its most controversial figures but retaining Henry Kissinger as Secretary of State. Nonetheless, little real movement occurred; there was scarcely time. When Ford announced that he would seek election in 1976, Ronald Reagan challenged him from the right. After a bitter and divisive primary fight, Ford gained the nomination, but Reagan owned the soul of the party. The Republicans prepared to lurch to the right; Ford's candidacy, win or lose, was but a temporary obstacle.

In fact, Ford almost won the election because the Democratic contender, Jimmy Carter squandered a huge initial lead. Carter then turned his narrow victory into the most unpopular presidency since World War II. The explanation lies in the elusive personality of Carter himself and in the injurious contradictions in the Democratic Party.

Carter commanded technical intelligence, much beyond many of his predecessors in the presidency. A competent submarine officer, he understood nuclear energy. A success in private industry in the peanut warehouse business, he also had a short but noteworthy political career in Georgia as governor. He was a meticulous and hard worker. As he noted in his memoirs, "From the beginning, I realized that my ability to govern well would depend upon my mastery of the extremely important issues I faced. I wanted to learn as much as possible and devoted full time to it. . . ."

The new President had broad but not deep political support. His political home base was the New South coalition of whites and blacks who accepted interracial politics. He wore his "born again" Christianity openly and promised a moral administration (in obvious reference to Nixon). However, he had little familiarity or sympathy for the other traditional constituencies of the Democratic Party: organized labor, ethnic and Catholic voters in the large urban areas of the Northeast and Midwest. In fact, Carter won only because he garnered 90 percent of the black vote and a respectable percent of white voters in the southern states.

The new President also had serious failings some of which had to do with the image he projected. The public came to believe that his sincerity was a mask. Also damaging was his amateur's attitude toward politics. Elected as an outsider, he was unschooled in national political leadership. As he warned about the "mess" in Washington, "You can't expect any better from political leadership that is bogged down in Washington for the last twenty-five or thirty years, deriving their advice, their counsel, their financial support from lobbyists, and special interest groups. . . . We can't run this government or this administration . . . from the White House Rose Garden"—a remark that would later haunt him.

Being an outsider also put Carter at something of a disadvantage with the media. As some Presidents have discovered to their dismay, the news media and Congress quickly exploit weakness. Thus, the huge Democratic majority in the Senate and House evaporated in factional infighting between contending wings of the party. The press was unflattering in its portrayal of the President, and Carter had the misfortune to be visited by serious economic problems and bad luck in foreign policy that might have disabled even a more astute politician.

In 1976, Carter won 40.8 million votes to 39.1 for Ford. The Democrats seized a commanding lead in the House, 292 to 143, and in the Senate, 61 to 38. Carter's campaign promises were extensive, but vague: Restore honesty to government; promote family values, nuclear disarmament, and a new national harmony. He promised to commit government to reflect "the high moral character of the American people."

His appointments, however, gave a mixed signal. He selected Washington insiders Cyrus Vance as Secretary of State and Joseph Califano as Secretary of Health, Education, and Welfare. He chose Patricia Harris, a black woman, to head Housing and Urban Development. Indeed, a substantial portion of lower administrative positions went to women and blacks. Civil rights leader Andrew Young became chief United Nations delegate. Zbigniew Brzezinski, a tough anti-Communist, won the post of National Security Adviser. Carter's personal staff was primarily Georgians: Hamilton Jordan as White House Chief of staff and Burt Lance as head of the Office of Management and Budget.

Carter's strengths and weaknesses emerged during his initial struggle to create a sound energy program. Any politician assumes that the first months in office decide the tone and quality of leadership. For a president, this honeymoon period can mean significant achievements. Carter, citing the disarray of Ford's energy policy called conservation of gas and petroleum supplies a national emergency. He proposed an ambitious major program in April 1977. It was intellectually sound—like much of what Carter attempted—but politically flawed. On April 18, the President addressed the nation, calling the energy crisis the "moral equivalent of war." If this smacked of hyperbole and exaggeration, the plan was nonetheless comprehensive and ambitious. It included a tax on gas-guzzling automobiles, a new tax on gasoline, and tax credits for home energy conservation. Carter also pressed for freer prices on natural gas.

By August, the energy bill had sailed through the House, but the Senate stalled it, debating the deregulation of natural gas prices. Finally, a year later, the program emerged as five related acts to reward home energy conservation, persuade electrical generating companies to switch to coal, mandate automobile efficiency, and increase natural gas prices. However, the sticky question of freeing oil prices from regulation remained.

Actually, Carter vacillated on this last, tough question. As he told the American nation in his April address, he understood their suspicions that energy companies were plotting to withhold oil and gas to raise prices. "You may be right," he said, "but suspicions about the oil companies cannot change the fact that we are running out of petroleum." This was a curious position for a national leader to take. If a conspiracy existed, then Carter should have acted. If not, he should have defused the issue. Instead, he shifted ground, urging Americans to live a simpler, more frugal life—as if to say that Americans should blame themselves.

Similarly, he held himself aloof during a long and bitter coal strike of the winter of 1977–78, suggesting that he had no policy. At the end of 1978, energy did become a national crisis, when Iran cut production from 5.5 million barrels a day to 1.5 million, promoting a world shortage. A revolution in January 1979, overthrowing the Shah of Iran, a loyal friend and long-time ally of American policy, further disrupted the oil trade. Higher prices and gasoline lines reappeared. Once again, many Americans believed that greedy companies engineered shortages to force the complete decontrol of oil prices. If this was indeed their policy, it succeeded. Carter proposed a limited decontrol of oil prices, although he matched it with a new windfall profits tax. In perspective, Carter's energy policy may be judged a relative success; but many Americans disagreed at the time. Worse, energy policy became knotted up with foreign policy issues beyond the control of the President.

A different sort of energy crisis in the spring of 1979 also undermined American confidence. A nuclear reactor at Three Mile Island generating plant near Harrisburg, Pennsylvania, narrowly escaped a complete "meltdown." A meltdown could have released lethal amounts of radiation into the earth, water, and atmosphere. The accident seriously contaminated the plant site, and thousands of nearby residents temporarily evacuated their homes. New public doubts about nuclear energy damaged an already troubled industry. One lesson was clear—there were no quick solutions to energy shortages.

The new President faced other immense economic problems. In some respects, the Carter administration differed little from the Ford government. Like his predecessors, Carter fought the twin evils of inflation and slow growth. But stagflation resisted his cautious policies. The early resignation of OMB director Lance, whose personal bank dealings touched off an investigation and accusations of improper practices, led to a shaky start. By 1978, inflation had

Jimmy Carter's plain and frugal style of dress reflected his deeply held views that the president should set realistic (and lower) expectations for the nation.   *(Ken Hawkins/ Sygma)*

heated up significantly to 7.7 percent per annum (driven upward by oil prices and large budget deficits).

Indecision plus difficulties with Congress gave the impression of an administration in disarray. The jangled nerves of public confidence showed dramatically in the victory of Proposition 13, a referendum passed in California in 1978. This regulation, approved by general ballot, slashed personal property taxes. Citizens in other states introduced similar measures. The message could not be mistaken: If federal and state governments refused to limit expenditures and taxes, the people would—whatever the consequences.

Carter's reaction was quixotic, but much in character: He retreated into moralisms and symbolism. During the summer of 1979, besieged by another gasoline shortage, rapid inflation, and slow growth, he retired to the presidential retreat at Camp David, Maryland. Public opinion polls had lurched to a 26 percent approval of his leadership. Obviously, he had to assert control, but in a speech for national television, he blamed a host of vague and intangible causes for a spiritual crisis of "national malaise." Although the concrete proposals in his talk made good sense—strong measures for energy conservation and a federally funded investment corporation to aid large businesses in danger of bankruptcy—he lost the sympathy of much of his audience by dwelling on spiritual crisis.

In foreign policy, Carter exhibited the same skills and flaws. For example, he rejected secret diplomacy, intrigue, and support for right-wing dictatorships. His tried to promote human rights. As he announced during the campaign, "There is only one nation in the world which is capable of true leadership among the community of nations, and that is the United States of America." Henceforth, he proclaimed, the United States would support or criticize nations according to their standards of domestic freedom. But just as it had during the presidency of Woodrow Wilson sixty years earlier, this moral emphasis sometimes conflicted with the necessities of alliances and hard choices. Other nations, particularly the Soviet Union, deeply resented the assumption that the United States could judge their internal affairs.

Still, there were major successes. A Panama Canal Treaty signed by Carter and approved by the Senate provided for eventual return of the Canal Zone to Panama and guaranteed user privileges to the United States. This act earned significant praise from Latin American nations who saw it as a major step in the abandonment of the previous U.S. policy of intervention. But in the United States the treaty became a *cause celèbre* for the right wing which charged that Carter had sold out American interests.

A second success represented the high point of the Carter administration. In March 1979, Israel and Egypt signed a general accord to end almost thirty years of warfare that began in 1948 with the creation of the Israeli state. Israel gained recognition from Egypt. In return, Israel promised to return Egyptian territory seized during the 1973 Yom Kippur War. Even more interesting was the process of negotiation. In late 1978, Carter invited Israel's prime minister Menachem Begin and President Anwar Sadat of Egypt to Camp David. He took a serious risk in doing so. The President acted as host, go-between, cajoler, and leader in the difficult parley. His triumph won a victory for moralism in international relations. Carter was justly pleased that this peace had been achieved by three leaders representing three different religions—a Christian, a Jew, and a Moslem, two of them born in the Middle East, in the cradle of western religions.

Other problems, however, could neither be pried open by Carter's moral fervor nor his human rights policy. Successful negotiations of a Soviet-United States SALT II agreement, signed in June of 1979, limited weapons systems, but the treaty died in the Senate. It fell victim to a vocal conservative minority that demanded higher defense expenditures and a cessation of negotiations with the Russians. It failed partly because the Russian invasion of neighboring Afghanistan in late 1979 enraged many lawmakers.

Despite Camp David, the Middle East undid Carter's presidency. Before his overthrow, Shah Mohammed Riza Pahlevi of Iran had been a constant friend of the United States. He had led his nation toward western-style modernization, but his methods were often brutal. The social disruptions and political frustrations of rapid change radicalized the population of Iran. Some demanded a form of Marxist rule, but a more significant element favored a radically conservative Islamic fundamentalist state. A shakey coalition controlled by this latter group seized power in early 1979. When the Shah of Iran entered the United States for medical treatments, the Iranians demanded his immediate deportation, but the United States refused, unable to turn away an old ally. Infuriated, Iranian militants and students seized the American Embassy and took fifty-three U.S. hostages, again demanding the return of the Shah.

Caught in a double bind, Carter could not accede. The radical students, encouraged and supported by the Ayatollah Khomeini, the behind-the-scenes power of the new Iranian theocracy, denounced the United States as a "Great Satan." After fruitless negotiations, Carter approved a secret rescue mission, but the ill-planned and badly equipped venture failed. Months dragged on while the nightly news reminded the American public that no progress had been made. Like the war in Vietnam, the hostage crisis became a television staple.

While Carter concentrated on the Iranian crisis, Senator Ted Kennedy of Massachusetts challenged him for the nomination of the Democratic Party in the spring of 1980. Carter pursued a "rose garden" strategy—refusing to leave the White House during the crisis. This tactic certainly heightened American anxieties about the hostages. Not that Kennedy could generate much enthusiasm; his campaign floundered before it started because he could not satisfactorily explain the auto accident and drowning of Mary Jo Kopechne on July 18, 1969, on Chappaquiddick Island off Cape Cod. Kennedy had been driving the car and he could not adequately explain how the accident had happened or account for his strange behavior after it. Moreover, Kennedy's invocation of liberalism did not excite the electorate. After a series of bruising primaries, Carter recaptured the nomination.

But the victory drink was spoiled. Carter's presidency, so full of promise and yet so unsuccessful, convinced many Americans to vote for a dramatic change. Carter could not reunite the Democratic Party. The stage was set for the brilliant campaign of Ronald Reagan.

Ronald Reagan's rise to the presidency belongs to the age of mass media. From a modest background in northern Illinois, Reagan grew up in an insecure and unstable family, in a nation shattered by the Depression of 1929. Reagan discovered a political hero in Franklin Roosevelt, whose speech patterns and cadences he later copied. After school at Eureka College, he found a job as a baseball announcer. However, his ambition remained acting, and in 1937, he won a small part in "Love Is on the Air." His career launched, he made several mediocre films and a few good ones. In perhaps his best picture, *King's Row*, he played a pilot who had lost his legs. Then as George Gipp in *Knute Rockne—All American*, he found his stride. Marriage to actress Jane Wyman in 1940 was a typical Hollywood romance—much celebrated and short.

If Reagan's acting won few accolades, he nonetheless, rose quickly in the rough and highly ideological world of Hollywood politics in the 1940s and 1950s. He led a fight against Communist influence in the movie industry but remained free of the excesses of some anti-Communist crusaders. After his divorce in 1948, he married Nancy Davis, an aspiring actress, but by then neither actor had much future in films. So in 1954, Reagan signed on with General Electric as a dinner circuit speaker and television host to sell G.E.'s products and free-enterprise philosophy. Reagan did both exceedingly well, and by the early 1960s, he had built a strong following on the right. His good looks, humor, and obvious sincerity disarmed critics who might otherwise have been appalled at some of his narrow views of the world. Even his tendency to exaggerate only confirmed his seriousness.

In 1966, Reagan won the governorship of California on a platform with his favorite planks: more morality and less government and a promise to stop university demonstrations. Although his diminished majority in 1970 suggested some voter displeasure at failure to deliver on promises, by then his political career had entered a new phase: He was a celebrity of new-right national politics.

The road from extremist politics toward the political center was fraught with compromise, but by 1980, the American electorate prepared to meet Reagan half way. Aided by evangelical Christian groups and new-right organizations that collected money and voters on his behalf, Reagan campaigned for more defense spending, lower income taxes, cuts in welfare spending, and ending inflation. He pledged to work for family values and other symbolic measures. Having personally experienced the failures of laissez-faire capitalism, a difficult family life as a child, and a divorce, he radiated faith in traditional institutions that only adversity can generate.

President Carter, who could not galvanize the Democratic constituencies, lacked the means to defend his administration. His only strong suit was fear of Reagan's inexperience and belligerence in foreign policy, which disappeared when the challenger convinced the public he was competent, sincere, and honest. Reagan repeatedly asked a question that encouraged Americans to trust his leadership: "Are you better off than you were four years ago? Is it easier for you to go and buy things in the stores than it was four years ago? Is there more or less unemployment in the country than there was four years ago? Is America as respected throughout the world as it was?"

Although votes for John Anderson, of Illinois, skewed the result, Reagan still won with 50.7 percent to Carter's 41 percent. Equally important (although the House remained Democrat, 243 to 192),

Republicans seized control of the Senate with 53 seats to 47. The most numerous block in the electorate as in 1980, however, stayed home. Of all eligible voters only 28 percent selected Ronald Reagan. The candidate had succeeded in capturing an American electorate polarized between Sunbelt and Frostbelt, between opponents and supporters of women's rights and abortion, between retired and current workers, and between races.

The new President did not speculate about this complex result. Buoyed by his skill as a "Great Communicator," he took the economic agenda of the new-right and sold most of it to the traditional working majority of Republican presidents—conservative southern Democrats and Republicans. Only a revision of economic priorities, he declared, could respond to the economic crisis of the day. On inauguration day, inflation stood at 13 percent a year, with a prime lending rate of 20 percent. More than 7 percent of the work force was unemployed. Like Nixon and Carter, he blamed Washington: "Government is not the solution to our problem; government is the problem." A generation disgusted by Watergate, confused by Vietnam, and antagonistic to the Great Society welcomed these words. Instead of government, Reagan promised to return to a timeworn principle: "Work and family are at the center of our lives, the foundation of our dignity as a free people."

Reagan's cabinet choices contained several surprises. For the post of Labor Secretary, Reagan broke an old tradition. Instead of appointing a labor man, he chose James Donovan, a construction company operator from New Jersey. James Watt, an opponent of conservationists and a leader of the "Sagebrush Revolt" in the far West went to Interior. General Alexander Haig won the spot of Secretary of State, and Democrat Jeane Kirkpatrick, an intelligent and hawkish political scientist, became chief U.N. delegate. Casper Weinberger went to Defense, where he quickly showed himself a skilled advocate of military spending. Donald Regan, chair of Merrill Lynch brokerage firm, took the position of Secretary of the Treasury. Together with OMB head David Stockman, he and the White House staff designed Reagan's economic policies. Altogether, they were skilled, intelligent, and highly ideological.

Reagan set cutting taxes and social spending as his first priority. His program, as the Secretary of Treasury announced, "relies on the oldest and most proven economic principles known to this country. It restores our faith in the private enterprise system, in personal ini-

Ronald Reagan and James Watt in the spotlight. Despite Watt's resignation under a cloud as interior secretary, President Reagan remained untouched by the controversy. (Atlan/Sygma)

tiative, in individual prerogative and in the traditions of personal saving and investment that have built everything from log cabins to high-rise apartments."

In the first dramatic months of his presidency, Reagan pushed hard for his promised income tax cut. Calling the current economic situation "the worst economic mess since the Depression" and labeling the previous decades a period of economic failure, he asked Congress for a 30 percent cut in tax rates over three years. He also proposed a massive budget shift of funding into defense and out of such social programs as guaranteed student loans, food stamps, and job-training programs. Beneath the poor, he promised to spread a safety net to catch the truly needy.

Despite initial stalling in Congress and then a curious attempt by the Democrats to outbid the President in tax giveaways to business, the budget passed in August of 1981 with a 25 percent tax cut in individual rates and expenditures skewed toward the military. David Stockman later confessed that the program meant nothing more than traditional Republican "trickle down" economics. The role of government in the American economy was not diminished by this budget. Indeed, over the four years, government expenditures as a percent of the gross national product increased slightly. What did diminish was the federal obligation to invest in human resources, especially for poorer Americans.

Reagan's brilliant legislative triumph occurred in the context of a dramatic attempt on his life on March 30, 1981. After an address at a Washington hotel, Reagan quickly passed through a crowd standing at the entrance, but not fast enough. John Hinckley Jr., a deeply disturbed young man, trying to reenact a moment from the film *Taxi Driver* to impress its young star, Jody Foster, fired at the President with a 22-caliber revolver. He hit a police officer and Press Secretary James Brady. One of the bullets ricocheted and struck the President in the chest. The presidential limousine sped Reagan to George Washington Hospital for treatment.

Oblivious to the gravity of his situation, Reagan cheerfully quipped one-liners to the medical staff: "Please tell me you're all Republicans." His blithe courage, undiminished by danger, revealed a man whose private personality matched his public optimism and sincerity. This demonstration had a decisive effect on public opinion, earning him respect, which he quickly invested in support for his tax and budget programs.

Other parts of his deregulation and antiinflationary programs fell into place. James Watt charged into the Interior Department intent on turning it into a kind of resource investment brokerage firm, consigning wilderness areas and scenic offshore oil sites for commercial exploitation. Like Reagan, he too was a devotee of the quick-draw quip, but his outrageous statements and resource giveaways became a serious liability to the administration.

Anne (Gorsuch) Burford, head of the Environmental Protection Agency administered water cleanup funds with, apparently, everything in mind but the purpose of cleaning up dangerous chemical dumps. Her politicalization of the office and favoritism toward industry ended in a Congressional investigation and her resignation in March 1983. But these scandals did not tarnish the image of Reagan, whom Colorado Democratic Representative Pat Schroeder called the "Teflon President." No political miracle worker, Reagan earned this position because he treated the presidency as head of state or chairman of the board, letting his appointees take the responsibility and blame for policy.

Despite firm promises of growth and a decline in inflation and unemployment, Reagan's economic policies at first had an opposite result because they were inherently contradictory. The tax cut failed to stimulate savings, investment, or growth because high interest rates, designed to cut inflation, plunged the nation into the worst recession since the 1930s. From the summer of 1981 through late 1982, the economy lurched downward, dragging Western Europe and the underdeveloped economies with it. American unemployment reached almost 11 percent in December 1982, or more than 12 million workers concentrated among blue-collar jobs in the industrial states and exaggerated among blacks, the young, and the unskilled. A swath of the American industrial world from Minnesota through Pennsylvania resembled the dark days of the 1930s, with huge crowds gathering at the announcement of a few job openings. This resulted in minor gains for the Democratic party in the 1982 elections with 26 new members, but the Senate lineup remained the same.

If the language and theory behind Reagan's economic policies sounded new, their content and effects were not. Severe recession, as it had in the past, reined in runaway prices. Oil demand and costs fell sharply. Upward pressure on wages declined, particularly in such major industries as auto manufacturing, where workers accepted salary cuts in return for security. Being in less demand, raw materials cost less.

Reagan's cure for the recession also came from the standard tool-box of economic measures. Continued high spending for such entitlement programs as medicare and veterans' payments, for servicing the national debt, and for huge new defense expenditures, built a budget deficit in 1982 of 117.4 billion, and 195.4 billion in 1983. These astounding sums befuddled conservatives, who demanded a constitutional amendment to balance the budget. For the time being, they refused to indicate how to achieve the balance. Even the President supported this limitation, although it would not take effect until the end of his second term.

In effect, the federal government, as it had since the 1930s, spent its way out of the recession. Interest rates remained high, although certainly a relief from the peak of 20 percent in 1980. Growth rebounded in early 1983 and gathered momentum until moderating over the summer of 1984 and into 1985 (some of the "growth" made up lost ground). By the election of 1984, the administration could rightly point to a revived economy. Its promotion of income redistribution toward the upper economic ranks was widely recognized, but of marginal importance to most Americans.

Put another way, a "Republican" shock to the system knocked down inflation, and a "Democratic" deficit restored growth. But the administration exaggerated the side effects of both policies. Unemployment (7.5 percent) and interest rates (14 percent) remained

Real Disposable Income by Fifths of the Population, 1980 and 1984*

Fifth of Population	1980		1984	
	Average Disposable Income per Family	Percent Share	Average Disposable Income per Family	Percent Share
Bottom	$6,913	6.8	$6,391	6.1
Second	13,391	13.2	13,163	12.5
Third	18,857	18.5	19,034	18.1
Fourth	24,886	24.5	25,724	24.5
Top	37,618	37.0	40,880	38.9

*All figures in 1982 dollars.
Source: *Urban Institute*.

high through the summer of 1984 although interest fell sharply by mid-1985. Budget deficits soared, casting a shadow on future economic growth. The President agreed to "revenue enhancements" (taxes) in 1983 and a minimal down payment on the deficit of 1984. Another troublesome phenomenon was the inflated value of the dollar vis à vis major world currencies, caused by high U.S. interest rates. The expensive dollar made it possible to buy cheaply abroad, but made U.S. products very expensive. The result was a record trade imbalance of $107.6 billion in 1984, and a significant lessening of domestic production. Nonetheless, such budgetary imbalances did not become a decisive issue in the November election.

On social issues—questions of class, race and gender—Reagan moved more cautiously. His evangelical and right-wing supporters hoped to retard or undo some of the changes in these areas since World War II. In general, the President agreed that the federal government should stay out of the business of creating equality. He supported traditional values, some of which implied more inequality. Translated into policy, this meant supporting antiabortion and prayer in public school amendments. Still, the President kept his distance from the evangelical right by freezing them out of important appointments.

In the area of civil rights, the administration indicated that it opposed new legislation and hoped to slow the enforcement of older statutes. Temporarily, it even blocked extension of the voting rights legislation of 1965, which protected voters in the South, although public pressure reversed this stand. The administration discarded means of enforcing school desegregation, such as busing. Even his appointment of Sandra Day O'Connor to the Supreme Court, a major advance for women's rights, ultimately aided the conservative cause. Although the evangelical right wing opposed her appointment, Reagan's strategy proved effective, for her consistent votes helped shift the Court to the right.

In foreign affairs, Reagan's ideology detoured traditional strategic thinking. His single-minded vision of a world divided between good (the United States) and the "evil empire" of the Soviet Union renewed fears of an arms race and nuclear war. It provided arguments for Soviet hawks, who had a similar, if reverse view of good and evil. Reagan's incautious comment in August 1984 before a radio broadcast suggests that the President believed in this division of good and evil. He joked that Congress had outlawed the Russians, and "American bombers were on the way." This unfunny remark, suggested an obsessive concern about the Soviets—and a very dated view of modern war. More important evidence than an occasional Freudian slip was the absence of any serious negotiations on disarmament and a defense budget of $135 billion in 1980 that shot up to $214 billion in 1983.

By the spring of 1982, blustery talk in the administration about surviving a nuclear holocaust helped force a shift in tone, if not policy. Thomas Jones, a deputy Undersecretary of Defense, commented in a widely quoted statement about building bomb shelters: "If there are enough shovels to go around, everybody's going to make it." New talks, dubbed START, began but quickly stalemated because of intransigence on both sides. Finally, after the election of 1984, and a charge of leadership in the Soviet Union bringing Mikhail S. Gorbachev to the helm, new negotiations were begun in 1985.

A policy of negotiating from strength and suggestions of winning a nuclear war worried several European NATO allies. Preparations to place Cruise short-range nuclear missiles in Germany, England, Italy, and the Netherlands ignited a temporary, mass protest movement, which subsided in 1983 without halting the installations. An American effort to disrupt the building of a Soviet natural gas pipeline to Western Europe by blocking sales of turbine and construction materials backfired and offended allies. Calling for equality of sacrifice, they rightly pointed out that the Reagan administration had lifted the embargo on U.S. sales of grain to the Soviet Union, which the Carter Administration had raised in response to the Russian invasion of Afghanistan in 1979.

Policy in Latin America had mixed results. The Falkland Islands crisis of April 1982 caught the administration between two allies. Claiming title, Argentina seized the British occupied islands off its shores. Prime Minister Margaret Thatcher ordered in the British navy and air force. At first, the United States took a neutral posture, but then it supported the Thatcher move. After a costly naval and air engagement, the Argentinians were routed. The British recaptured the islands. Eventually, the right-wing generals who had promised victory were overthrown, and a democratic government was installed in Argentina. It was an unforeseen but happy consequence.

Elsewhere in Latin America, the Reagan administration relied heavily upon arms and force. In the fall of 1983, the President ordered the invasion of the tiny island republic of Grenada after a coup had replaced a moderate leftist with a hard-line faction. Stores of arms and Cuban advisors were found on the island. Many of the island residents and most other Caribbean nations applauded this tough action.

A far more complex situation mired American policy in Central America. For decades, the tiny nations of the area had attempted to construct political stability upon the quicksands of poverty. A revolution in Nicaragua brought a left-wing government to power, one that looked to Cuba and the socialist governments of Europe for support. Nicaragua also supported rebels in neighboring El Salvador, a nation torn between guerrilla revolutionaries and a dictatorship of extraordinary brutality. In this complex situation, the Reagan administration applied pressure at two points. It urged the government of El Salvador to stop its terrible violations of human rights (with some limited success), while it bolstered the armed forces to fight the rebels. In the early spring of 1983 the President dispatched several thousand troops to nearby Honduras for joint maneuvers, which turned out to be a permanent garrison. Employing the CIA, the administration financed Nicaraguan rebels fighting to overthrow the government. These efforts resulted in serious economic damage to Nicaragua and convinced a vascillating Congress to shut off aid for clandestine warfare temporarily in 1984 and then restore it in 1985.

The most difficult situation proved to be the Middle East. In June 1982, Israel invaded Lebanon to rid its borders of harassment by the Palestine Liberation Organization (PLO), which freely operated there. Israel succeeded militarily, but the Lebanese government collapsed, and the nation broke into warring Christian and Moslem factions. To promote peace, the Reagan Administration stationed about 2,000 troops in an enclave near the Beirut airport, but terrorists took advantage of the thinly guarded bivouac and drove a truck full of bombs into the compound, killing 239 American troops. Thus, costly error spotlighted an incautiously devised policy.

In the midst of these difficulties, the President replaced his Secretary of State. General Haig's flamboyant style and his hostile relations with key administration figures, such as Jeane Kirkpatrick, hurried his downfall. George Schultz, former Secretary of the Treasury under Nixon, replaced Haig. The policies remained much the same, although Shultz proved to be a better team player.

Ronald Reagan took this mixed record to the American electorate in 1984 for ratification. His opponent, Walter Mondale, struggled to respond to it. In a series of grueling primary contests, Mondale bested Senator Gary Hart of Colorado and the Reverend Jesse Jackson of Chicago, the first serious black candidate for president. Mondale chose as his running mate Representative Geraldine Ferraro, the first woman to be nominated for such an office in a major political party. Nonetheless, Ronald Reagan set the agenda, basing his campaign on the economic recovery and low inflation. Candidates Mondale and Ferraro based their campaign on family values, the huge federal deficit, and social fairness. They warned of terrible consequences if Reagan's economic and foreign policies continued, but even the enthusiastic response to Ferraro's candidacy did not shake confidence in the buoyant leadership of the President. On November 7, 1984, he won a second term, and the chance to be the first president to serve two full terms since Eisenhower.

This landslide election underscored a developing shift in American politics and social policy. The postwar economic boom of the 1940s through the 1960s had financed a revolution in social policy. Major advances for veterans, women, blacks and other social minorities had been possible without an extensive redistribution of income. In the parsimonious and confusing 1970s, national policy gradually drifted away from this commitment. The first Reagan administration confirmed this broad trend, and the second promised more of the same.

The landslide victory of Ronald Reagan in 1984, in which he garnered a majority of votes from every major group in American society except blacks, Jews, and orientals, built a remarkable bridge between the forces of change and ideological conservatism in American society. Not accidentally, Reagan gained a huge majority among young voters. He spoke directly to their culture (as an actor and movie star, he had helped invent their world). Happily at ease with himself, personally tolerant, and with a suggestion of the glitter of Hollywood, he did not threaten young voters—even though a great many of them opposed his conservative views on women's rights, abortion, nuclear war, and education. He built a coalition, not of social groups, organizations, and classes, but a confabulation of reality and ideology. Whether or not this would ultimately lead to a political realignment remained uncertain. The only clue was the profound racial division that emerged in the balloting.

Yet beneath politics, the dynamics of change in American society continued relentlessly during these years. New life-styles coexisted with the reaffirmation of traditional institutions. Beneath the clichés about relying on old virtues, a new sort of society was emerging with new problems and new promises. Increasingly, the decline of older institutions shaped this world into a society of autonomous, even isolated, individuals. At the same time, however, the new society was, more than ever, a mass society, defined by mass culture, mass communications, and dependent on a world economic order. Confronted with this, both liberals and conservatives struggled to defend traditional values and policies as they understood them. Yet progress and change remained relentless. Old problems and old inequalities reappeared in unanticipated new guises.

How to confront this new world remained, as it always had, a political problem. The question which the Reagan administration posed was what sort of solution would be tried. Would Americans construct a national consensus based on public or private solutions? Would government remain the primary institution for solving social and economic problems? This was a choice in emphases, perhaps, but it was a choice that had not been faced so clearly since the end of World War II. Nor did it ever have quite so much meaning.

Suggested Reading

The historical contours of the period following World War II have begun to emerge with some clarity in recent years. Two major divisions now seem apparent: from 1945 to about 1968 and from 1968 onward. Because the events referred to in this book are so recent, some of the historical questions have not yet been sharply defined. However, a surprisingly large amount of fine work has already been done, much of which suggests that the period from 1945 to 1968 represents an extraordinarily prosperous and progressive time and possibly even an exception to much previous American history.

One explanation for the economic stability after the war is suggested in Otis Graham's *Toward a Planned Society* (1976), which discusses the increasing tendency of the American government to undertake central economic planning. Gunnar Myrdal's *An American Dilemma: The Negro Problem and Modern Democracy* (1944) indicates the seriousness of the problem of race relations that society was called upon to confront after the war. Keith Olson's *The G.I. Bill: Veterans and the Colleges* (1974) is a good study of the role of this important legislation in revolutionizing higher education in America. Susan Hartmann, in *The Home Front and Beyond: American Women in the 1940s* (1982), adds an important perspective on the fascinating question of the effects of war on women. Changes in the American family have been discussed by a number of authors. A good, short account is Barry Farber's *Family and Kinship in Modern Society* (1973). Richard A. Easterlin offers an interesting perspective on the sudden increase in the birthrate after the war in his *American Baby Boom in Historical Perspective* (1962). The revolution in American medicine that followed the war is ably sketched in James Bordley and A. McGehee Harvey's *Two Centuries of American Medicine: 1776–1976* (1976). A fascinating study of changes in public attitudes is George H. Gallup's *The Gallup Poll: Public Opinion, 1935–1971* (1972). Some of the difficult concepts and arrangements in postwar economics are clarified in Alfred E. Eckes, Jr.'s *A Search for Solvency: Bretton Woods and the International Monetary System, 1941–1971* (1975). A fine account of the Roosevelt presidency during the war is James Mac-Gregor Burns's *Roosevelt: The Soldier of Freedom* (1970).

The Cold War has been the subject of much debate. Historians have argued over the degree of responsibility that the Soviet Union and the United States should share for initiating and perpetuating this hostile confrontation. John Lewis Gaddis's *The United States and the Origins of the Cold War, 1941–1947* (1972) is a fine, comprehensive account. Stephen E. Ambrose, in *Rise to Globalism: American Foreign Policy Sine 1938* (1971), argues that since the late 1930s, the United States has increasingly taken an interventionist position in world affairs. Lloyd C. Gardner's *Architects of Illusion: Men and Ideas in American Foreign Policy 1941–1949* (1970) is a critical essay on the ideology of policymakers. The complicated policies surrounding the creation and use of the atomic bomb—and the effects of these policies—are admirably documented in a fine book by Martin J. Sherwin, *A World Destroyed: The Atomic Bomb and the Grand Alliance* (1975). Gregg Herken, in *The Winning Weapon: The Atomic Bomb in the Cold War, 1945 to 1950* (1981), makes an interesting case that there were no real atomic secrets to be guarded. A very useful source is Hans L. Trefousse's *The Cold War: A Book of Documents* (1965). An interesting popular account of the Cold War may be found in Carl Solberg's *Riding High: America in the Cold War* (1973). Adam B. Ulam, in *Expansion and Coexistence: Soviet Foreign Policy, 1917–73* (1974), provides a comprehensive account of Soviet intentions during this period.

The memoir literature of foreign-policy figures is particularly interesting and literate. Two of the outstanding works are Dean Acheson's *Present at the Creation: My Years in the State Department* (1969) and George F. Kennan's *Memoirs: 1925–1950* (1967). Also interesting is *Private Papers of Senator Vandenberg*, by Arthur H. Vandenberg, Jr. (1952). A controversial book describing the darker side of diplomacy is Allen Weinstein's *Perjury!: The Hiss-Chambers Conflict* (1978). Weinstein makes a case for the guilt of Alger Hiss, accused of passing secret documents to the Russians in the late 1930s. In the same vein, Ronald Radosh and Joyce Milton, in *The Rosenberg File: A Search for the Truth* (1983), provide significant evidence that Julius Rosenberg was guilty of passing atomic information to the Russians and that the FBI implicated his wife to force him to confess.

Assessment of the Truman presidency has already undergone at least one revision. Viewed unfavorably by many of his contemporaries, Truman has been given high marks by later historians. A good place to begin reading is with Truman's own *Memoirs* (1955). This work is full of interesting anecdotes and gives a sample of the president's feisty style. Alonzo L. Hamby in *Beyond the New Deal: Harry S Truman and American Liberalism* (1973), judiciously assesses the President's relationship to liberalism. Bert Cochran's *Harry Truman and the Crisis Presidency* (1973) is a very readable, iconoclastic account. Robert J. Donovan in two volumes has provided a very readable account of the Truman presidency—*Conflict and Crisis: The Presidency of Harry S Truman, 1945–1948* (1977), and *Tumultuous Years: The Presidency of Harry S Truman* (1982). Special issues surrounding the Truman administration have been covered by Arthur F.

McClure, *The Truman Administration and the Problems of Postwar Labor,
1945–1948* (1969). John Snetsinger, in *Truman, the Jewish Vote and the
Creation of Israel* (1974), delineates the president's ambiguous policy toward that new nation. Richard S. Kirkendall's *Harry S Truman, Korea, and
the Imperial Presidency* (1975), is a good discussion of Truman's policies.
William Berman, in *The Politics of Civil Rights in the Truman Administration* (1970), traces the administration's activities in this field. Richard
Lowitt provides a balanced account of the *Truman-MacArthur Controversy*
(1967). Truman's record on civil liberties has been challenged by two writers: David Caute, in *The Great Fear: The Anti-Communist Purge Under
Truman and Eisenhower* (1978), and Anthan F. Theoharis, in *Seeds of Repression: Harry Truman and the Origins of McCarthyism* (1971).

Changes in urban and suburban life were widely studied in the postwar
period. Several contemporary books offer a great deal of insight into the
suburban culture of the 1950s. The most important is David Riesman's
The Lonely Crowd: A Study of the Changing American Character (1950).
William H. Whyte, Jr.'s, *The Organization Man* (1956) is a fascinating
study of suburban culture and Whyte's revulsion by it. J. D. Salinger's *The
Catcher in the Rye* (1951), a very controversial novel, captures the tone of
much of the youth revolt that began in the 1950s. Herbert Gans, in *The
Levittowners: Ways of Life and Politics in a New Suburban Community*
(1967) argues that the new suburban culture did *not* display the vapid conformity described in much of the literature of the era. Two other books
explore his question: Richard L. Rapson's collection *Individualism and
Conformity in the American Character* (1967) and Scott Donaldson's *The
Suburban Myth* (1969). Vance Packard's *The Hidden Persuaders* (1957) is a
fascinating, contemporary document that identifies advertising as the basic
element in the conformist culture of the 1950s.

A good study of how segregation in housing helped create separate
spheres of urban and suburban culture is Charles Abrams, *Forbidden
Neighbors: A Study of Prejudice in Housing* (1955). A very interesting and
acerbic biography by Robert A. Caro, *The Power Broker: Robert Moses and
the Fall of New York* (1974), details the impact of highways and the highway
lobby on America's first city. Ralph Ellison's *Shadow and Act* (1964) is a su-
perb collection of essays on black issues in America during this period.
There are a great many discussions of the impact of black music on the
mainstream of American popular culture. Among the best and most readable is Carl Belz's *The Story of Rock* (1969).

In recent years the reputation of Dwight Eisenhower has improved. Historians now judge him to be an enlightened conservative. The best general
account of his presidency is Charles C. Alexander's *Holding the Line: The
Eisenhower Era, 1952–61* (1975). Robert H. Ferrell's edition of *The Eisenhower Diaries* (1981) sheds important new light on this complex man. These
should be read in conjunction with Eisenhower's memoirs, *The White
House Years* (1963–1965). A good collection of documents is Robert L.

Branyan and Lawrence H. Larsen's *The Eisenhower Administration: A Documentary History* (1971). An interesting popular biography is Steve Neal's *The Eisenhowers' Reluctant Dynasty* (1978). Stephen E. Ambrose's exhaustive biographical volumes should also be consulted. These are, *Eisenhower: General of the Army, President-Elect, 1890–1952* (1983), and *Eisenhower: The President* (1984). One of the most controversial issues of the Eisenhower administration, the desegregation decision, is handled exhaustively by Richard Kluger, *Simple Justice* (1975). James R. Killian, Jr., discusses the important issue of science in these years in his memoir, *Sputnik, Scientists, and Eisenhower* (1976).

Two particularly interesting biographies add to the literature of this era. They are James T. Patterson's *Mr. Republican: A Biography of Robert A. Taft* (1972) and John Bartlow Martin's two-volume *The Life of Adlai E. Stevenson* (1977). Earl Warren's *The Memoirs of Earl Warren* (1977) provides useful information about and insights into this Supreme Court justice who did much to alter America's social conscience.

Issues of power, productivity, and communications made up a vast subject in postwar writing. An early account of automation is John Diebold's *Automation: The Advent of the Automatic Factory* (1952). Howard Boone Jacobson and Joseph S. Soucek discuss the automation controversy in their work *Automation and Society* (1959). Ralph Parkman's *The Cybernetic Society* (1972) is an interesting update of the issue. Discussions of the increasing concentration in the American economy are numerous. Among the more interesting books on this subject are Richard J. Barber's *The American Corporation; Its Power, Its Money, Its Politics* (1970) and Neil H. Jacoby, *Corporate Power and Social Responsibility: A Blueprint for the Future* (1973). As in all of his books, John Kenneth Galbraith, in *The New Industrial State* (1971), is witty and provocative.

Two books in particular offer contrasting views of the potential impact of nuclear warfare on American society. The first, Herman Kahn's *On Thermonuclear War* (1960), argues the feasibility of survival after such a catastrophe. In the second, Arthur I. Waskow and Stanley L. Newman, *American in Hiding* (1962), the authors discuss what they view as the deplorable effects of large-scale civil defense projects. Marshall McLuhan, in his *Understanding Media: The Extensions of Man* (1964), suggests that modern communications, not nuclear power, have most radically transformed modern society.

The Kennedy-Johnson years have been the subject of much disagreement. Historians have disputed the impact of Kennedy's presidency in particular. Some, such as Arthur M. Schlesinger, Jr., in *A Thousand Days: John F. Kennedy in the White House* (1965), contend that the young president must be placed in the pantheon of America's great leaders. Two of Kennedy's advisers share something of this view: Pierre Salinger, in *With Kennedy* (1966), and Theodore C. Sorensen, in *Kennedy* (1965). Other writers are less enthusiastic. Henry Fairlie, *The Kennedy Promise: The Pol-*

itics of Expectation (1973), is an interesting account. The Kennedy family is submitted to a scathing review by two reporters, Peter Collier and David Horowitz, in *The Kennedys: An American Drama* (1984). David Halberstam's *The Best and the Brightest* (1969) is an exhaustive and revealing discussion of the foreign policy that led to defeat in Vietnam. Jim F. Heath, in *Decade of Disillusionment: The Kennedy-Johnson Years* (1975), and Bruce Miroff, *Pragmatic Illusions: The Presidential Politics of John F. Kennedy* (1976), deflate the claims of Kennedy's supporters.

Some of the special issues of the Kennedy administration are well covered in Hobart Rowen's discussion of economics, *The Free Enterprisers: Kennedy, Johnson and the Business Establishment* (1964), and Carl M. Brauer's *John F. Kennedy and the Second Reconstruction* (1977), in which the author documents the president's civil rights activities.

Some of Kennedy's own writings make interesting reading—for example, *Profiles in Courage* (1961). It is difficult to understand Kennedy without some insight into his family. A readable biography of his father is David Koskoff's *Joseph P. Kennedy: A Life and Times* (1974). Arthur M. Schlesinger, Jr., provides a very favorable account of the president's brother in *Robert Kennedy and His Times* (1978). James MacGregor Burns has written an important biography of Edward Kennedy: *Edward Kennedy and the Camelot Legacy* (1976).

Aside from the general works listed above that touch on the Johnson administration, other books specifically assess the Johnson years. Readable and interesting is Doris Kearns's psychological study and biography, *Lyndon Johnson and the American Dream* (1976). Robert Caro, in his biography *The Years of Lyndon Johnson* (1982), is unsparing in his revelations and criticism of the future president's weaknesses. Eric Goldman, resident White House intellectual, has an interesting account, *The Tragedy of Lyndon Johnson* (1969). Frank Cormier, a reporter, provides fascinating details of Washington in *LBJ: The Way He Was* (1977). The origins and implementation of Johnson's most important domestic legislation are discussed in a government publication, Stephen Goodell and Bennet Schiff's, *The Office of Economic Opportunity During the Administration of President Lyndon B. Johnson, 1963–1969* (1973).

Social and political movements of the 1950s and 1960s have preoccupied many observers. A good beginning point is Arthur M. Schlesinger, Jr.'s *Vital Center: The Politics of Freedom* (1949). William F. Buckley's *God and Man at Yale: The Superstitions of "Academic Freedom"* (1951) is a good conservative response to liberal ideas about the nature of modern thought. The function of religion in America is brilliantly described by Will Herberg in *Protestant—Catholic—Jew: An Essay in American Religious Sociology* (1960). A special issue of *Daedalus* magazine (Winter 1967) contains a broad discussion of the role of religion in American society. Roderick P. Hart, in *The Political Pulpit* (1977), delineates the movement of evangelical religion into the political arena.

The major advance in social relations during the 1950s and 1960s came in the recognition of the rights of black Americans. The central figure in this cause was Martin Luther King, Jr. Probably the best biography of this leader is David Lewis's *King: A Critical Biography* (1970). A very favorable essay on the Student Nonviolent Coordinating Committee is Howard Zinn's *SNCC: The New Abolitionists* (1965). Good source material and articles may be found in a work edited by August Meier and Elliot Rudwick, *Black Protest in the Sixties* (1970). Black self-consciousness helped to strengthen other varieties of self-consciousness in this period. An interesting discussion is contained in Arnold Dashefsky's edited work, *Ethnic Identity in Society* (1976).

Radical student politics had a major impact on American society during the 1960s. Assessment of the principal organization of the New Left—Students for a Democratic Society (SDS)—differs. A sympathetic account is contained in Kirkpatrick Sales' *SDS* (1973). Irwin Unger, in *The Movement: A History of the American New Left, 1959–72* (1974), is more critical. A good sample of New Left ideas can be found in Abbie Hoffman's *The Conspiracy* (1969), which discusses the trial of several leftist leaders for their activities at the 1968 Democratic National Convention in Chicago. Two new books give a very different perspective to the radical movements of the 1960s. Wini Breines argues that the New Left grew out of a particular community and culture in *Community and Organization in the New Left, 1962–1968: The Great Refusal* (1982). Quite the opposite tack is taken in Joseph Conlin's amusing *The Troubles: A Jaundiced Glance Back at the Movement of the Sixties* (1982).

American culture also changed profoundly during the 1960s. An interesting account of one of the earliest rebels is Dennis McNally's *Desolate Angel: Jack Kerouac, the Beat Generation, and America* (1979). Morris Dickstein, *Gates of Eden: American Culture in the Sixties* (1977), is an excellent essay on the connections between radical movements and American culture during this era.

Most of the history of the 1970s is, as yet, unwritten. There are, however, a number of important books on the women's movement. Any study should begin with Betty Friedan's landmark, *The Feminine Mystique* (1963). William H. Chafe's *Women and Equality: Changing Patterns in American Culture* (1977) is a good short history that concentrates on the recent period. Anne Koedt, Ellen Levine, and Anita Rapone, in a volume entitled *Radical Feminism* (1973), provide a sampling of radical feminist writings. The National Commission on the Observance of International Woman's Year Report, *To Form a More Perfect Union* (1976), indicates a high degree of government support for women's rights. Another important issue of the 1970s—the older population—is well covered in William Graebner's *A History of Retirement: The Meaning and Function of an American Institution, 1885–1978* (1980). Herman P. Miller's *Rich Man,*

Poor Man (1971) contains an important discussion of income distribution in the United States.

Economic issues had extraordinary importance during the 1970s and early 1980s, and the writing on them is enormous and controversial. One important general book is by Robert L. Heilbroner and Lester C. Thurow, *Five Economic Challenges* (1983). An interesting compendium of articles on the "new" economy of the 1980s is contained in Michael L. Wachter and Susan M. Wachter's *Toward a New U.S. Industrial Policy?* (1981). Ira C. Magaziner and Robert B. Reich in *Minding America's Business* suggest that the United States is rapidly losing its competitive edge in international trade due to unwise investment practices. A case in point is the automobile industry where, as Emma Rothschild demonstrates in her work, *Paradise Lost: The Decline of the Auto-Industrial Age* (1973), one of America's most important industries has been permanently diminished by competition. One of the greatest problems of the 1970s was shortages of basic raw materials. This is the subject of Steven B. Hunt's *The Energy Crisis: A Critical Analysis of the Energy Policy of the United States* (1978). Much of the best literature on economics and economic policy remains in periodical form. Of special interest are the essays of Andrew Hacker. Two of these appeared in the *New York Review of Books*: "Farewell to the Family?" (March 18, 1982), and "Where Have the Jobs Gone?" (June 30, 1983).

A question that many political observers asked during the 1970s was: Had there been a significant realignment of parties and constituencies during the period? An interesting overview is provided by Richard J. Barnet in *The Lean Years: Politics in the Age of Scarcity* (1980). In his influential book *The Rise of the Unmeltable Ethnics: Politics and Culture in the Seventies* (1971), Michael Novak convincingly discussed the coming disintegration of the Democratic Party coalition. One observer who hoped that the growth of the Republican party would also imply a shift to the right was Richard A. Viguerie, who argued strongly in *The New Right—We're Ready to Lead* (1981) for a new and radical conservatism. Several important articles by political scientist Walter Dean Burnham judiciously consider whether or not such a shift has taken place. One of these is "The Eclipse of the Democratic Party" in *Democracy* (July 1982).

Overall histories of the 1970s and early 1980s are, of course, just now appearing. There are, however, several interesting works on at least part of the era. George C. Herring in *America's Longest War: The United States and Vietnam, 1950–1975* (1979) provides significant detail and background to the end of that bitter struggle under the Ford Administration. Jonathan Schell's *Time of Illusion* is a critical and politically committed discussion of the Nixon era. The redirection of American foreign policy is the subject of Seyom Brown's *The Crises of Power: An Interpretation of United States Foreign Policy during the Kissinger Years* (1979).

Histories of the presidents who presided during this period underscore the impression of political instability and confusion. The most fascinating character is, of course, Richard Nixon. Since his early career, he has been dogged by controversy. His own *Six Crises* (1962) and his *Memoirs* (1978) are important and illuminating. Garry Will's *Nixon Agonistes: The Crisis of the Self-Made Man* (1970) is an irreverent but delightful book. Carl Bernstein and Bob Woodward's *All the President's Men* (1974) is the best book on Watergate, by the two reporters who unearthed much of the incriminating evidence. One of Nixon's key players was adviser, and later Secretary of State, Henry Kissinger. Seymour M. Hersh is unremitting in his criticism of Kissinger in his exposé *The Price of Power: Kissinger in the Nixon White House* (1983). Kissinger's memoirs, *White House Years* (1979), are just as unremitting in their self-justification, but they still provide a number of interesting insights into policymaking. The short, caretaker administration of Gerald Ford has been treated adequately in two works: John Osborne's *White House Watch: The Ford Years* and reporter John J. Casserly's *The Ford White House* (1977).

Jimmy Carter has provided two glimpses into his presidency, one at the beginning of his administration and one at the end: *Why Not the Best* (1977) and *Keeping Faith: Memoirs of a President* (1982). The latter book, in hardback, is published in a format to resemble a hymnal.

The phenomenon of Ronald Reagan will undoubtedly intrigue American historians for many years to come. There is much to be explained—his extraordinary success and the origins of his ideology, for example. Lou Cannon's early biography *Reagan* (1982) is thus far the best account. Robert Dallek in *Ronald Reagan: The Politics of Symbolism* (1984) is more ambitious but less successful. A shocking discussion of nuclear policy during the first Reagan administration is Robert Scheer's *With Enough Shovels: Reagan, Bush and Nuclear War* (1983).

Index

About the Author

James Gilbert received his B.A. from Carleton College and his M.A. and Ph.D. from the University of Wisconsin. He has taught at Teachers College, Columbia University, the Centre for Social History at Warwick University, Coventry, England, and at the University of Maryland. In 1978, he was chosen Distinguished Scholar-Teacher at Maryland. In 1968 he published *Writers and Partisans*. His other books include *Designing the Industrial State* (1972) and *Work Without Salvation* (1978). In 1977 his "Wars of the Worlds" was named the best article of the year by the Popular Culture Association. He has been a Fellow of the Woodrow Wilson Foundation and the National Endowment for the Humanities.

A Note on the Type

The text of this book is set in 10/12 Caledonia, a typeface originally designed for Linotype by W. A. Dwiggins. It belongs to the family of types, called "modern" faces, that are characterized by the pronounced contrast between the thick and thin strokes in each letter. Caledonia is similar to Scotch Modern but its letters are more freely drawn.

This book was set via computer-driven cathode-ray tube and composed by Eastern Graphics, Binghamton, New York. It was printed and bound by The Maple Press Co., York, Pennsylvania.